Democracy in Senegal
Tocquevillian Analytics in Africa

Democracy in Senegal
Tocquevillian Analytics in Africa

Sheldon Gellar

DEMOCRACY IN SENEGAL
© Sheldon Gellar, 2005.

First published in 2005 by
PALGRAVE MACMILLAN™
175 Fifth Avenue, New York, N.Y. 10010 and
Houndmills, Basingstoke, Hampshire, England RG21 6XS
Companies and representatives throughout the world.

PALGRAVE MACMILLAN is the global academic imprint of the Palgrave Macmillan division of St. Martin's Press, LLC and of Palgrave Macmillan Ltd. Macmillan® is a registered trademark in the United States, United Kingdom and other countries. Palgrave is a registered trademark in the European Union and other countries.

ISBN 1–4039–7026–2
ISBN 1–4039–7027–0

Library of Congress Cataloging-in-Publication Data

Gellar, Sheldon.
    Democracy in Senegal : Tocquevillian analytics in Africa / Sheldon Gellar.
        p. cm.
    "Workshop in Political Theory and Policy Analysis, Indiana University."
    Includes bibliographical references and index.
    ISBN 1–4039–7026–2—ISBN 1–4039–7027–0 (pbk.)
    1. Democracy—Senegal—History. 2. Political culture—Senegal—History.
3. Senegal—Politics and government. I. Indiana University, Bloomington.
Workshop in Political Theory and Policy Analysis. II. Title. III. Series.

JQ3396.A91G43 2005
320.9663—dc22   2005042973

A catalogue record for this book is available from the British Library.

Design by Newgen Imaging Systems (P) Ltd., Chennai, India.

First edition: September 2005
10 9 8 7 6 5 4 3 2 1

Printed in the United States of America.

*To the Senegalese people for their hospitality,
sense of honor, and love of liberty*

CONTENTS

PREFACE

I have written this book because I love Senegal and believe in Africa's future.

My interest in Tocqueville began in 1984 when I was a visiting scholar at Indiana University's Workshop in Political Theory and Policy Analysis headed by Vincent and Elinor Ostrom. Until then, it had never crossed my mind to think of Tocqueville's work as relevant to Africa. Vincent Ostrom made me realize that Tocqueville, in writing about America, was not just doing a case study but elaborating a methodology—what Ostrom calls Tocquevillian analytics—for studying democracy. After reading *Democracy in America* carefully for the first time, I turned to another of Tocqueville's masterpieces, *The Old Régime and the French Revolution*. In writing about the development of the centralized state and the devastating effects of state tutelage in destroying local initiative in France, Tocqueville seemed to be accurately describing what I had seen in Francophone Africa. Tocqueville hated extreme administrative centralization, impersonal bureaucracies, and the centralized state's control over the economy and daily life because they implicitly denied the great diversity among human societies and sought to impose the same uniform rules for everyone.

Over time, I began to understand the validity of Tocqueville's ideas about freedom of association and the art of association as bulwarks against tyranny, but even more importantly, as preconditions for the establishment of self-governing communities. The more deeply I delved into Tocqueville, the more I appreciated the breadth and pertinence of his analysis of the role of laws, religion, language, culture, and mores in the transition from aristocratic to democratic societies.

Tocqueville had something to say on almost every topic including slavery, equality, the status of women, genocide of the American Indian, and even how to govern colonies.

My interest in Africa began in 1958, when I came to Paris as a graduate student at the *Institut d'Études Politiques* (Science Po). General De Gaulle had just come to power; France was embroiled in a bloody colonial war in Algeria; and Guinea had just become the first and only Black African French colony to choose independence. During my two years in Paris, the many Africans I met were more concerned with independence and economic development than democracy.

Senegal attracted me because I had studied at IRFED, a development-training institute in Paris run by Father L. J. Lebret, a Dominican priest who advised Pope John XXIII on development issues and served as economic advisor to the Senegalese government. Inspired by Lebret, I chose Senegal as the subject for my doctoral dissertation.

I first went to Senegal in November 1962 to do fourteen months of fieldwork. On the boat from Marseille to Dakar, I met Ismaila Dia, a young Muslim aristocrat from Fouta Toro who was returning to Senegal after finishing his pharmaceutical studies in France. Ismaila took me into his family, introduced me to Senegalese society, and became my African *"grand frère."* Ismaila was a devout Muslim with a genuine interest in other religions that we both shared.

Unlike Tocqueville who never returned to America, I have been back to Senegal many times over the past forty years and have personally witnessed many of the changes described in this book. As an academic researcher and international development consultant, I have had the privilege and pleasure of having been to every one of Senegal's *départements* (the equivalent of our states) which afforded me the opportunity to observe Senegal's great physical and climatic diversity. During my travels, I have observed and talked with aristocrats, former slaves, and praisesingers (griots); farmers, herders, and fishermen; mechanics, domestics, taxi drivers, and petty traders; foresters, agricultural extension agents, and state bureaucrats; journalists, judges, and lawyers; doctors, pharmacists, and university professors; feminists, human rights advocates, and literacy specialists; ministers, mayors, deputies, and local government officials; marabouts, priests, and Christian missionaries; writers, actors, and musicians; and lots of young people in urban neighborhoods.

When I visited my first Senegalese village accompanied by a French cooperative specialist and a Senegalese official, the village chief did all the talking while the young men sat quietly in the back. Women were absent from the meeting. The village chief was deferential to the state official and listed the problems of the village, which he expected the state to solve. Forty years later in the same village, I saw quite a different picture. Not only were women present at the meeting, they also spoke up and were not afraid to contradict the village chief when they disagreed. Young men also intervened to articulate their concerns and demonstrate what their village had done to improve conditions. Although still respected, the village chief no longer dominated the meeting.

In 1963, Ismaila would speak only French in his pharmacy to his customers and refused with some disdain to use Wolof, Senegal's *lingua franca*. He felt obliged to give money to the family griot and to take care of the former slaves attached to his family. Forty years later, his own children spoke Wolof as their first language; he answered in Wolof to customers who couldn't speak French; and he was willing to grant former slaves and low caste people from his village a voice in community affairs back home. Times had changed.

In 1968, I spent four months in Dakar during a political crisis that shook the foundations of the regime. Senegal had become a one-party state and allowed few outlets for the people to express their grievances or to affect government policy. Thirty years later I served as Democracy advisor to the USAID mission in Senegal for fifteen months. I personally witnessed the explosion in associational life, the maturing of a free press, and the march toward a more open political system. I also experienced the efforts of party and state officials to hold back the tide of change and to preserve their privileges and control over the people. I also saw donors designing projects without consulting the people they were intended for and creating new organizations that quickly faded away after the project was over because they were not compatible with traditional modes of organizing.

My most recent trip to Senegal was in 2004. Many Senegalese expressed their disappointment with the new regime after the 2000 presidential elections ousted Abdou Diouf from office and brought Abdoulaye Wade to power. They complained that Wade was trying to retain too much power in his own hands, that he was favoring his own family, and that corruption was still rampant. What I found was that Wade, despite all the power he had, could not impose his will on the people. The people had become better informed. On several occasions, he had to cancel policies and modify statements when he saw that public opinion was against him.

Although originally conceived in the nineteenth century, Tocquevillian analytics provides a fresh and comprehensive methodology to study the processes of democratization in Africa. This book draws on the lessons that I have learned from Tocqueville and my experiences in Senegal and other African countries. It offers Tocquvillian analytics as an alternative methodology to the largely ahistorical and state-centered approach used by many Western scholars studying democratization processes today. Like Tocqueville who used America to illustrate and sharpen his ideas about the evolution of democracy in France and Europe, I am using Senegal to begin an examination of the current state of democracy in Africa and its prospects for the future. Like America, is this small West African country exceptional? Perhaps. Its relatively long independence history of participation in electoral processes and modern democratic institutions make Senegal unusual. However, many of the positive traits found in Senegal—for example, religious and ethnic tolerance, a taste for liberty, and a vibrant associational life—that constitute the foundations for a democratic culture can be found elsewhere in Africa.

Skilled in the art of association, Africa's peoples are in the process of forging their own version of the democratic revolution that began in America. The Senegal case suggests that the peoples of Africa have an immense reservoir of self-governing capabilities and growing taste for freedom that bodes well for the future of democracy and contradicts the prevailing pessimism concerning the African continent. The positive aspects supporting democracy in Senegal need to be reinforced and expanded while overcentralization, suppression of basic freedoms, and religious and ethnic intolerance need to be resisted.

The organization of the book and the chapter titles reflect an effort to highlight the concepts and language that Tocqueville used in his own

work—for example, point of departure, democratic despotism, art of association, spirit of religion, local liberties, and so on. Each chapter is introduced
by a pertinent quote from Tocqueville.

This book owes much to many people. I owe a great debt to Vincent
Ostrom who encouraged me to apply Tocquevillian analytics to Africa,
supported my writing endeavors, and pushed me to integrate my material.
The work began in 2000 at the Harry S. Truman Institute for the Advancement
of Peace in Jerusalem where I was a Research Associate in the Africa Unit.
I thank the Truman Institute for their support. At the Workshop, Vincent and
Elinor Ostrom welcomed me into their community of international schol-
ars and provided a pleasant and stimulating environment in which to finish
this book. I also appreciate the collegiality of Workshop Associates Barbara
Allen, Aurelian Craiutu, Marilyn Hoskins, Sam Joseph, Filippo Sabetti,
Amos Sawyer, Sujai Shivakumar, Jamie Thomson, and Jim Wunsch who have
shared their scholarship, comments, and enthusiasm for Tocqueville with me.
Thanks also to Martin Klein, Babacar Kanté, and Pathé Diagne for their
helpful comments on the manuscript.

I would also like to acknowledge those American and European scholars
whose work has stimulated my thinking about Senegal. They include
Jonathan Barker, Linda Beck, Cathy Boone, Lucie Colvin, Jean Copans,
Christian Coulon, Lucie Creevey, Donal Cruise O'Brien, Philip Curtin,
William Foltz, Wesley Johnson, Martin Klein, Irving Markowitz, Paul
Pélissier, David Robinson, Frederick Schaeffer, Carrie Sembène, Bernhard
Venema, Richard Vengroff, and Leonardo Villalòn.

Senegalese scholars, writers, politicians, and development practitioners
have contributed tremendously to my understanding of Senegalese history,
culture, and politics. I owe much to Boubacar Barry, Abdoulaye Bathily,
Jacques Bugnicourt, Sidy Cissokho, Mamadou Dia, Pathé Diagne, Abdoulaye-
Bara Diop, Momar-Coumba Diop, Makhtar Diouf, Mamadou Diouf,
Jacques Faye, Babacar Kanté, Penda Mbow, Malick Ndiaye, Emmanuel
Ndione, Mamadou Niang, Ousemane Sembène, Pape Sène Léopold Sédar
Senghor, Fatou Sow, Cheikh Tidjiane Sy, Ibrahima Thioub, and Babacar
Touré. I would also like to extend special thanks to Ismaila Dia and Famara
Sagna whose friendships have endured for more than forty years, and to
honor the memory of the late Pape Babacar Mbaye, a Senegalese deputy
whose courage, integrity, and commitment to democratic ideals serves as a
wonderful model to Senegal's younger generation of politicians.

Gayle Higgins, Patty Lezotte, Sarah Kantner, and David Price from the
Workshop staff and Eric Coleman provided invaluable support in preparing the
manuscript for publication. I also would like to thank David Pervin of Palgrave-
Macmillan for his encouragement and willingness to publish a book on Africa
with Tocqueville in the title. Heather Van Dusen and Erin Ivy provided production support while Maran Elancheran did a meticulous job of copy-editing.

Finally, I would like to acknowledge the generous financial support
offered by the Earhart Foundation and the Indiana University Workshop in
Political Theory and Policy Analysis that enabled me to complete this book.

MAP OF SENEGAL

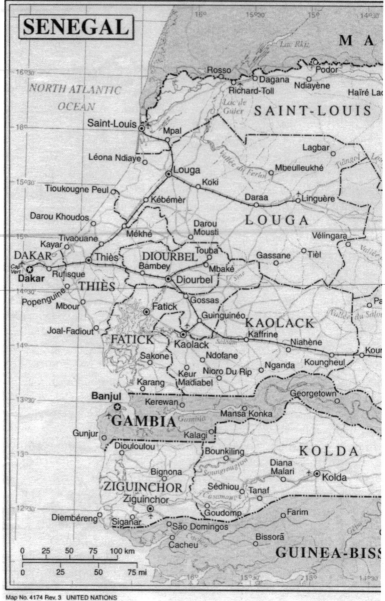

Map No. 4174 Rev. 3 UNITED NATIONS
January 2004

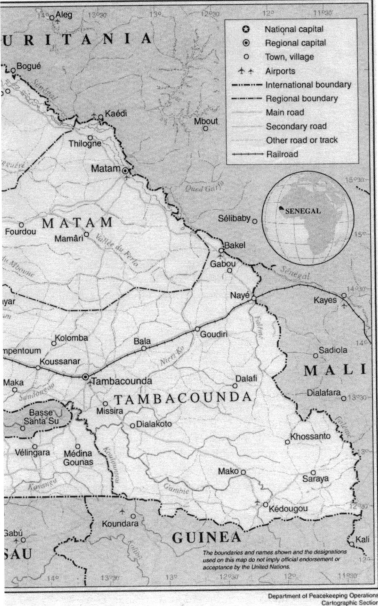

ACRONYMS AND
ABBREVIATIONS

AJ	And Jef
AJAC	Association des Jeunes Agriculteurs de Casamance
ALMA	Association pour la Liaison et le Développement des Agnams
ARC	Alliance des Radios Communautaires du Sénégal
ASC	Association Sportive et Culturelle
ASESCAW	Association Socio-Educative Sportive et Culturelle, L'Amicale du Walo
BDS	Bloc Démocratique Sénégalais
BMS	Bloc des Masses Sénégalaises
BPS	Bloc Populaire Sénégalais
CER	Centre d'Expansion Rurale
CNCR	Conseil National de Concertation des Ruraux
CNTS	Confédération Nationale des Travailleurs Sénégalais
CONGAD	Conseil des Organisations Non-Gouvernementales d'Appui au Développement
COSEF	Conseil Sénégalais des Femmes
CPP	Convention People's Party
ENA	École Nationale d'Administration
ENAS	École Nationale de l'Administration du Sénégal
ENDA	Environnement et Développement du Tiers-Monde
FAIS	Fédération des Associations Islamiques du Sénégal
FAL	Front Pour l'Alternance
FC/TI	Forum Civil/Transparency International
FEANF	Fédération des Etudiants d'Afrique Noire en France
FNS	Front National Sénégalais
FONGS	Fédération des Organisations Non-Gouvernementales du Sénégal
FSD	Front pour le Socialisme et la Démocratie
GIE	Groupement d'Intéret Economique
HCRT	Haut Conseil de la Radio-Télévision
IFAN	Institut Fondamental d'Afrique Noire
LD-MPT	Ligue Démocratique-Mouvement Pour le Parti du Travail
MAC	Mouvement Autonome de Casamance

MFDC	Mouvement des Forces Démocratique de la Casamance
MMUD	Mouvement Mondial pour l'Unicité de Dieu
NGO	Non-Governmental Organization
ONCAD	Office National de Coopération et d'Assistance Pour le Développement
ONDH	Organisation Nationale des Droits de l'Homme
ONEL	Observatoire National pour les Elections
PAI	Parti Africain de l'Indépendance
PBS	Positive Black Soul
PDS	Parti Démocratique Sénégalais
PIT	Parti de l'Indépendance et du Travail
PRA-Senegal	Parti du Regroupement Africain-Senegal
PRSI	Parti Républicain Socialiste Indépendant
PS	Parti Socialiste
PSS	Parti de la Solidarité Sénégalaise
PSS	Parti Socialiste Sénégalais
PUR	Parti de l'Unité Républicaine
RADDHO	Rencontre Africaine pour la Défense des Droits de l'Homme
RDA	Regional Development Agency
RND	Rassemblement National Démocratique
SAED	The State Water and Irrigation Agency
SES	Syndicat des Enseignants du Sénégal
SFIO	Section Française de l'Internationale Ouvrière
SMDR	Sociétés Mutuelles de Développement Rural
SUDES	Syndicat Unique et Démocratique des Enseignants du Sénégal
UDS	Union Démocratique Sénégalaise
UNACOIS	Union Nationale des Commerçants et Industriels du Sénégal
UNSAS	Union Nationale des Syndicats Autonomes de Sénégal
UNTS	Union National des Travailleurs Sénégalais
UPIS	Union pour le Progrés Islamique au Sénégal
UPS	Union Progressiste Sénégalaise
UTLS	Union des Travailleurs Libres de Sénégal

CHRONOLOGY OF EVENTS

Eleventh Century	War Jabi, ruler of Tekrur converts to Islam
Twelfth to Fourteenth Century	Rise of the Mali Empire as the dominant power in western Soudan
	Founding of Djolof Empire which absorbs Tekrur and controls Baol, Walo, Cayor, Fouta Toro, and Sine
Fifteenth Century	First European contact with Senegal by Portuguese explorers (1445) Koli Tengela installs Denianké dynasty in Fouta Toro
	Decline of the Mali Empire
Sixteenth Century	Decline of Djolof Empire and breaking away of former vassal states of Cayor, Baol, Walo, and Sine to establish independent monarchies
Seventeenth Century	Establishment of trading ties with France, England, and Holland
	Rise of the Atlantic slave trade Founding of Saint-Louis in 1659 by the French War of the marabouts against the aristocratic orders in Fouta Toro, Walo, Djolof, and Cayor
Eighteenth Century	Height of the Atlantic slave trade Muslim Revolution in Fouta Toro in 1776
	French Revolution breaks out in Paris (1789)
	Saint-Louis sends *cahiers de doléances* to to French National Assembly
	Lebu break away from Cayor and establish Republic on Cap Vert peninsula (1790s)
Nineteenth Century	Umar Tall receives title of Grand Khalife of West Africa for the Tijani order (1825)
	Slavery abolished in French Senegal (1848)

Senegal sends deputy to French National Assembly in 1848

Faidherbe becomes governor of French Senegal in 1854 and begins conquest of the interior

Cap Vert peninsula annexed by French (1859)

Umar Tall driven out of Fouta Toro Ma Ba defeated in 1867 by Bour of Sine

Defeat and death of Lat Dior in 1886

French and English sign treaty fixing boundaries of Senegal and the Gambia (1889)

Saint Louis, Gorée, Rufisque, and Dakar become Communes and their inhabitants Citizens End of the Almamate in Fouta Toro (1891)

Destruction of the old aristocratic order Rise of the Sufi Brotherhoods

Twentieth Century

Malick Sy establishes Tivaouane as capital of his Tijani order in 1902

Ahmadou Bamba establishes Mouride order Dakar becomes capital of French West Africa (1902)

French take steps to eliminate slavery (1903)

Blaise Diagne becomes first Black African deputy in 1914

Death of Malick Sy in 1922 and Ahmadou Bamba in 1927

Lamine Guèye creates Senegalese Socialist Party in 1929

Suppression of democratic institutions by Vichy regime following the fall of France in 1940

Twentieth Century
(Postwar Era)

Fourth Republic abolishes distinctions between Citizens and Subjects in 1946

Establishment of Bloc Démocratique Sénégalais (BDS) by Senghor and Dia in 1948 to combat Lamine Guèye's Socialist Party BDS becomes majority party (1951–1952) with support of Sufi religious leaders and former Subjects

Universal suffrage granted (1956)

First Senegalese executive established in 1957

Degaulle comes to power (May 1958) and offers self-government or independence to African colonies

Union Progressiste Sénégalaise (UPS) captures all eighty seats in National Assembly (1959)

Senegal becomes independent in 1960

Twentieth Century (Postindependence Era)

Demise of Mamadou Dia in December 1962

Senegalese Second Republic established as strong presidential regime (1963)

Elimination of legal political parties (1966) and emergence of Senegal as one-party state

Rise of state bureaucracy and state tutelage over economic and associational life

Movement toward political liberalization (1974–1980)

Abdou Diouf becomes president in peaceful transition after Senghor resigns in 1981

Abdou Diouf restores unlimited multiparty system in 1981

Islam becomes increasingly important in shaping Senegalese society

Outbreak of separatist insurgency in Casamance in 1982

Rise of independent press

Reform of electoral system in 1991

Blossoming of associational life

Emergence of independent radio in 1994

Decentralization code in 1996 expands powers of local government

Opposition parties make steady gains

Younger marabouts more active in politics

Abdoulaye Wade defeats Diouf in 2000 presidential elections

New 2001 constitution reinforces presidential power while expanding political rights

Wade moves to consolidate his power (2000–2002) through his party's control over National Assembly and most local government bodies

Media, civil society, and public opinion check

Wade's authoritarian tendencies

CHAPTER ONE

Tocquevillian Analytics in Africa

> A great democratic revolution is taking place in our midst; everybody sees it, but by no means everybody judges it in the same way.[1]

In March 1957, Ghana became the first Black African country to gain its independence from a colonial power. To commemorate this momentous event, *Life* magazine featured a picture of Ghanaian judges grandly attired in powdered wigs and black robes on its cover. Democracy in Africa, in those days, seemed to be simply a matter of the new nations adopting Western models and forms of democracy.

During the early 1960s, Western observers were generally optimistic about Africa's democratic future. Free, competitive elections preceded the granting of independence in most of the new African states formerly under French, British, and Belgian colonial rule. When the winners took power, most co-opted or eliminated their opponents and established authoritarian one-party regimes in the name of national unity. Starting in 1966, a spate of military coups pointed to the fragility of Africa's new states. By the mid-1980s, twenty-five African countries had succumbed to military rule while only a handful of multiparty regimes had survived. The future of democracy in Africa looked bleak.

During the 1990s, Africa saw the end of apartheid and white minority rule in South Africa while one-party regimes and military rule throughout the continent gave way to multiparty systems in more than a dozen African countries starting with Benin. However, during this same period, Africa also experienced genocide in Rwanda, bloody civil wars in Algeria, Angola, Mozambique, Guinea-Bissau, Sudan, and Zaire; predatory warlords plundering their countries in Somalia, Liberia, and Sierra Leone; and the restriction of political liberties despite the holding of multiparty elections. Although the violence ended or subsided in many parts of Africa in the early years of the third millennium, democracy in Africa remained fragile and its future uncertain despite the increase in the number of electoral democracies throughout the African continent since 1990.

Is Africa part of the modern Democratic Revolution that began with the American and French Revolutions? If so, why has democracy had such a problem taking hold in Africa? What are its prospects for democracy in the future? How should one study democracy in Africa?

Although social scientists and democratic theorists often refer to the work of Alexis Tocqueville (1805–1859) in their analyses of American and European societies, they rarely apply his methodology and insights to the study of democracy in the non-Western world.[2] Yet, the questions and issues raised by Tocqueville in his studies of France and America are just as crucial for understanding the development of democracy in Africa. How does the weight of the past affect the evolution of new political institutions and political behavior? What are the relationships among equality, freedom, and democracy? To what extent does centralization destroy the capacity for local initiative and self-governance? What conditions are needed to nurture the flourishing of self-governing communities? What safeguards are needed to preserve freedom and to prevent democracies from evolving into dictatorships?

Waves Apart: Tocqueville and Huntington on Democracy and the Democratic Revolution

In *Democracy in America*, Tocqueville pointed to the American experience as the harbinger of a democratic revolution that would eventually encompass Europe and the Western world, transforming aristocratic orders into democratic orders. When Tocqueville wrote his masterpiece, America was the only democracy in the world. Since then, democracy has been consolidated throughout Europe and much of the Western world and spread to the non-Western world.

In *The Third Wave: Democratization in the Late Twentieth Century*, Samuel P. Huntington cites Tocqueville as having been the first to identify the worldwide trend toward democracy and describes the evolution of modern democracy as proceeding in waves[3] and eventually spreading to the non-Western world.[4]

While Huntington and Tocqueville both maintained that democracy was the wave of the future and vulnerable to setbacks and reversals, especially in countries where democracy had not been firmly entrenched, they presented different definitions and approaches toward the study of democracy. With his emphasis on liberty, equality, popular sovereignty, and self-governance as the foundations of democracy, Tocqueville offered a broader vision of democracy than Huntington and other contemporary analysts who see democracy as based more narrowly on universal suffrage, free periodic elections, and multiparty competition.

Though Tocqueville and Huntington both regarded popular sovereignty as expressed through universal suffrage to be an essential feature of democratic regimes, they differed sharply as to what that meant and how it was to be applied. For Huntington, popular sovereignty gave the people the right to choose and oust rulers through the ballot box and operated primarily at the national level. Tocqueville visualized popular sovereignty as directly exercised by and with the people through their participation in politics and self-governing institutions at all levels of society, not just in national elections.[5]

Tocqueville also had a radically different conception of the state and the role of the state in a democratic order than Huntington, who accepted a Hobbesian concept of the state giving the state the monopoly of political authority over all those living in a given territory, that is, the nation-state.[6] Tocqueville rejected the idea that political authority needed to be concentrated in the state. For Tocqueville, such concentration of power was detrimental to the new democratic order and could easily lead to tyranny.

Whereas Tocqueville regarded the centralized state as a source of despotism, Huntington saw the centralized state as essential for political modernization in developing societies and advocated a strong central state to insure order and political stability. Weak central governments were bad governments. Hence, whatever strengthened central government institutions was good for the country and the public interest.[7]

Huntington argued that democracy in developing nations had to be built from the top down by national elites in charge of a strong state that could preserve order and effectively deal with primordial claims. He saw modern democracy as taking place uniquely within the framework of the nation-state.[8]

In *Democracy in America*, Tocqueville used the American example to demonstrate that a decentralized form of the state was possible in a democratic order.[9] In America, Tocqueville discovered that the absence of administrative centralization and the existence of multiple and diffuse sources of political authority permitted citizens to participate directly in the management of public affairs to deal with tangible problems in their communities. The practice of citizen participation in local self-government described and advocated by Tocqueville as a concrete manifestation of popular sovereignty had little in common with notions of participation stressing citizen involvement in selecting national rulers and articulating opinions and interests that might or might not be taken into consideration by central government.

The kind of democracy envisioned by Tocqueville promoted self-government and the active participation of citizens in the management of local affairs. People learned how to work together and how to be self-governing within the framework of family, neighborhood, village, and other community-based institutions. For Tocqueville, these institutions needed to enjoy a high degree of autonomy from the state in order to flourish. Free self-governing institutions and associations at the grassroots level also provided a bulwark against state tyranny.

Huntington, on the other hand, tends to regard subnational group identities and communities based on religion, ethnicity, kinship, and local loyalties as potential dangers to order and political stability and obstacles to political modernization. His mistrust of subnational community identities— the primordial forces—reflects a pessimistic view of human nature that implies that human beings, if left to their own devices, will be constantly at war with each other and are incapable of self-governance, hence the need for a strong sovereign state to preserve the peace and maintain order.

Unlike Tocqueville, Huntington justifies using a minimal and procedural definition of democracy based on free, fair, and open elections because it makes it easier to classify political systems.

> To some people . . . "true democracy" means *liberté, égalité, fraternité,* effective citizen control over policy, responsible government, honesty and openness in politics, informed and rational deliberation, equal participation and power and various other civic virtues. These are, for the most part, good things and people can, if they wish, define democracy in these terms. Doing so, however, raises all the problems that come up with the definitions of democracy by source or by purpose. Fuzzy norms do not yield good analysis. Elections open free and fair are the essence of democracy, the inescapable sine qua non.[10]

However, classifying a regime as either democratic or authoritarian tells us little about how the regime functions, the degree of freedom enjoyed by its populations, or its prospects for the future.

Tocqueville himself never provided a precise and consistent definition of democracy. Its meaning depended upon the context in which he wrote. He sometimes referred to democracy as a political regime characterized by popular sovereignty and, at other times, as a type of society based on equality of social conditions.[11]

For Tocqueville, the Democratic Revolution marked the transformation of aristocratic orders based on birth and privilege into societies where political, social, and legal equality prevailed. Tocqueville regarded human equality as both a fact and article of faith that implied that all human beings had the capacity for self-government regardless of their social status at birth. Equality made democracy feasible. Unlike Tocqueville, Huntington had little to say about equality in discussing democracy.[12]

Tocqueville insisted on liberty as essential to an authentic democracy and the most important safeguard against tyranny. For Tocqueville, the remedy to the flaws of democracy was more liberty rather than more order.[13] Although Huntington clearly considers political freedom to be an important component of democracy, he, nevertheless, maintained that order was the first priority and a prerequisite for freedom.[14]

Tocqueville brooded over the viability of democracy and its capacity to preserve freedom. For Tocqueville, *Democracy in America* was not merely a case study of an exotic experiment on the North American continent; it also examined the viability of democratic societies under circumstances of increasing conditions of equality among mankind.[15] Democracies could easily degenerate into democratic despotism when too much power was concentrated in the hands of a single person, political institution, bureaucratic administration, or when the "tyranny of the majority" discarded the rights of the minority.

The wave of the future, democracy, did not necessarily have to turn out right. Tocqueville was deeply concerned with the viability of democracy and its capacity to preserve freedom. He argued that democracies could easily degenerate into democratic despotism. Democratic despotism would occur when too much power was concentrated in the hands of a single person, political institution, bureaucratic administration, or when the "tyranny of the majority" discarded the rights of the minority. Tocqueville's native France, which went through much turmoil and suppression of political freedoms gained during the early years of the French Revolution, provides an excellent example of the difficulty of maintaining the viability of young democracies lacking traditions of political freedom.[16] Many of the new African states that emerged after obtaining their independence experienced similar kinds of problems in sustaining democracy. Tocqueville's concerns about the viability and quality of democracy are still relevant today for looking at the future of democracy everywhere.

Tocqueville's multilayered concept of democracy and the issues and concerns he raised are particularly important for understanding the movement toward democracy and the prospects for sustaining it in Africa.

Brilliantly applied in his monumental study of democracy in America, Tocquevillian analytics provides a more powerful and comprehensive tool for understanding the processes of democratization and constitution of order in Africa than the concepts used by Huntington and others pursuing similar lines of analysis in postcolonial societies which have shed little light concerning the causes of the failure of the nation-state model and why democracy has had such a difficult time taking hold in Africa.

Tocquevillian analytics requires going well beyond Huntington's top-down approach to the analysis of democratization processes focusing on national elites, central government, elections, and the nation-state. When applied to Africa, Tocquevillian analytics looks at the environment, history, institutions, ideas, and diversity of African peoples. It places Africa within the mainstream of world history as societies passing from aristocratic to democratic orders. It also requires looking at African peoples and communities, their social state and capacity for self-governance, their efforts to work together to solve common problems, and the forces that obstruct or move them forward on the road to democracy.

In applying Tocquevillian analytics to the study of democracy in Senegal, this book hopes to offer an alternative and more comprehensive mode of analysis to the study of democratization processes and demonstrate how Tocqueville's methodology can help us to a better understanding of the dynamics and diversity of African peoples and their struggle for democracy and self-governance.

In *Democracy in America*, Tocqueville identified mores (manners and customs, habits of the heart and mind); laws (institutional arrangements); and environmental factors (geography and climate) as the three main factors shaping American democracy. In various forms, they also constitute the heart of Tocquevillian analysis.

Tocquevillian Analytics in Africa

The main components of Tocquevillian analytics encompassing his broadly based comparative historical methodology that can effectively be applied to Africa, in general, and Senegal, in particular, can be summed up as follows:

Contextual Components

1. *The impact of the physical environment in shaping political, economic, and social structures and relationships.* Tocqueville was acutely aware of the importance of physical environment in shaping the organization of societies. America's abundant natural resources and the availability of land facilitated the development of equalitarian social structures and a high degree of mobility. The physical environment also had a major impact in shaping the development of political institutions and relationships within and among societies in Africa. The flat savannah country facilitated transportation and trade in the west Sudan, the rise of large-scale empires, and the spread of Islam while societies in the dense tropical forest zones, where communication was more difficult, were generally more egalitarian, smaller in size, and more self-sufficient.

2. *The importance of history in shaping national character and institutions.* To understand a society's character, Tocqueville argued that one needed to go back to its origins. Unfortunately, many studies of Africa start with independence or the colonial era, downgrade the importance of history, and consider indigenous traditions preceding contact with the West as irrelevant or obstacles to democracy. Tocqueville would have found much that was familiar in Senegal's, and much of precolonial Africa's, history and aristocratic social structures since Europe's aristocratic traditions and social structures endured for many centuries. However, other parts of Africa have had quite different histories, political institutions, and social structures that may have been less familiar to Tocqueville. The features of Africa's acephalous and pastoralist societies differ markedly from those in highly centralized and stratified African societies. Precolonial history, political institutions, and social structures still affect African attitudes toward government, other ethnic groups and communities, and institutional arrangements in the postcolonial era. Differences in the colonial regimes—French, British, Belgian, and Portuguese—and the degree of colonial oppression and repression of indigenous institutions have also played an important role in shaping national political institutions and attitudes of Africans toward government after independence.

3. *The importance of laws, especially property rights and inheritance laws in shaping political, economic, and social structures.* Tocqueville noted that the aristocratic order in Europe was based on land and property rights. Property rights systems in America favored more egalitarian distribution of land than the primogeniture system prevailing in Europe. In Africa, communal ownership

of land and prohibitions against alienating communal land helped to preserve communitarian structures at the village level. Colonial laws expropriated large tracts of land, which was transferred to the state or the white settler population. Property rights and access to natural resources continue to constitute a major arena of African politics.

Sociocultural Components

1. *The degree of social equality in society and the extent to which there is movement toward greater equality.* Tocquevillian analytics examines the state of social equality within a given society and its influence on political institutions, behaviors, and mores. Although Tocqueville generally used national societies as the unit of analysis, he also looked at regional and local differences concerning the state of equality within larger national societies. Precolonial Africa had a wide range of societies ranging from highly egalitarian to highly aristocratic societies. Caste and slavery were important elements in many parts of precolonial Africa. Different types of colonial regimes affected the relative degree of social equality, some weakening, and some strengthening precolonial forms of inequality. Colonial regimes also introduced new forms of inequality based on racial criteria and the creation of a new political elite based on knowledge of the language and institutions of the colonizer.

2. *The importance of mores, customs, and values (culture) in shaping political institutions and political behavior.* Tocqueville was acutely aware of the importance of values and norms determining social status and people's behavior toward each other in society. Mores, customs, and norms vary widely throughout Africa, affecting attitudes toward authority, strangers, gender, and different age groups in society. Traditional notions of caste, honor, loyalty, justice, clientship, and hospitality continue to affect political behavior and expectations concerning political institutions and other groups and communities.

3. *The central role of religion and religious institutions in shaping political attitudes, institutions, and relationships.* Unlike Marxists and many modernization theorists, Tocqueville did not see religion as the opium of the masses or atavistic and destined to decline with the spread of a scientific worldview. Tocqueville believed that faith in God was an inherent feature of humanity and that religious values like human equality, tolerance, and peace supported a democratic culture. Different forms of traditional religions, Islam, and Christianity continue to deeply affect the values and behavior of African societies, which remain profoundly religious.

4. *The crucial role of language as an instrument for promoting mutual understanding and group identity.* Highly sensitive to the importance of language in defining group identity, Tocqueville described how English became the dominant language in America and contributed to forming a distinctly

American identity among different nationalities. He also pointed to differences in the use of language in aristocratic and egalitarian societies. In Africa, language forms one of the most important foundations of group identity. Ethnic identity was often based on the particular language people spoke. Because of the presence of hundreds of different languages in Africa, many Africans were multilingual and often used a common lingua franca to communicate with strangers and their maternal language at home. Under colonial rule, Western education and mastery of the language of the colonizer gave Africans higher political and social status.

Political Components

1. *The importance of popular sovereignty and constitutional choice in the design of political institutions.* Tocqueville maintained that popular sovereignty and the ability of people to make their own laws through constitutional choice were key elements in modern political systems. He also noted that formal rules providing for democratic institutions and liberties would not necessarily be applied by rulers nor invoked by people in societies without liberal democratic traditions. Most precolonial societies exercised a certain degree of constitutional choice in organizing their political orders. These political orders were based on customs or charters elaborated by representatives of different groups in society. Under colonialism, indigenous African societies lacked the freedom to establish a new political order. At independence, the leaders inherited colonial state structures and adopted liberal Western constitutions based on European models with little consultation with the people. One-party states, military regimes, and personal dictatorships violated the political and civil rights guaranteed by their country's constitution and gave their people little say in making the laws and rules governing their lives.

2. *The identification of the concentration of power in centralized governments and bureaucracies as restricting freedom and initiative and leading to despotism and dependency.* Tocqueville regarded concentration of power in the hands of a single person, political institution, or bureaucracy as an obstacle to democracy. Many precolonial African societies lived under highly centralized monarchies, particularly during the heyday of the slave trade. Colonial regimes in Africa established highly centralized autocratic state structures that were Africanized by those coming to power after independence. Concentration of personal power and overcentralization subverted democracy in most of the new African nations.

3. *The importance of local liberties and the constitution of self-governing communities as vital to democracy.* Tocqueville asserted that local liberties gave communities the right to manage their own affairs and reinforced their taste for liberty. He was concerned that an all-powerful central government would attempt to control all aspects of social and economic life, thus stifling freedom and

local initiative. Many societies in precolonial Africa were self-governing communities that fiercely defended their independence. The imposition of colonial rule often led to the demise of local liberties and the imposition of "decentralized despotism."[17] During decolonization and after independence, African political elites placed more emphasis on gaining control of national level institutions rather than seeking to reestablish local liberties and decentralized democratic governance.

4. *The crucial role of political and civil liberties, especially freedom of association and the press as bulwarks against tyranny.* Tocqueville believed that freedom of association and freedom of the press were more important than holding free and periodic elections in preserving freedom and protecting minorities against the tyranny of the majority. He also believed that the "art of association" was the key to creating stable, self-governing communities in the democratic era. Associational life was highly organized in precolonial Africa, usually around gender, age-sets, and occupation. Most colonial regimes sharply restricted freedom of association, freedom of the press, and other civil liberties for their African subjects. In many colonies, Africans were subjected to forced labor, forbidden to organize political parties and trade unions, or to publish independent newspapers. The absence of civil liberties permitted forced labor and other abuses of civil liberties. In postcolonial Africa, military regimes and one-party states restricted political and civil rights and placed local government and civil, economic, and cultural associations under the tutelage of the state or the dominant party. In many African countries, freedom of association and the press permitted people to organize and criticize the governments and enabled them to apply pressure for greater democratization.

Tocqueville attacked the eighteenth century *philosophes* and revolutionaries for creating "an imaginary ideal society in which all was simple, uniform, coherent, equitable, and rational."[18] He recognized that the best of societies has its flaws and weaknesses. During the 1960s and 1970s, African elites adopted ideologies and development models that were poorly suited to Africa. In Senegal, the postindependence debates among the intellectuals advocating Negritude, African Socialism, and different varieties of Marxist ideologies had little meaning for most Senegalese and little to do with how the country was actually organized and functioning or how it should be organized.

Tocqueville did not believe that any one model of democracy could be applied universally and made it clear that the triumph of democracy would depend upon the application of principles rather than the export of models of democracy. While he proclaimed that America was the most advanced of democracies, Tocqueville insisted that the American model with its federal institutions could not be easily adopted in Europe. Tocqueville respected the great diversity of humanity and the need for different societies to find viable institutions that incorporated old and new mores, values, and customs in such a way so as to make the best of what he considered the universal movement toward greater equality. In Africa, where communal values are still strong, the face of democracy will vary as African societies experiment with mixes of old and new political institutions that reflect diverse traditions, value systems, and physical environments.

Because of its long precolonial aristocratic past and early experience with Western-style democratic institutions, Senegal provides an excellent starting point for applying Tocquevillian analytics to the study of the evolution of democracy in Africa.

The reader should not interpret the use of Tocquevillian analytics to trace the evolution of democracy in Senegal as an effort to portray Senegal as an African replica of American democracy. Senegal's aristocratic past, communitarian traditions, and attachment to Islam stand in marked contrast to America's individualism, attachment to Protestant Christianity, and lack of feudal traditions. And while profoundly influenced by French Jacobin and republican political traditions and institutions, democracy in Senegal is not simply an effort to emulate French democracy. This is especially true at the grassroots level where the Western concept of democracy is a relatively new one.

Démocratie and *Demokarassi*: Democracy in Senegal

As anyone who has studied comparative literature knows, translations from one language to another, in the best of cases, are imperfect.[19] The same words and concepts wind up having different and multiple meanings, connotations, and usages when translated from one language to another or even from one society to another using the same maternal language. English versions of Tocqueville's work translate *liberté* sometimes as freedom and sometimes as liberty depending on the context. Freedom and liberty also have different meanings and connotations in English. Freedom has been defined as "liberation from slavery or restraint from the power of another." Liberty has been defined as "the power to do as one pleases" or "freedom from arbitrary or despotic control."[20]

The word "democracy" has multiple meanings and usages in different languages and societies.[21] As used by the ancient Greeks, it referred to rule by the people. However, slaves and foreigners who comprised the majority of the population were not considered as part of the people. As used by Tocqueville, democracy could either refer to social equality or to a political system based on the doctrine of the sovereignty of the people. Contemporary political scientists generally call regimes that have free, competitive multiparty elections democracies. Some put adjectives before the term and refer to political, economic, and social democracy and make distinctions between liberal and illiberal democracies.[22] Other political scientists have referred to quasi-democracies, semi-democracies, and clientelist democracies.[23] Before the demise of communism and the end of the Cold War, communist regimes referred to themselves as people's democracies and claimed that they placed greater emphasis on economic rights and eliminating economic inequality than bourgeois democracies where the ruling classes used the façade of political equality and civil rights to cloud the people's awareness of the vast economic inequalities between capitalists and workers.

The Western-educated African elites who organized political parties and competed in multiparty elections during the last days of colonial rule adapted the language of Western democracy. In most instances, the constitutions of the new African states, written in the language of the colonizer, guaranteed basic liberties and incorporated similar institutional forms of democracy found in the West. The language, norms, and formal institutions of democracy inherited from the colonial power by the Western-educated African elite who took power were based on Western models that had developed over long periods of time in very different political, cultural, and economic contexts.[24] In most cases, they had little meaning for the great majority of the population who had different histories and traditions of governance. As a consequence, the gap between Western-educated elites and rural grassroots populations concerning the meaning of democracy is widespread throughout Africa.

In most cases, the values, norms, and institutions contained in the constitutions were ignored and gave way to rationalizations to justify the establishment of nondemocratic systems. One of the major reasons for the vulnerability of Western-style democracy in Africa was the fact that the majority of the populations neither understood nor internalized the language and models of democracy presented by the elites. This was to be expected since few Africans during the autocratic phases of colonial rule had any experience of, or exposure to, modern democratic institutions, enjoyed political and civil rights common to citizens in a democracy, or benefited from access to civic education open to citizens in societies committed to universal education.

Even in countries like Senegal where Western democratic traditions dated back to more than a century before independence, the concept of democracy and degree of internalization held by the Western-educated French-speaking elites differed markedly from the great majority of the population who were not fluent in French.[25] For many years, the contents of the French term *démocratie* as used by Senegal's French-speaking elites referred to equality before the law, freedom of association, a free press, and the holding of fair and open elections.[26] During the 1980s and 1990s, Senegalese political opposition leaders placed great emphasis on *alternance* (the ousting of the regime in power through the ballot box) as the most significant component of *démocratie* in Senegal. Because one party held power since independence and allegedly used its control over the state apparatus to ensure victory in the elections, opposition leaders claimed that Senegal was not a true *démocratie*. The victory of Abdoulaye Wade and the opposition in the March 19, 2000 presidential elections was greeted with euphoria by opposition parties who previously had little faith in the ability of the regime in power to conduct elections fairly. The losers took some consolation in the fact that by accepting their electoral defeat, their country had improved its image as a democratic nation in the eyes of the world.

Over the years, the concept of democracy has spread beyond the Western-educated elites. Rural African definitions and concepts of democracy incorporate traditional African communitarian values, often affirming a taste for what Tocqueville called "local liberties."[27]

In Senegal, people at the grassroots level have coined new definitions for democracy in their own language that reflect indigenous communitarian values while incorporating notions of free elections, freedom of association, and other civil liberties. In Wolof, Senegal's *lingua franca* that is spoken or understood by 80 percent of the population, the concept of *demokaraasi* places the emphasis on such values as consensus in decision-making, solidarity, and mutual reciprocity in sharing resources and evenhandedness in treating everyone fairly.[28]

The term *demokaraasi* incorporates standards for evaluating the presence of democracy in electoral institutions. Thus, one stresses that voters in the same social networks—family, village, neighborhood, religious community—should agree on candidates and policies to be supported; support elected officials who provide material benefits; and insist upon evenhanded distribution of benefits by elected officials whether through public or private channels. *Demokaraasi* can also be extended to refer to participation on the part of members of the community in common works of benefit to the whole community and the willingness to equitably share the fruits of their efforts. As we shall see, the myriad of village development associations that have sprung up throughout Senegal in recent years clearly reflect a strong commitment to the values of *demokaraasi*.

The concept of *demokaraasi* is particularly prevalent in villages and local communities where people prefer to come to a consensus on the candidate or party of their choice in order to reinforce local solidarity. Elected officials are expected to share resources with their constituents and to distribute them fairly. These values can coexist with a high degree of social inequality and dependency. With the spread of greater social equality, however, Senegalese feel less compelled to follow the lead of their social superiors and more willing to initiate and accept competition, conflict, and factionalism. The communitarian values inherent in the Wolof notion of *demokaraasi* also work to promote reconciliation after conflict and reduce the likelihood of these conflicts ending in violence.

Applying the methodology used by Tocqueville to describe, analyze, and compare the dynamics of French and American democracy to Senegal will hopefully contribute to a deeper understanding of the forces fostering or blocking the promotion of freedom and democracy in Senegal and, by extension, to other parts of Africa.

CHAPTER TWO

Point of Departure

> If we could go right back to the elements of societies and examine the very first records of histories, I have no doubt that we should there find the first cause of their prejudices, habits, domineering passions and all that comes to be called the national character.[1]

Much of the current literature on the processes of democratization in Africa fails to incorporate an analysis of precolonial political institutions, cultures, and patterns of behavior and their impact on current efforts to build and consolidate democratic institutions. Studies of the transition to democracy in Africa usually begin with independence or colonial rule. Tocqueville knew better than to start his study of democracy in America with the American Revolution. He went back to the beginning of European colonization of North America. To understand the march toward democracy in France, he did not begin with the period immediately leading up to the French Revolution. He went back seven hundred years in French history.

Physical Configuration of Senegal

Senegal's physical configuration had a great influence in shaping its historical development. Its geographical location brought it into contact with the great medieval empires of western Sudan, North Africa, and Islamic civilization and, later, western Europe. The strong interest in and openness to foreign cultures and international politics, so characteristic of contemporary Senegal, thus is no new phenomenon.

Geographically, Senegal lies entirely in the zone between the Sahel and the Guinean forests. Senegal is part of the historical region of Senegambia, which took its name from the Senegal River in the North and the Gambia River further to the south.[2] Both the Senegal and Gambia Rivers originate in the Fouta Djallon Mountains in Guinea and flow into the Atlantic. The heartland of Senegal lies in the large plain between these two important river basins.

The location of its northern borders on the fringe of the desert put Senegal into contact with North Africa and Islamic civilizations more than a millennium ago. For several centuries, most of Senegal fell under the hegemony of the Ghana and Mali Empires[3] dominating the western Sudan and controlling the overland trade and trade routes between North Africa and West Africa. Its western borders on the Atlantic Ocean and proximity to Europe facilitated ties and trade with Europe dating back to the fifteenth century when the Portuguese became the first European power to discover Senegal.

Senegal's Atlantic coastal strip extends from Saint-Louis on the mouth of the Senegal River down to the Gambia. Before the arrival of the Europeans and the rise of the Atlantic slave trade, few Senegalese lived in the coastal areas. Most of Senegal's indigenous populations lived in the Senegal River Valley and in the heartland north of the Gambia River. The Senegal and Gambia Rivers linked Senegal's Atlantic littoral with the interior and became important trade arteries, especially after the expansion of the Atlantic slave trade in the seventeenth century.

Senegal's tropical climate with its short rainy season, long dry season, and light shallow soils gave birth to agrarian economies in the Senegalese heartland, built around millet, a drought-resistant cereal requiring relatively little rainfall and a short growing season. Free from the tsetse fly, northern Senegal could raise cattle, horses, donkeys and camels, as well as sheep and goats.

In precolonial times, the Senegal River Valley stood out as an important producer of millet for the region. Annual flooding of the Senegal River provided an additional crop and transformed the area within the flood recession plain close to the Senegal River into the most valuable and coveted piece of land in the Valley.[4] Proximity to the desert to the north and the Ferlo to the south led to fruitful economic exchanges between its sedentary and nomadic populations. Senegal's three major ethnic groups, the Wolof, Halpulaar, and Serer, all had deep historical roots in this region. The nomadic Moors in what is now Mauritania also had close ties with the populations in the Senegal River Valley.

Historically, southeastern Senegal and the Casamance region, cut off from the heartland by the Gambia River, have been marginal to the mainstream of Senegalese history.[5] The southwestern corner of Senegal, known as the Lower Casamance and occupied primarily by the Diola and other acephalous peoples had physical features quite distinct from those found in northern Senegal. There, abundant rainfall and high humidity, dense mangrove swamps and forests, and alluvial soils gave rise to a unique agrarian economy and civilization built around rice, which differed markedly from the agrarian economies north of the Gambia River.[6]

The abundance of land relative to the size of the population facilitated frequent migrations and led to the emergence of a different kind of land tenure system than that found in Europe.[7] Unlike feudal Europe where the peasantry was tied to land conquered and owned by the nobility, in Senegal, the peasantry had the freedom to come and go as they pleased and to found or settle in new villages. The first occupants of villages became the custodians and managers but not the owners of land in newly established villages. Their descendants allocated community land to villagers and strangers in exchange for modest symbolic and/or material rents. Families and entire villages moved regularly in response to internal disputes, war, or changing ecological conditions.

The abundance of land and flat terrain facilitated a high degree of mobility and migration in precolonial Senegal where populations moved freely. Mobility has been an important characteristic of the Senegambia for many centuries. Precolonial mobility generally involved a southern movement of peoples seeking better-watered lands and the movement of defeated competitors for royal power. With land now scarce, mobility and migrations have taken different forms. In contemporary Senegal, this can be seen in the rural exodus toward Senegal's larger cities and the growing Senegalese diaspora now living and working outside of Senegal's borders in other parts of Africa, western Europe, and North America.

Today, the physical configuration of contemporary Senegal bears little resemblance to that of the distant past when Senegal had virgin forests, plentiful land, more fertile soils, and higher levels of rainfall. The southward advance of the Sahara desert, declining rainfall, deforestation, and widespread soil erosion has undermined Senegal's environmental base and contributed to the acceleration of the rural exodus. Despite the movement to towns, cities, and abroad, many urbanized Senegalese still remain attached to their ancestral lands and historic roots. This phenomenon is reflected in the presence of a myriad of associations that maintain regular ties and provide financial and material support to the village of origin of their members.

Origins of Senegal's Peoples and Polities

The common stereotype of Africa in the West is one of a continent without history, populated by savage tribes and isolated from civilization until the coming of the Europeans.[8] In fact, Senegal and much of west Africa were detribalized, organized into self-governing communities, states, and empires that had regular contact with North Africa and the Muslim world many centuries before the coming of the Europeans.

The origins of Senegal's diverse African societies, like the European societies in western Europe, go back many centuries before the emergence of American society. Since African societies were essentially oral civilizations, which did not keep written records, their origins are more difficult to document. Nevertheless, a wealth of oral history and traditions coupled with materials written in Arabic by Muslim visitors to the region has permitted the reconstruction of Senegalese history within a broader west African context.

Senegal has six major ethnic groups, which make up nearly 95 percent of its population—Wolof, Halpulaar, Serer, Diola, Mandinka, and Soninke. All the main ethnic groups, with the exception of the Diola and a segment of the Serer, evolved into aristocratic societies divided into orders and castes and were eventually incorporated into monarchies. The very origins of Senegal's different ethnic groups remain steeped in legend and it is difficult to corroborate hypotheses. Based on his analysis of the similarities in the language and culture of ancient Egypt and those found in Senegal and other parts of west Africa, Cheikh Anta Diop, the late Senegalese historian and cultural nationalist, has argued that most of Senegal's peoples originated in the Nile River Valley before emigrating to West Africa.[9] The Halpulaar inhabitants of the Senegal River Valley trace their origins to the Middle East.[10] Oral traditions maintain that the movement of Berber tribes into southern Mauritania in the eleventh century stimulated the migration of Tukulor, Fulbe, Wolof, and Serer to the south. Other oral traditions maintain that Mandinka and Socé coming from the east during the heyday of the Ghana Empire originally inhabited the heartland between the Senegal and Gambia Rivers.

Despite the murkiness of the origins of Senegal's peoples, a lot is known about the political and social organization and evolution of Senegal's populations since the beginning of the second millennium. At that time, Tekrur, situated in the Middle Senegal River, was the most prominent of Senegal's precolonial African states and the home of several of Senegal's major ethnic groups.[11] Thanks to its strategic location Tekrur prospered from the trans-Saharan trade between North and West Africa, which involved gold and slaves moving north, and cowries, salt, and weapons coming south. During the eleventh century, War Jabi, Tekrur's Tukulor ruler, converted to Islam. The great majority of the Tukulor population followed their ruler's example and became the first major Senegalese ethnic group to embrace Islam en masse. Tekrur became an important center for Muslim clerics and missionaries settling throughout West Africa. During the thirteenth century, Tekrur lost its independence and became a vassal state of the Mali Empire in the east. The kingdom of Gajaaga located on the Upper Senegal River Valley was founded by Soninke from ancient Ghana.[12]

Further south, the Wolof, according to oral tradition, was unified under the leadership of the legendary Ndiadiane Ndiaye who was chosen by the Wolof of Djolof as their ruler (*bourba*).[13] Ndiaye then proceeded to conquer the Wolof states of Walo, Cayor, and Baol and integrate them into the Djolof Confederation/Empire toward the end of the thirteenth century. Some oral traditions maintain that the areas comprising the Wolof states were first occupied by Socé and Mandinka who came from the east and settled in the area from the lower Senegal River to the Gambia River.

The Serer migrated south from the Senegal River Valley into the area south of the Wolof kingdoms. They had no complex political institutions until they came into contact with Mandinka migrants moving north from the Gambia. The majority of the Serer were incorporated into what became Sine and Saloum, which were founded and ruled by members of a Mandinka royal dynasty.[14] With the decline of the Mali Empire, different Mandinka royal lineages set up small-scale kingdoms along the Gambia River with Gabou as the largest and most important in the region.[15]

Senegal's precolonial monarchies were influenced by the Sudanic state system instituted under the multiethnic Mali Empire. Tributary societies under the hegemony of the Mali Empire retained their rulers and political and cultural autonomy. The Keita lineage that ruled Mali made no effort to impose an official language, culture, or religion on the different peoples under their jurisdiction. Administration of tributary peoples was highly decentralized; local political entities were permitted to run their own affairs as long as they paid their taxes, supplied soldiers, and declared their allegiance to the ruler. Boundaries remained fluid, expanding and contracting according to the military strength of the ruler. Local political entities cherished their freedom and broke away when they could.

The decline of the Mali and Djolof Empires in the fifteenth century eventually led to the breakaway of what were formerly tributary states and the establishment of independent monarchies throughout the Senegambia. In the early part of the sixteenth century Koli Tengala Ba, a Fulbe adventurer, established his hegemony over Tekrur that came to be known as Fouta Toro and founded the Denianké dynasty that ruled until 1776. By the end of the sixteenth century, Walo, Cayor, Baol, Sine, and Saloum had managed to obtain their independence from Djolof hegemony and Gabou in the south had become independent of Mali.

The newly independent monarchies sought to assert greater authority over the regional and local *lamanats*, which had previously enjoyed a high degree of autonomy. The evolution toward centralized monarchies was accelerated by the development and expansion of the Atlantic slave trade that began in the sixteenth century and reached its peak in the late seventeenth and eighteenth centuries. During this period, monarchs built up the military caste of royal slaves and nobles (*ceddo*) attached to the court at the expense of the provincial nobility. Rulers used the military to raid neighboring territories to obtain slaves for the Atlantic slave trade. They sold the slaves in exchange for guns and imported luxury goods. With the increase in violence, rulers came to be more dependent upon the *ceddo* who collected taxes for the monarch, fought his wars, and pillaged the countryside.

Some of the monarchies began to undergo major transformations during the eighteenth century. The revolution led by Muslim clerics from the Halpulaar aristocracy (*torodo*) overthrew the Denianké royal dynasty in Fouta Toro in 1776 and established a new regime headed by a Muslim cleric chosen by the *Grands Electeurs* of Halpulaar society. Elsewhere, the Lebu, a subgroup of the Wolof, broke away from the hegemony of Cayor and established a mini-republic in the Cap Vert peninsula.[16] In the mid-nineteenth century, Muslim religious leaders like Ma Ba and Umar Tall attempted to establish theocratic states while resisting the beginning of the French conquest of Senegal.

Most analyses of Senegal's precolonial aristocratic monarchies cover the period between the breakup of the Djolof and Mali Empires and the French colonial conquest during the nineteenth century. One school of historical analysis depicts Senegal's precolonial monarchies as despotic polities built and maintained primarily through violence.[17] The nobility, their allies among the *jambur*, and the crown slave warriors dominated and exploited the commoners (*baadolos*). Despite differences in social status by birth, the nobility and crown slave warriors constituted a sort of predatory military class (*ceddo*) who plundered and pillaged their own people. This school of analysis attributes the reinforcement of violence and exploitation as largely the result of the European-initiated Atlantic slave trade and the integration of the region into the international capitalist system. Proceeds from the slave trade, taxes levied on local communities, and booty from pillaging constituted the main sources of revenue for the monarchies.

A second school of analysis, while also highly critical of the *ceddo* dominated monarchies, saw the intensification of violence and centraliza-tion in the monarchies as a rupture or aberration from the ideological and moral foundations underlying the formation of traditional African political systems.[18] This approach asserted that traditional African concepts of power led to the creation of larger political units in pluralistic confederations that unified different self-governing ethnic, religious, and territorial communi-ties under the banner of the ruler. Although giving their allegiance to the sovereign ruler, each of the constituent communities enjoyed a large degree of autonomy to manage its own affairs while their leaders participated in decision-making at the central level.

Rulers were selected from an electoral college consisting of representatives of the different orders, religious communities, and ethnic minorities, and could be deposed if they abused their power or violated traditional norms. This perspective depicted the precolonial polities as constitutional monar-chies bound by institutionalized checks and balances. If dissatisfied with the results, losers from the contending royal dynasties could choose to go into exile. When dissatisfied with the ruler, the kingmakers sometimes brought back an exiled prince from one of the eligible dynasties to replace the offending monarch. In the earlier days of the monarchy, the representative of the *jambur* notables was the second personage in the realm and had a decisive role in choosing the ruler. In time, the representative of the *ceddo* military slave caste eclipsed the representative of the *jambur* notables in influence

The ideal ruler maintained peace and justice in the land and defended the people from external attacks. Oral traditions state that the Wolof of Djolof chose Ndiadiane Ndiaye as their ruler because he was a wise man who knew how to bring peace by fairly and successfully arbitrating land disputes among warring parties. The ruler was also held responsible for the prosperity of the people. Drought, famine, and invasions of locusts indicated that the ruler was in disfavor with the local divinities and could be used as grounds to depose him.

Both schools agreed that centralizing rulers succeeded in replacing independent heads of different orders with men loyal to themselves. Thanks to the growing dependence of rulers on force, the head of the crown slave warriors often became the principal kingmaker. Disgruntled contenders from different royal dynasties who rejected the official choice made by the electoral college often used force in an attempt to impose themselves as ruler. Candidates to the throne attempted to increase their prestige and bolster their chances by amassing a large entourage of dependent clients whom they generously rewarded in exchange for their loyalty. Rulers often used their right to allocate unused royal land to reward their clients and to consolidate political alliances.

Clientelism became one of the most characteristic features of Wolof aristocratic monarchies. Patron–client relationships created asymmetrical social ties between rulers and nobles and their dependents from the lower orders and casted elements of society. The entourage of the ruler included *griots* that preserved the genealogies of royal dynasties, sang the praises of the ruler, and led his troops into battle with their drumming. Although griots were considered to be too impure to be buried in the ground along with other members of society, many became very wealthy, thanks to the generosity of their patrons. Rulers attached the most skilled artisans in the realms to their entourages and showered them with gifts. Crown slaves with exceptional military prowess also became part of the ruler's entourage, serving in the palace guard and holding high political and administrative positions. Though slaves by birth and socially inferior to freemen, the best warriors among the crown slaves could amass great power, wealth, and possess their own slaves. However, their slave status precluded them from ever aspiring to rule. Although Islam did not become the official royal cult in any of the Wolof monarchies, rulers sought to include Muslim clerics (marabouts) in their entourage and relied on their blessings and protective amulets. Some rulers received a modicum of Islamic education. Nobles from royal lineages who had aspirations to the crown attempted to build up large entourages to enhance their prestige and support their claims to power and develop alliances with other noble families through intermarriage.

Social State and Mores of Senegal's
Aristocratic Societies

Prior to the rise of the monarchies and the development of castes and orders, African societies in Senegal were primarily small-scale, agrarian societies organized into self-governing communities. The eldest descendants of the founder generally assumed the role of village chief while male family heads sat on the village council. People founded villages by clearing new land. Village chiefs allocated community lands to villagers and strangers. In time, with the expansion of the lineage, the eldest descendants of the original founder, or those who cleared large tracts of unoccupied land, assumed the title of *lamane* (Master of the Land) and allocated unused community lands over broader stretches of territory transcending the village. The land belonged to local divinities and could not be alienated. Lineages rather than individuals exercised usufruct rights over community lands. The *lamane* distributed land not as an individual but as the leader of the collectivity. Family heads allocated land within the family. Exploitation may have been individual but usufruct rights were collective. Before the consolidation of the monarchies, the *lamanes* stood at the top of the social hierarchy. The relative importance of the *lamanes* was derived from the size of the area under their management and the number of people in their community. From their ranks came most of the rulers in the early days of the monarchies.

Village economies were based on agriculture. Some groups specialized in fishing, hunting, and herding activities. Other groups became blacksmiths, woodworkers, and weavers. The blacksmiths were the most important group of artisans in the village economies because they made farming tools and weapons and were believed to possess mystical powers. Slaves did not constitute a major group in society before the rise of the monarchy.

The emergence and consolidation of castes and orders in Senegalese society coincided with the rise of monarchies. Social status became determined primarily by birth. However, unlike Europe where there was a high correlation among ascriptive social status, political power, and wealth, in Senegal, slaves could become important political personages while casted people could amass considerable wealth.

Tocqueville singled out the Anglo-Americans, in general, and the Puritans, in particular, who settled in New England as the prototype of America's new egalitarian society. In the Senegalese context, the Wolof who constitute the largest ethnic group in Senegal, and whose language has become the country's lingua franca, can serve as a prototype of precolonial Senegal's aristocratic societies.[19] Other ethnic groups incorporated into Senegal's precolonial monarchies like the Halpulaar, Mandinka, Soninke, and to a lesser extent, Serer had similar social hierarchies based on caste and orders.[20]

Orders and castes among the Wolof dated back to the twelfth century. Wolof society consisted of freemen, slaves, and casted people (*neeno*).[21] The *neeno* were divided into three main caste divisions, which in turn were subdivided into more specialized groups in the following hierarchical order:

(1) *Jef-lekk* who worked in specialized manual trades—blacksmiths, jewelers, and metalworkers; leatherworkers, woodcutters and woodworkers, and weavers. Blacksmiths, jewelers and metalworkers had the highest social status among the artisans and made weapons for the army, farm implements, and jewelry.

(2) *Sab-lekk* (griots) who were made up of several sub-groups such as genealogists, praise singers, singers, and musicians. Masters of language, they exercised great influence through the power of their words. As genealogists, they could legitimize or delegitimize one's claim to royal or noble status. Their praises could enhance the prestige of their patrons while their taunts could diminish the reputation of rivals of their patron.

(3) *Noole*, who served in the royal court as courtesans, court jesters, and spokespersons for the crown. Although at the very bottom of the caste system, the noole played an important role. Like the fool in *King Lear*,

they could say unpleasant but true things to the ruler and get away without being punished. The rulers used them to communicate with visitors and the public and to serve as the messenger of bad news.

Intermarriage between persons of caste and non-casted persons was forbidden. Caste members usually married those within their own ranks. They usually lived apart from the non-casted population. Slaves often lived in their own villages or in wards within villages.

Wolof society could be divided into two basic orders, those who were free and those who were slaves.

Wolof society had five distinct orders:

(1) The nobility (*garmi*) who consisted of actual and potential holders of royal power and their relatives. Multiple royal lineages existed in all of the Wolof monarchies.

(2) The notables (*jambur*) who had an intermediary status between the nobility and the common people. The *jambur* usually came from the families of *lamanes* and village chiefs. Although not eligible to become rulers, they often held important political and administrative positions, especially at the regional and local level.

(3) The commoners (*baadolo*) who were farmers and herders. Although freemen, they were regarded as subjects with little power.

(4) The slaves of the crown (*jaami bur*) who served the ruler. Crown slaves provided the bulk of the ruler's army and constituted the palace guard. The best fighters among them often attained high political office and amassed great wealth. Although by birth of lower social status than the commoners, their leaders had higher political and economic status. Non-military slaves worked for their royal masters in productive activities, for example, agriculture and mining. Unlike the *ceddo*, they worked hard and were not treated very well.

(5) Domestic slaves (*jaami baadolo*). Fewer in number than the crown slaves, the domestic slaves did not engage in military activities but worked as farmers, herders, and servants. In time, they became part of the extended family of their masters. Unlike chattel slaves in the West, domestic slaves with the permission of their masters, could marry, be granted land which they could farm for themselves, and form their own villages.

Another category of slaves were the trade slaves captured in wars and raids on neighboring territories. In most cases, trade slaves were sold within a few months of capture and constituted the most important export commodity of Senegal's precolonial monarchies.

Tocqueville observed that each caste in aristocratic societies had its own opinions, duties, mores, and lifestyles.[22] Lower castes and orders were expected to be humble, subservient, and loyal vis-à-vis their social superiors; the nobility was expected to be courageous in war and generous to those of lower status under their control. Despite differences in status determined by birth, different elements in aristocratic society nevertheless developed strong affective ties to each other. The noble owned the land on which his serfs worked. Serfs had to work for their noble masters and did not have the option to leave. The nobility owned the land and clearly had the power to exploit the serfs who worked their land. Relationships between serf and lord, originally based on involuntary ties, were reinforced by ideologies and mores which induced serfs to accept their lot, the biological and moral superiority of the nobility, and to take solace in basking in the reflected glory of their masters.

While mores and lifestyles of royalty and the nobility in Senegal's precolonial monarchies resembled those of their peers in French and European aristocratic societies, social structures differed markedly because political power in Senegal was dissociated from ownership of property. Political power derived from military might and one's status at birth, not from ownership of land. Unlike the French and European peasantry, the *baadolo*, Senegal's free peasant farmers, were never serfs tied to land owned by the nobility. Although often victims of raids and pillaging that cost them part of their crops and loss of their animals, the *baadolo* remained freemen who usually maintained permanent usufruct rights to the land allocated to their families by the *lamanes* and village chiefs.

The correlation among political power, social status, and wealth also differed considerably in France and Europe and in Senegal. In France, those at the bottom of the social hierarchy like the serfs were also those who were the poorest and most powerless elements in society. In Senegalese aristocratic society, griots and skilled artisans were often wealthier than the peasant commoners while crown slaves could amass great wealth and power. Local and regional notables had less wealth and political influence than the leading crown slave warriors in the ruler's entourage. Senegal's precolonial aristocratic societies had no equivalent social group that resembled the nascent French bourgeoisie, which clearly had more status, wealth, and political influence than serfs and artisans. Nor did Senegal's free peasants have the same hunger for property rights as emancipated serfs and small landholders did in France in the years before the French Revolution. Although Senegal did not have a European-style commercial bourgeoisie, it did have groups of Dioula, Halpulaar, Luso-African, and *métis* traders, most of whom were engaged as middlemen in the slave trade or merchants dealing in kola nuts, salt, and other traditional African commodities.[23]

Aristocratic mores in Senegal did not permit the nobility to exploit its social inferiors. Nobles aimed their exploitation primarily at the *baadolo*, who were also freemen like the nobles. Tradition dictated that nobles be generous to those of inferior status, especially to casted people in their personal entourage. Nobles often felt obliged to accede to the requests of their clientage. Extravagant generosity was considered to be a great virtue and stinginess a shameful vice among the Senegalese nobility.

Relationships between the *baadolo* and the nobility also differed sharply from those between serfs and nobles in French and European society.

Senegal's commoners did not farm the land owned by the nobles nor were they forced to work for them. Often victims of their raids and pillaging, the commoners had little affection for the *ceddo* nobility or for monarchs who did not protect them. The *baadolo* had closer affective ties with, and loyalty to, their village chiefs and *lamanes* to whom they paid modest annual rents than to the monarch and his provincial and local representatives who levied taxes.

The Wolof placed values such as honesty, wisdom, justice, integrity, honor, modesty, moderation, self-mastery, self-respect, civility, hospitality, generosity, loyalty, social responsibility, justice, and peace at the center of their morality system.[24] The ideal *jambur* or notable who incarnated these values was wise, irreproachable in his behavior, and loved peace, justice, and the good. Members of the Councils of Elders used to bear the title of *jambur*.

In contemporary Senegalese society, many of the mores associated with Senegal's aristocratic societies before the colonial conquest are still alive and orienting political and social relationships despite the destruction of the monarchies by the French more than a century ago. Those in power sometimes exhibit old *ceddo* modes of behavior, for example: amoral behavior, indifference to the public good, ostentatious consumption and gift-giving, and living beyond one's means. Other Senegalese espouse traditional *jambur* values and patterns of behavior and tend to be pious, modest, frugal, self-sacrificing, hardworking, and community-oriented.

Thus far, our analysis of the social state and mores of Senegal's precolonial aristocratic societies and monarchies has omitted the place and influence of Islam and Muslim religious leaders in the old political order destroyed by colonial contact. The ascendancy of Islam and its impact on the evolution of aristocratic society merits a section of its own.

Islam and Senegal's Aristocratic Societies

Unlike Christianity in western Europe, Islam in Senegal's aristocratic societies was, with rare exceptions, not the official or majority religion. Muslim clerics or marabouts could be divided into two distinct categories, those who became fully integrated into the ruler's court, performing both religious and political functions and those who while performing religious functions maintained their distance and a certain degree of autonomy.[25]

In the eleventh century, Tekrur became the first monarchy in Senegal to fully embrace Islam. A new era of non-Muslim rule began when Koli Ba conquered Tekrur and imposed an animist Fulbe dynasty that lasted until Tukulor marabouts led a successful rebellion against Denianké rule in 1776, the same year that America declared its independence. The Tukulor marabouts themselves constituted an aristocratic order (*torodo*). After defeating the Denianké royal dynasty and the *ceddo* nobility, they became the dominant group in Fouta Toro and established a theocratic regime headed by an Almamy chosen by a restricted electorate consisting of the heads of the dominant maraboutic families. Unlike Muslim clerics elsewhere in Senegal, the *torodo* were at the top of the political and social hierarchies and had great economic power, thanks to their control over the fertile flood recession lands of the Senegal River. Although the *torodo* accepted the institution of domestic slavery, they opposed the Atlantic slave trade, the selling of commoners into slavery, and the failure to liberate slaves who had converted to Islam. While the *torodo* of Fouta Toro opposed slavery and the *ceddo* nobility, they retained a highly rigid and hierarchical social structure.

In the Wolof monarchies, Islam never became a royal cult despite the fact the rulers welcomed Muslim religious leaders and integrated them into their court and society. In the fifteenth and sixteenth centuries, some rulers and part of the nobility adopted Islam while the rest of the people remained pagan. In the seventeenth century, the aristocracy began to move away from Islam while more commoners began to practice the new religion.

During the height of the slave trade in the seventeenth and eighteenth centuries, some Muslim leaders supported the cause of the commoners and adopted positions critical of the *ceddo* aristocracy.[26] They thus attacked the selling of Muslims into slavery as a violation of Islamic law. Late-seventeenth century rebellions in Walo, Cayor, Djolof, and Fouta Toro by Muslim clerics failed to overthrow the aristocratic order and establish theocratic states.

The marabouts had a social status equivalent to that of the *jambur*. Many came from outside Wolof society and were members of other ethnic groups—primarily Mandinka from the Gambia region, Moors from Mauritania, and Halpulaar from the Senegal River Valley. They often served as advisors to the ruler and provided amulets and blessings for protection. Some marabouts opposed the *ceddo* because of their drinking and pagan practices. In time, they became the main defenders of the *baadolo* commoners who were the main victims of *ceddo* exactions and pillaging. When the French began their conquest of the Senegalese interior in the mid-nineteenth century, the marabouts sided with the rulers against the French. When the monarchies collapsed after a series of crushing military defeats, the marabouts picked up the pieces and established their moral and spiritual authority over the Wolof populations who converted to Islam.

Islam exercised less influence in the Serer monarchies of Sine and Saloum.[27] Though the Serer welcomed the marabouts to their realm, they steadfastly clung to their traditional African religions. When Ma Ba launched a jihad to establish a purer form of Islam in the areas north of the Gambia River, the Serer resisted and killed him. Their opposition to Ma Ba and the Wolof monarchies looking to maraboutic support in their struggle with the French led the Serer to seek alliances with the French. The influence of the precolonial rulers lasted longer in the Serer monarchies that signed treaties with the French. At the beginning of French rule, most Serer had not been converted to Islam. However, a small number of Serer, living in communities near the Atlantic coast having long ties with European traders had converted to Christianity. Léopold Sédar Senghor, Senegal's first president, was a direct descendant of these Serer Christians.

During the second half of the nineteenth century, alliances between the French, who were to establish their rule over most of Senegal by the end of the century, and the aristocracies in place successfully resisted efforts by Ma Ba and Umar Tall, to establish theocratic states. Although Tall recruited large numbers of men from his native Fouta Toro to fight for him, his main conquests and successes took place further east.[28]

The peoples least touched by Islam were the Diola, Balante, Bassaris, and other acephalous societies living on the periphery of the precolonial aristocratic monarchies. The Diola, in particular, resisted all efforts at Islamisation and efforts by Mandinka rulers in the Casamance and Gambia regions to subjugate them.

Western Influences on Senegal's Precolonial Societies

Despite four centuries of contact between Europe and Senegal, from the time the first Portuguese arrived on Senegal's shores in 1445 and the French colonial conquest in the second half of the nineteenth century, Western influences had surprisingly little impact on the peoples of Senegal. While trade with Europeans and the Atlantic slave trade had contributed to the centralization of the aristocratic monarchies, the strengthening of the *ceddo*, and an increase in the number of slaves in Senegalese society, contact with Europe brought no major changes in political and social institutions and mores.

The Portuguese left a legacy of a handful of trading settlements on the Atlantic coast with Portuguese names—Rufisque, Portudal, and Joal and a tiny population of Christians with Portuguese names like da Costa and da Souza who were descendants of Portuguese traders and African women. The Dutch who occupied a tiny barren and unoccupied isle off the Cap Vert peninsula called Gorée left no trace after being pushed out by the French in 1667. The English who took over French settlements in Senegal for short periods of time during the periodic wars between France and England also left few marks on the peoples living within the present boundaries of Senegal.[29]

Of all the European powers, the French, who eventually became the colonial masters of Senegal, had the most influence on Senegal's precolonial societies for three reasons. First, they had more contact with Senegalese than other Europeans. Second, they established permanent settlements on Senegalese territory on Gorée Island and at Saint-Louis on the mouth of the Senegal River. Third, and most important of all, these settlements were incorporated into a political entity known as the colony of French Senegal that was considered to be an extension of metropolitan France.

While the French had the most contact with Senegal's precolonial societies, their influence on Senegalese institutions and culture, nevertheless, remained extremely limited because French Senegal was inhabited primarily by the French and Afro-Europeans who were the descendants of unions between French men and African women. Saint-Louis was the administrative capital. As trade with the interior increased, Saint-Louis grew and attracted an increasingly larger number of Africans. Before the French

Revolution, the majority of the African residents of Saint-Louis were slaves or bondsmen. The Afro-Europeans adopted French culture and Christianity and had the same political rights as Frenchmen. These rights were, of course, limited. When the French proclaimed the abolition of slavery during the height of the French Revolution, this edict was never applied to Senegal. Following the French revolution of 1848, the Republic once again abolished slavery in all of France's overseas colonies.

Although some Senegalese today proudly point to a long tradition of enjoying political rights and Western-style democratic institutions dating back to the French Revolution, in fact, these rights did not begin to be exercised by indigenous Senegalese before the establishment of the Third Republic in the 1870s. Even then, the French, who since the French Revolution had proclaimed the gospel of equality and the need to abolish all privileges and inequalities based on birth, resisted applying the gospel, even to the tiny number of black African Senegalese who lived in the old French colony of Senegal.

Between the French Revolution and the establishment of French sovereignty over all of Senegal, none of the existing aristocratic monarchies and acephalous societies attempted to adopt new European political institutions. During this period, the debate going on in Senegalese societies was over whether one should maintain traditional aristocratic institutions or embrace Islamic theocratic institutions.

As we see in chapter 3, the French accelerated the march toward greater equality in Senegal not by introducing new political institutions and laws but by using their military might to crush, domesticate, and level Senegal's formerly independent aristocratic polities.

CHAPTER THREE

The Old Order and Colonialism

They used the debris of the old order for building up the new.[1]

Although not an epic event like the French Revolution, the French colonial conquest brought about revolutionary changes in Senegal's aristocratic societies. Political entities like Fouta Toro, Baol, Djolof, Cayor, Sine, Saloum, Gajaaga, and Gabou, which had functioned continuously for several centuries as sovereign polities in dealing with Europe, disappeared. (See Map 3.1.)

The imposition of French sovereignty leveled Senegal's aristocratic societies by stripping their old rulers of their royal prerogatives, disarming the *ceddo* nobility, and formally abolishing slavery. Colonialism also promoted "equality" by according the same low political status to kings, nobles, commoners, casted groups, and slaves.

Conflicting Opinions of Colonialism

In his analysis of the French Revolution, Tocqueville presented opposing interpretations and evaluations of this seminal event.[2] Some asserted that the French Revolution not only destroyed the old order but also undermined all order and led to anarchy. Admirers of the French Revolution saw it as leading to the rejuvenation of France and the creation of a new human race based on noble ideals—liberty, fraternity, and equality. Tocqueville himself had a more complex interpretation, which did not see the Revolution in black and white terms. Tocqueville asked probing questions about the nature and impact of the Revolution: What was its true significance, its real nature, its permanent effects? What exactly did it destroy and what did it create?

A myriad of opinions also exists concerning the impact of colonialism on indigenous societies. The official ideologies of the French colonizers emphasized the civilizing mission of their enterprise.[3] They saw themselves as bringing the benefits of French civilization to the backward peoples of Africa by liberating Africans from the tyranny of feudal aristocracies.

28

Map 3.1 Precolonial states of Senegal and distribution of major ethnic groups, ca. 1850

Ethnic Groups

Wolof
Fulbe
Serer
Lebu
Tukulor
Bambara
Sarakollé
Mandinka
Diola

The egalitarian ideals of the French Revolution justified the abolition of slavery and assimilationist policies that transferred French democratic institutions and educational systems to the colonies. In practice, outside of Senegal, assimilationist policies in France's Black African colonies were rarely implemented. By the mid-1880s when Europe began the scramble for Africa, Jules Ferry, the French prime minister, was justifying French imperialism on the ground that superior races had the right to rule over inferior races. By 1900, French colonial ideologies and practices had begun to stress the innate cultural differences between Frenchmen and Africans and display a greater willingness to accept traditional authority as long as it was subservient to the French.

More recently, modernization theorists have stressed the benefits of colonialism as reflected by the introduction of Western education, rational state bureaucracies, and democratic political institutions.[4] Their interpretation often regards colonialism as a "School for Democracy" because certain democratic institutions were introduced under colonial rule.[5]

Karl Marx and his ideological successors regarded colonialism as an objectively progressive force because it destroyed the old feudal structures, which were deemed more backward than capitalist structures.[6] At the same time, they portrayed colonized peoples primarily as victims of Western imperialism. Twentieth century Marxists associated with dependency theories have stressed the exploitative aspects of colonialism and have argued that colonialism kept colonial peoples backward while creating patterns of political, economic, and cultural dependence that have been perpetuated after independence.[7]

The conflicting opinions about the impact of colonialism contained in both the modernization and Marxian dependency schools of thought described African societies as influenced almost exclusively by external forces beyond their control introduced by the West. Often lacking knowledge of African history and precolonial societies, they rarely succeeded in providing accurate answers to questions raised by Tocqueville concerning the extent to which the old order was destroyed and a new order created.

Until the end of World War II, French colonial rule in Senegal bore a curious resemblance to familiar precolonial patterns of administration and governance. In many regions, the French relied heavily upon the old *ceddo* aristocracy to administer the countryside and collect taxes. The French built their new order organized by the French colonial state on the ruins of the old.

Colonial Conquest and
the Shattering of the Old Order

The military conquest of the interior began in 1854 when Louis Faidherbe, a French military officer, was appointed governor of Senegal. At that time, the French only controlled Saint-Louis, the island of Gorée, and some fortified posts along the Senegal River. Faidherbe believed that through conquest he could impose more enlightened and humane institutions on the subjugated regions.[8] Faidherbe and the French also had more mundane reasons for launching the conquest; they no longer wanted to pay customs and other levies to African rulers for trading in the interior.

Faidherbe began by defeating the Moors of Trarza who controlled the gum trade along the Senegal River, annexing Walo in 1855, driving Umar Tall, the Islamic reformer, from Fouta Toro in 1857, and establishing French hegemony over the Senegal River region. In 1859, he established a military base in Dakar and quickly annexed the entire Cap Vert peninsula, which had been under the control of the Lebu Republic. Over the next four decades, France extended its sovereignty over all of Senegal's hinterland. By 1900, France had firmly established its rule over the territory encompassed by the republic of Senegal today.

The second half of the nineteenth century was a period of tremendous upheaval in Senegal. Although the French military conquest gave the *coup de grace* to the old aristocratic monarchies, their power and authority had already been weakened by the end of the Atlantic slave trade and periodic revolts by the marabouts.[9]

The extent and speed of collapse of the old order in Senegal's precolonial monarchies depended largely upon the extent of their collaboration with the French and success in defending their regimes against radical Muslim reformers.

The Tukulor *torodo* aristocratic families in Fouta Toro, who sided with the French against Umar Tall and Abdou Bocar Kane, retained much of their authority in their home territories.[10] After the French eliminated the Almamate in 1891, the heads of pro-French aristocratic families were often named as canton chiefs and given considerable leeway to administer their districts with a minimum of supervision by the French colonial administration. French rule did little to alter Fouta Toro's rigid caste structure and traditional mores. After the subjugation of Fouta Toro, its aristocratic families saw the value of French education as crucial for consolidating their privileged position within the French colonial administrative system.

The Serer kingdom of Sine too underwent few political and social changes as a result of the French conquest compared to the rest of the country.[11] In 1867, the *Bour* of Sine defeated and killed Ma Ba in battle and aligned his kingdom with the French in successfully resisting forced Islamization. Despite French efforts to undermine the authority of the *Bour*, Sine retained the right to name its own ruler.

The *Bours* of Sine and Saloum and Mandinka rulers in the Casamance signed protectorates and treaties with the French formally recognizing French sovereignty while allowing them to retain their titles. In return, the French promised that they would honor the traditional rules for selecting the ruler and make no changes in the habits, customs, and institutions of the country. But in the end, the French reneged on their promises by intervening to depose rulers deemed inimical to French interests and to insure that rulers to their liking would succeed the old rulers when they died. In time, the French stripped the old monarchs of their titles and divided their realm into smaller administrative units that no longer coincided with precolonial boundaries.

Military conquest led to the rapid collapse of the old order in the Wolof monarchies of Cayor, Djolof, and Baol, which had fought hard to stop the French takeover of their country.[12] After Lat Dior's defeat and death in 1886, the French broke up Cayor and Baol into cantons. The violent death of its rulers and the decimation of the *ceddo* nobility in its battles with the French led to a major political crisis and leveling of Wolof society, followed by the rapid rise of maraboutic authority that filled the leadership vacuum left by the destruction of the old ruling class and *ceddo* nobility.

The French military conquest and destruction of the old order had a major impact on the *ceddo* crown slaves. Most turned to the land for a living. Some remained in the entourages of former rulers and aristocrats who had been appointed as officials in the colonial territorial administration and served them as bodyguards and tax collectors. French colonial officials often looked the other way when canton chiefs and their *ceddo* entourage intimidated the populations in the areas under their jurisdiction into making contributions to their coffers. Such practices further undermined the legitimacy of the old aristocrats with the people.

The imposition of French rule contributed to the leveling of Senegal's African societies by undermining without destroying the institution of domestic slavery. Although the French Constitution abolished slavery in 1848, the prohibition against owning slaves applied only to French citizens and to the areas under French sovereignty. Throughout most of the nineteenth century, the French took few steps to end slavery on the grounds that the law abolishing slavery did not apply to territories having protectorate status.[13]

Victor Schoelcher's speech in the French Senate denouncing the continued existence of slavery in areas under French sovereignty led to a change in policy and a crackdown on slave trading in Senegal. The immediate result was the massive migration of slave-owning Fulbe out of the areas under direct French administration. French concern for promoting peanut production also led them not to emancipate slaves in the 1880s and 1890s, in zones where most of the peanuts were produced by slaves. In 1903, the governor-general of French West Africa instructed the courts not to recognize slavery at all and in 1905, a decree forbade making anyone a slave or trading in slaves. Despite the new rules, domestic slaves continued to exist, not so much as the property of others, but as a low-status group within a hierarchical social system.[14] At the same time, many former slaves now had the freedom to move. Some slaves originating in areas outside Senegal returned to their homes while others founded new villages.

Despite the destruction of the old political order, common social patterns continued. Noble families continued to support retainers and show largesse to their social inferiors, albeit on a much more limited scale. Griots still sung the praises of nobles who felt obliged to shower them with franc notes;

former slaves continued to show great deference to their old masters and performed many chores for them; individuals of caste origins still could not marry outside their group. With fewer patrons to support them, many casted artisans moved to the new towns where they practiced their old skills or learned new ones in the manual trades.

The *baadolos* or commoners saw some improvement in their situation under French rule. Though still coerced into paying taxes, they were no longer subject to periodic raids and violence by the ceddo.

The *jambour* rural notables, for example, village chiefs and former *lamanes,* who generally had larger landholdings and the right to allocate unused community land also benefited from the development of the cash-crop economy in Senegal. In sparsely populated areas of the peanut basin, the rural notables began to lend land to seasonal migrant farmers coming from Guinea, Mali, and the Gambia in exchange for three or four days of labor service in their fields.

The construction of the Dakar–Saint-Louis and Dakar–Niger railroads, the preference given to peanut production, and the decision by the *métropole* to make Dakar the administrative and economic capital of French West Africa shifted the main locus of the colonial economy from the Senegal River region to the peanut basin, which encompassed the former monarchies of Djolof, Cayor, Baol, Sine, and Saloum.[15] The decline of the Senegal River region led to a large outflow of its populations into the new towns and other areas of Senegal. At the same time, the development of the peanut economy led to large migrations of population into the less sparsely populated areas of the peanut basin. The main beneficiaries of this movement were the maraboutic authorities.

Religion and the New Colonial
Order: The Spread of Islam

In Senegal, Islam had been gaining ground steadily before the colonial conquest, largely because it had sided with the commoners against the *ceddo* nobility. Marabouts who kept their distance from the old rulers gained in popularity. During the second half of the nineteenth century, Islam also became closely associated with the resistance to French rule.

Religious considerations were not a major factor in France's opposition to Islamic reformers. The French were not crusaders, seeking to bring Christianity to Africa. They fought Islamic reformers because they constituted a major obstacle to the expansion of French control over the interior.[16] While the French defeated the militant Islamic reformers and warriors fighting to set up their own theocratic states, they were not able to— nor did they seek to—undermine the spiritual authority of their successors.

Influential marabouts had to be watched closely to insure that they would not incite their followers to revolt against French rule. Ahmadou Bamba, the founder of the Mouride Brotherhood, was twice sent into exile by the French because they feared his growing popularity among the Wolof masses disoriented by the collapse of the old monarchies. After Bamba formally issued a statement asking his followers to accept French authority and collaborated with them in recruiting troops for the French army, the French left him alone and gave him a free hand to build up his following.

The French Third Republic that completed the conquest and subjugation of Senegal was thoroughly secular in orientation. The French thus made no efforts to convert Senegal's Muslims to Christianity. On the contrary, French policy deliberately kept Christian missionaries out of predominantly Muslim areas. As a result, Christian missionaries and schools were concentrated largely within the confines of the old French colony of Senegal and in areas and among groups like the Serer and the Diola that had fiercely resisted Islamization prior to the colonial conquest.

By destroying the power of the *ceddo* forces who had been the main opponents of maraboutic authority, the French military conquest and subjugation of Senegal helped facilitate the spread of Islam. After the consolidation of French rule, some French colonial officials saw the rapid expansion of Islam, especially among the Wolof, as a nationalist reaction against French domination and a form of passive resistance. Others saw the spread of Islam as filling a political and spiritual void left by the collapse of the old aristocratic political order. The denigrating of traditional African religions as pagan and inferior to the religions of the book by both the French and the marabouts also moved many practitioners of traditional religions to formally embrace Islam.

After several decades of colonial rule, the marabouts became one of the main pillars of the French colonial system while distancing themselves from direct association with the French colonial administration.[17] The marabouts preached the doctrine of rendering unto Ceasar what was Caesar's, which kept the French happy and led to a system of mutual accommodation.

Maraboutic authority became expressed largely through the creation and consolidation of Sufi Brotherhoods whose influence was felt throughout Senegal and not just among the Wolof. The Sufi Brotherhoods offered an alternative to both European influences and the violent *jihads* led by Islamic reformers.

Until the mid-nineteenth century, the most important Sufi order in Senegal had been the Qadiri Brotherhood whose origins date back to the eleventh century. Founded in the eighteenth century in Morocco, the Tijani Brotherhood came to Senegal via Moorish marabouts and later through Umar Tall, who received the title of Grand Khalife of West Africa while on pilgrimage to Mecca in 1825.[18] The Tijani movement spread rapidly after the colonial conquest, particularly among the Halpulaar and Wolof populations.

Much of the Halpulaar population of Fouta Toro identified with the Tijani branch founded by Umar Tall. Two predominantly Wolof branches of the Tijani Brotherhood emerged among the Wolof. Malick Sy, who enjoyed very good relations with the French, founded the Tivaouane branch and attracted Wolofs from Cayor and the new towns. Malick Sy emphasized the importance of Islamic education and drew followers among the Senegalese urban elite and rural notables. He preached the need to create new social relationships based on equality and mutual aid among believers and created several rural villages to implement these ideals. The son of a marabout and blacksmith, Abdoulaye Niasse, the founder of the Kaolack-based branch of the Tijani Brotherhood was one of the rare Senegalese religious leaders of low-caste origins. Like Malick Sy, he stressed the importance of Islamic education. His followers were concentrated in Saloum and Rip, which had once been under the control of Ma Ba.

Ahmadou Bamba, the founder of the Mouride Brotherhood, was a contemporary of Malick Sy and Abdoulaye Niasse. Until he began his own Brotherhood in 1902, he had been affiliated with the Qadiri Brotherhood.[19] The Mourides attracted the former partisans of Lat Dior and the remnants of the old Wolof order that had resisted the French.

Although disdaining European culture and keeping his distance from the French, Bamba eventually allayed their fears by accepting French authority and encouraging his followers to grow peanuts, the mainstay of the French colonial economy. His followers consisted largely of former slaves, warriors, artisans, and some nobles. Bamba's lieutenants established an efficient movement that organized thousands of followers to move to the new pioneer zones to the east where they grew millet as their food crop and peanuts for the market. The French encouraged this movement by allocating thousands of hectares of land to the Mouride leaders for distribution to their followers.

The Mouride Brotherhood encompassed a complex set of relationships that reflected a blend of old and new patterns of social behavior. On the one hand, there was a leveling of social status based on birth. Followers who submitted to maraboutic authority had the same relationship to their marabout, whether noble, commoner, or slave. The work ethic of the Mourides also contradicted the disdain that the old aristocracy had toward manual labor. Artisans became respected members of Mouride communities and the Mourides attracted a disproportionate share of artisans because of their positive attitudes toward manual labor.

Maraboutic families also often maintained certain practices identified with the aristocracy. For example, they attempted to enhance their social status through intermarriage with the daughters of the old nobility. The rites of submission, which tied the follower to the marabout, stressed the inequality of the relationship between marabout and talibé and resembled patterns of submission and subservience between ruler and subjects prevalent under the old Wolof monarchies. *Talibés* bowed and lowered their voices and their eyes in addressing their marabouts. On the other hand, submission was entirely voluntary. If dissatisfied, the *talibé* had the option to break his ties with his marabout.

Although their relative importance within Senegal had diminished, the influence of Qadiri Brotherhoods remained strong in the Casamance among the Mandinka and Islamized elements of the Diola, in Cap Vert, parts of the Fleuve, and near Tivaouane where Cheikh Bou Kounta, a Moor from a distinguished line of marabouts, founded a new branch of the order in 1885. Kounta stressed the importance of work and working for the marabout and tended to attract large numbers of former slaves.

The trauma touched off by the turbulent times of the French conquest also led to the development of a new Sufi order among the Lebu of Cap Vert, whose founder, an illiterate miracle worker, proclaimed himself to be a reincarnation of the prophet Mohammed. Unlike the learned founders of other Senegalese Sufi Brotherhoods, Limamou Laye had only a rudimentary Islamic education and could not read and write in Arabic. He denounced the quest for material wealth and championed African culture and the Wolof language.

The spread of Islam was a response to the colonial conquest and a continuation of the Islamization of the country that had begun earlier. It led to important transformations in Senegalese society and created new forms of ruler–ruled relations. Senegalese forms of Sufism demonstrated a clear mistrust of the state and temporal authority especially when that authority was exercised by foreigners and non-Muslims. The Sufi Brotherhoods in Senegal also strove to maintain their autonomy vis-à-vis the colonial administration and their temporal authority over their followers in the rural areas under their control.

The French Colonial State

Administrative Centralization and Colonial Autocracy

Although established by force, the imposition of French central administration over the populations of the interior during the early years of colonial rule had some parallels with how it was done in France under the French monarchy where aristocrats retained their rank and titles while all effective authority was gradually withdrawn from them.[20]

After the colonial conquest, some former rulers were allowed to retain their titles and were used by the French to maintain order and collect taxes. At the same time, the French made it clear that they were in charge and the sole legitimate authority in the colony. Those who remained in the administration became underlings in the colonial bureaucracy. The French *commandant*, the functional equivalent of the *intendant* under the monarchy and the prefect in postrevolutionary France, became the incarnation of French central authority in the field in Senegal.

Faidherbe, the brilliant military governor of Senegal, laid the foundations for Senegal's territorial administration in the 1850s.[21] He used Algeria, where he had served, as his model. This meant establishing a system in which French colonial officials would be assigned to specific regions and charged with supervising the local chiefs. He divided the colony into *cercles* and entrusted their administration to African chiefs who were recruited from the old aristocracy known for their submissiveness and willingness to comply with French orders. The title of *commandant*, given to the French military officer assigned to supervise the local chiefs, reflected the military and authoritarian character of the territorial administration.

Before 1900, French colonial officials in the field were hostile to the precolonial African aristocracy and their institutions. Colonial officials in most instances showed little respect to former rulers in their personal dealings. They embraced assimilationist colonial doctrines that declared the objective of French colonial policy to transfer French institutions and culture to the colonies to replace the allegedly more backward cultures they had encountered. However, assimilation was expensive and implied large investments in French education for African children and a dense French presence to directly oversee the colonized population. In the end, assimilation was simply not practical.

After 1900, most French colonial officials adopted the doctrine of association that stressed the major differences between French institutions and civilizations and those in the overseas African territories and the difficulty of transforming Africans into Frenchmen. While this approach fostered greater interest in learning more about local customs and languages and working through the old precolonial aristocracy, it justified a policy of paternal authoritarianism to preserve French domination. Jules Harmand, a major theoretician of the doctrine of Association argued that the conqueror by nature and function was an aristocrat and that his government by duty and necessity had to be despotic.[22]

French colonial officials espousing the doctrine of association opposed efforts to transfer French political institutions to the colonies. They preferred to work with submissive African aristocrats and rural notables whom they could manipulate rather than with Western-educated Senegalese citizens fully aware of their rights. As late as the 1920s, officials like Albert Sarraut, the French Colonial Minister, warned that the rapid spread of Western education and the establishment of universal suffrage would lead to anarchy and the end of France's civilizing mission.

The French made the rules and gave the orders. The Senegalese "auxiliary elites" in the colonial bureaucracy who served as clerks, bookkeepers, translators, and customs officials were expected to carry them out. French officials rarely delegated tasks to their subordinates. The autocratic bureaucratic style contributed to the development of a submissive culture among Senegalese in the lower echelons of the colonial bureaucracy. Rare was the person who dared to take responsibility for carrying out any task not being directly ordered by his superior or to present his own views without being solicited.

The heavy-handedness of the French colonial administration also discouraged local initiatives in the countryside since the only person authorized to make important decisions was the French *commandant*. Although the French set up *Conseils des Notables* at the *cercle* level, the local French commandant presided over the meetings and set the agenda. The *Conseils* had no deliberative or financial powers and accepted the plans and programs presented by the French commandant with little comment.

Operating on the same principles as the centralized administration in France described by Tocqueville, the French colonial bureaucracy was wary of local institutions and associations not under its direct control. As in France under the monarchy, the administration adopted a paternalistic stance that assumed that the rural populations were not capable of managing their own affairs.

Although autocratic and highly centralized, the French colonial bureau- cracy did not have sufficient human, financial and logistical resources to directly regulate the daily affairs of Senegalese in the interior. As late as 1926, Senegal's colonial service had only 63 administrators and civil servants, which amounted to one French official for every 20,000 Africans.[23]

Spending most of their time in district headquarters rather than on tour in the countryside, French colonial officials relied heavily on the canton chiefs to serve as their intermediaries with the local populations and regarded local authorities primarily as instruments for communicating and implementing policies dictated by the colonial state.

Rural Senegalese experienced an autocratic colonial administration that rarely solicited their views or that of their leaders. The people in the interior generally regarded the canton chiefs, who were often recruited from old aristocratic families or heads of the former crown slaves, as direct agents of the French rather than as their own leaders and spokesmen. For Senegalese subjects, the French colonial state was the manifestation of an alien occupying power.

For leadership, Africans in the countryside turned to maraboutic authority and village chiefs. Unlike the canton chiefs who were salaried officials and an integral part of the colonial administration, village chiefs did not have to be literate in French. Although their appointments had to be approved by the colonial administration, their authority derived from their inherited status as direct descendants of the founder of the village. The rural populations looked to the village chief to allocate communal land and to arbitrate disputes within the village.[24] Rural Senegalese generally avoided administrative channels or court structures set up by the colonizer, preferring to settle disputes among themselves without recourse to external intervention.

Colonial Boundaries: Setting the Stage for the Nation-State

In precolonial Senegambia, boundaries of African kingdoms were fluid and depended upon the ability of rulers to effectively control their populations. Rulers had a core area over which they exercised direct control. Plentiful land and low population densities raised the costs of controlling populations outside the core area and facilitated the option to exit on the part of those not satisfied with the existing ruler.[25]

The colonial boundaries of Senegal were artifacts created by French, British, and Portuguese colonizers who carved up and divided Senegambia into colonies and administrative districts after the 1884–1885 Berlin Congress laid down the rules for dividing the African continent. Since the exercise of state sovereignty depended upon effective occupation of a particular territory, the colonizer needed to set boundaries to demarcate the territory it would control and to keep other European powers from making claims on that territory. Territorial boundaries defining the limits of the colony resulted from the outcome of negotiations between colonial powers vying for control over territory in a given region.

The territorial boundaries of modern Senegal changed frequently during the period of colonial conquest and pacification. In 1850, the French colony of Senegal consisted of a few coastal settlements, parts of the Delta of the Senegal River, and tracts of land in the Casamance obtained by treaties with local chiefs. By the end of the century the territorial limits had been set, although it took somewhat longer before France could control all the populations under its sovereignty.[26]

In Senegal, colonial borders did not prevent the movement of populations across borders. For example, many Halpulaar who had deserted their traditional lands during the eighteenth and nineteenth century because of Moorish control over the north bank of the Senegal River returned to their lands during the twentieth century. In the Lower Casamance, the Floup, a branch of the Diola, who lived on both sides of the Senegal–Portuguese Guinea border maintained their traditional political and religious structures and showed little respect for borders in performing religious ceremonies and other community rites. The organization of most of France's West African colonies within the French West Africa Federation also facilitated movement across borders. Senegal's booming peanut economy attracted thousands of seasonal migrant workers coming from the neighboring colonies of French Soudan and Guinea.[27]

European mapmakers drew lines that arbitrarily divided existing political and ethnic communities and often disrupted previous patterns of interaction and symbiosis between nomadic and sedentary populations. Despite their artificiality, the territorial boundaries drawn up by the colonizer eventually became the boundaries of independent nation-states.

Citizens and Subjects

Tocqueville identified the dogma of the sovereignty of the people as the main principle underlying American democracy. The French colonizer evoked quite a different principle as the basis of colonial rule—that of the sovereignty of the metropolitan state and its right to rule over subjected peoples. This was made possible, not through a negotiated social contract between ruler and ruled but through brute military force.

The policies and behavior of the metropolitan colonial state contradicted French republican beliefs in equality and the rights of man. The French got around this by maintaining that the legal distinctions between citizens and subjects had nothing to do with racial criteria. Africans were subjects because their cultural inferiority and lack of French education, language skills, and knowledge of French institutions precluded them from exercising the rights and obligations incumbent on French citizens.

By a quirk of history, a tiny minority of Senegalese freemen and their descendants born in areas considered to be French soil acquired French citizenship, thanks to the assimilationist policies of the *Ancien Régime* that regarded French Senegal as an integral part of France. Following the French Revolution of 1848, Senegalese having lived five years on French territory automatically acquired French nationality and citizenship rights.[28] The areas considered to be French soil coincided with what came to be known as the Four Communes of Dakar, Gorée, Rufisque, and Saint-Louis.

Citizenship brought higher status and privileges to Africans who possessed it. Citizens were exempted from forced labor *corvées* and the *indigénat*, a system of summary justice that gave French administrators the power to fine and imprison African subjects without a hearing. When conscripted in the army, Senegalese citizens served in the same units as the French and enjoyed higher pay and better facilities than conscripted African subjects. Senegalese citizens also had the right to vote, run for office, and form political associations. French cultural assimilationist policies proclaimed the equality of man and superiority of French and European culture. Senegalese who mastered the French language, acquired French culture, and adopted French institutions were considered to be the equal of Frenchmen.

Ironically, the status of citizen for most Senegalese citizens derived not from meeting cultural standards set by the French, but by birth.[29] If born in the Four Communes, one could be a citizen without speaking, reading, or writing French. Theoretically, African subjects under French rule could become naturalized French citizens if they met a rigorous set of criteria stressing loyalty and service to France, a certain level of French education, and mastery of the French language. In practice, naturalization was discouraged and very few Senegalese born outside the Four Communes became citizens.

The legal existence of Senegalese citizens coupled with assimilationist policies providing French education and introducing representative political institutions modeled on those found in the French *métropole* laid the foundations for the creation of a Senegalese Western-educated elite steeped in French culture and French political traditions.[30] Enjoying their privileged position within the French colonial system, the Senegalese citizen-politicians developed a great affinity for the French model of democracy and a strong interest in metropolitan French politics.

Western-educated Senegalese citizens had a dual image of France. On the one hand, they identified with France's 1789 revolutionary equalitarian political traditions and championing of human rights. On the other hand, they often opposed what they considered to be an autocratic and undemocratic French colonial administration and colonial officials who did not regard Senegalese citizens as their equals.

The first Senegalese ethnic groups to acquire French citizenship were the Wolof and Tukulor in Saint-Louis and the Lebu on the Cap Vert peninsula.

Demographic growth accounted for the increase in the number of citizens of African origin in the Four Communes. In Faidherbe's day, the total population of the Four Communes was less than 19,000. By the end of the first decade of the twentieth century, the population of the Four Communes had more than tripled. The rapid expansion of the African electorate enabled Blaise Diagne, a Senegalese Black African, to be elected deputy in 1914, thus ending the domination of Senegalese politics by the French and *métis* elites who then constituted one-fifth of the total electorate.

Blaise Diagne, Senegal's first Black African deputy (1914–1932), actively recruited African troops to fight for France in World War I in return for guarantees that France would preserve the rights of the citizens of the Four Communes. The differential treatment between Senegalese citizens and subjects in the French army exacerbated tensions between these two groups. Subjects in the interior resented the higher pay, better living conditions, greater prospects for promotion to officers, and higher pensions enjoyed by the citizens. As in the past, slaves or former slaves constituted the bulk of the recruits from the subject population living outside the Four Communes. The participation of so many slaves and ex-slaves in the war effort led to their greater unwillingness to submit to traditional authorities when they returned home.

During the inter-war period (1920–1939), prominent citizen–politicians often defended the interests and rights of the subjects in their dealings with the colonial administration and canton chiefs largely recruited from the old *ceddo* aristocracy. Some like Lamine Guèye, French West Africa's first Black African lawyer, demanded that the rights of citizenship also be extended to Senegal's subjects. The Popular Front government (1936–1937) in France headed by Leon Blum, introduced colonial reforms making it easier for African subjects to become naturalized, restricted the use of forced labor, and permitted African subjects with elementary school degrees to join trade unions, thus reducing the legal barriers to subjects' exercising the political rights enjoyed by the citizens.[31]

On the eve of World War II, less than 5 percent of the total population had acquired the status and rights of citizens. Although the Western-educated elites among them aspired to political equality with the French, their quest for political equality did not mean their giving up values and lifestyles rooted in precolonial societies. Few Senegalese citizens sought to become Black Frenchmen. The other 95 percent of the population who were subjects had little knowledge of French democratic traditions. Except for the canton chiefs and notables aligned with the colonial administration, most subjects were more concerned about getting the colonial state off their backs.

World War II and Decolonization: Democratization and Independence

The autocratic system of French colonial administration continued right up to the end of World War II. It became even more repressive during the war when officials loyal to the Vichy regime in France governed Senegal and the rest of French West Africa from July 1940 until November 1942.[32] The Vichy regime abolished all of Senegal's democratic institutions and trade unions, squashed the rights of the Senegalese citizens, and stepped up the use of forced labor.

The war against Nazi Germany led to the discrediting of racist theories trumpeting white supremacy and made it impossible for France to continue colonial policies that denied political rights and liberties to the populations living in its overseas colonies. The domination of early postwar French governments by General Charles de Gaulle, who had launched the French resistance movement from Black Africa and left-wing political parties, led to extensive colonial reforms.[33]

The October 28, 1946 constitution of the Fourth French Republic radically changed the nature of relationships between France and its overseas colonies. The preamble to the constitution proclaimed that the newly established French Union, consisting of France and its overseas territories, would be founded upon the equality of rights and duties without distinction of race or religion. It also asserted that France would lead the overseas populations under its charge to a state of freedom in which they would administer themselves and conduct their affairs democratically.

Egalitarian and democratic principles became applicable to the former subjects who were granted the rights of citizens. Women were allowed to vote for the first time in France and this right was also extended to African women in the colonies. The Senegalese electorate steadily climbed from 46,000 in 1946 to over one million in 1956 after French lawmakers transformed the principle of universal suffrage into reality.[34]

Differences in the legal status of citizens and subjects disappeared. Laws were passed abolishing the hated system of native justice and forced labor. The legal gap between Frenchmen and Africans also narrowed. Laws were passed giving Senegalese civil servants holding the same rank as French colonial officials the same salaries and advantages. Labor laws passed in France granted African workers many of the rights and benefits enjoyed by Frenchmen in France and enabled them to join forces with metropolitan trade unions.

For Tocqueville equality of conditions, which included the right to choose one's rulers and to participate in the exercise of authority, was necessary but not sufficient to ensure democracy. There could be no democracy without political liberty. To ensure political liberty, one needed rules that permitted and guaranteed freedom of association and freedom of the press. Before the war, these had been enjoyed only by the tiny minority of citizens. During the postwar period, freedom of association extended to the former subjects led to a tremendous outburst of organizational energy that affected all sectors of Senegalese society.

The influence of the Senegalese Muslim Brotherhoods continued to grow in both the towns and countryside. Trade union membership boomed with Dakar's postwar spurt of economic growth and industrialization and the increase in the number of Senegalese working for the French colonial government as teachers, veterinarians, and health workers. Ethnic and regional associations flourished. Casted artisans also began to establish their own associations. Senegalese-run rural cooperatives emerged in the countryside that operated independently of the French colonial administration. Senegalese traders and merchants began to organize their own associations to defend their interests. The sharp increase in the number of Senegalese students attending high school in Senegal and universities in France led to the creation of highly politicized student associations.

The explosion of associational life coupled with the expansion of the electorate led to changes in the organization and structure of Senegal's political parties and the nature of election campaigns. Before World War II, political parties were less structured and revolved primarily around the personalities of those leading the party. These parties appealed to a much smaller electorate of citizens concentrated largely in the Four Communes.

With the expansion of the electorate, political parties now had to campaign all over the colony.[35] Lamine Guèye's Socialist Party, which had been dominated by the citizens of the Four Communes, had difficulty adjusting to the new situation and holding on to its status as majority party that it enjoyed during the early postwar period. It was eventually outmaneuvered and overcome by the _Bloc Démocratique Sénégalais_ (BDS) founded by Léopold Sédar Senghor and Mamadou Dia in 1948, which became Senegal's majority party in 1951–1952. The BDS appealed to the former subjects in the interior and won the support of some of the leading maraboutic authorities from the Tijani and Mouride Brotherhoods. The BDS also attracted the backing of many of the new voluntary associations that had sprung up after the war, for example, trade unions, transporter, trader and artisan associations, ethnic and regionally based groups, and urban neighborhood associations. The ascendancy of the BDS was due to its ability to make alliances with a wide range of locally based groups and to respect their autonomy.

The political reforms weakened the authority of French colonial administrators, who no longer wielded the same degree of power that they exercised before the war. The power and influence of the canton chiefs also declined drastically. The colonial administration still intervened in succession struggles within the major Tijani and Mouride Brotherhoods and continued to grant special benefits to prominent marabouts involved in peanut production. The French increasingly turned to the marabouts as a counterweight to the more radical urban elements in Senegalese politics highly critical of the French and demanding self-government and independence.

Although democratic electoral competition and the exercise of political liberties by Senegal's population hit their peak in the 1950s, the French still retained full control over Senegal's executive branch and administration with few democratic checks on their activities until the June 1956 _Loi-Cadre_. The same _Loi-Cadre_ law that established universal suffrage also marked a major step toward self-government by endorsing the establishment of popularly elected territorial executive councils, increasing the legislative powers of the territorial assemblies and reducing the prerogatives of the Governor-General and territorial Governors.

The triumph of the *Bloc Populaire Sénégalais* (BPS) in the March 1957 territorial elections and the creation of Senegal's first territorial government led by Mamadou Dia marked the end of a period of unbridled pluralism and the beginning of a movement toward unity and independence. The newly constituted BPS consisted of the old BDS plus a group of young radical intellectuals educated in France. In early 1958, Lamine Guèye's Socialists fused with the BPS to form the *Union Progressise Sénégalaise* (UPS).

The September 28, 1958 referendum gave France's overseas territories three options: integration into the French Republic; immediate independence; or self-government within the framework of a French Commonwealth dominated by France. After a bitter debate, the UPS chose the third option, thus precipitating the walkout of many of the younger radical intellectuals who wanted immediate independence. Under heavy pressure from the French and the marabouts, who feared that radical elements within the party would seek to undermine their authority, Léopold Sédar Senghor, the party leader, and his reluctant lieutenant Mamadou Dia convinced the UPS to opt for self-government in the referendum. Less than two years later, Senegal became an independent and sovereign state.

Slightly more than a century had passed between the time Faidherbe began his conquest of the Senegalese interior to independence. The colonial conquest had led to a leveling of precolonial Senegalese society by destroying the power of the old *ceddo* aristocracy and the institution of slavery and incorporating all of Senegal's population under French rule. Though touted as a school for democracy, colonial rule destroyed local liberties and did little to promote democratic values and self-government outside the Four Communes. Its modus vivendi with Sufi Brotherhoods insured both peace and the rapid spread of Islam. In according political and civil rights to only a tiny segment of the Senegalese population born in the Four Communes, colonial rule created a major but not unbridgeable gap between Western-educated Senegalese citizens and the rest of the population. While the post–World War II colonial reforms permitted Senegal's former populations to participate in democratic electoral politics and to organize new forms of political, social, economic, and cultural associations, these reforms coupled with greater access to Western education did not lead to the disappearance of precolonial mores and customs or the wide-spread adoption of Western-style individualism.

One of the major legacies of French colonialism was a highly centralized state and the concentration of power in the hands of the executive. Denied access to and having little control over the executive branch for so long, Senegalese politicians were highly critical of the French colonial state and administration and sought to reduce its prerogatives. However, Senegal's new rulers succumbed to the temptations of power and sought to establish a state apparatus that was even more centralized than the state structures they had inherited, often at the expense of their people's political liberties.

CHAPTER FOUR

Centralization and Democratic Despotism

Their imagination conceives a government which is unitary, protective, and all powerful, but elected by the people.[1]

The evolution of the postcolonial African states had many parallels with what happened in France during and after the French Revolution. While old rulers were replaced, centralization was intensified. The opposition was squashed and often accused of collaborating with foreign powers. Liberties proclaimed in constitutions affirming the rights of man were snuffed out or shunted aside.

Tocqueville attributed the success of American democracy to the fact that political liberties were already firmly entrenched in the American colonies when independence came and provided checks on democratic despotism. In France, the lack of experience of the people in exercising political liberties before the Revolution made it easier for Robespierre and his successors to establish despotic governments that ruled in the name of popular sovereignty and restricted the rights granted during the early phases of the French Revolution.

Shortly after obtaining self-government, the leaders of Senegal's dominant party established a de facto one-party state in which the ruling party governed the country for forty years. Attachment to democratic traditions dating back to the establishment of the Four Communes, traditional mistrust of those in power, and the influence of the Sufi Brotherhoods placed limits on authoritarian rule in Senegal. As a result, what Tocqueville referred to as democratic despotism was much milder in Senegal than in most African countries.

The Party-State, Centralization, and Democratic Despotism

In Africa, the establishment of one-party states was justified on the grounds that mass political parties represented the will of the people.[2] Parties that won elections by huge majorities often claimed to incarnate the popular will.

Kwame Nkrumah proclaimed that his Convention People's Party (CPP) was Ghana and that Ghana was the CPP.

For African mass parties that came to power just before independence, democracy implied centralization.[3] Once in power, strong political parties used the apparatus of the state to reinforce their hold on power and to restrict or eliminate opposition parties that they claimed undermined national unity. The party's claim to be the supreme embodiment of the popular will justified its claim to control the machinery of the state and to use it to strengthen the power of the new regime against its enemies. As a result, boundaries between party and state structures became blurred. The party-state became the norm in regimes headed by a dominant single party regardless of ideology or attitudes toward the former colonizer and the West.[4]

To decrease opposition participation, the UPS-dominated government changed the electoral law to create a single national constituency for the March 1959 national legislative elections that allocated all eighty seats in the National Assembly to the party winning the majority of votes. Its commanding victory enabled the UPS to consolidate its hold over government and move toward a one-party state. Between 1960 and 1966, one saw the progressive elimination of opposition parties in Senegal through co-optation, nonrecognition, and repression.

Movement toward centralization accelerated after Mamadou Dia's elimination from the political scene following the resolution of the political crisis of December 17, 1962 in Senghor's favor. As the undisputed leader of his party and head of government, Senghor promoted the centralization of state and party structures. He began by revising the 1960 Constitution in March 1963, to eliminate the office of prime minister and concentrate virtually all executive power in the hands of the president. Senghor argued that the 1960 Constitution had created confusion by dividing executive power between the president and the prime minister. Senghor organized a national referendum in March 1963 for the people to approve the new Constitution and legitimize the establishment of a strong presidential regime. Having won the plebiscite by an overwhelming majority, Senghor moved quickly to expand the powers of central government and the central organs of the UPS and to eliminate the political opposition.

The December 1, 1963 national presidential and legislative elections were the last national elections to be contested by opposition parties until 1978.[5] In 1964, the government outlawed the *Front National Sénégalais* (FNS), a coalition of supporters of Mamadou Dia, Cheikh Anta Diop, *Parti du Regroupement Africain-Sénégal (PRA-Sénégal)*, and the illegal *Parti Africain de l'Indépendance* (PAI). The legal opposition totally disappeared in June 1966 when PRA-Sénégal rallied to the UPS and its leaders rewarded with ministerial posts and places in the UPS Bureau.

Despite the elimination of opposition parties, Senghor insisted that Senegal was not a single-party regime but a "unified-party regime" that united all parties under the banner of the UPS. While accepting the principle of opposition parties, he insisted that they would have to serve as a loyal opposition. In justifying the banning or nonrecognition of radical nationalist and left-wing parties, Senghor often accused them of being subversive and directed from abroad by foreign powers.

As secretary-general of the UPS, Senghor strengthened the party executive at the expense of the party's regional unions. Senghor saw the UPS regional party unions as potential threats to his authority.[6] Senghor reduced the powers of the intermediary regional party institutions that served as checks on abuses of authority by the central party executive, which he dominated. While retaining the form, Senghor undermined the power of the Regional Party Unions by transforming them into a loose group of departmental party units headed by men loyal to him and with little influence or control over local party units. Centralization of party institutions led to the atrophy of local and regional party institutions just as Tocqueville had warned that centralization of state power would lead to the atrophy of local government. With electoral victory assured because of the absence of a legal political opposition, the party had no competition and, therefore, little motivation to mobilize its troops. Deprived of control over local government resources, local politicians had few incentives to work hard to build a local political base. Advancement in the party became increasingly dependent upon having Senghor's support and blessings.

In time, the party became less dynamic and relevant as the state became the main center of power. Although Senghor derived his political legitimacy as national leader of the party that won every national election,[7] he maintained his influence and power through his control over the state, which became the predominant institution in the Senegalese party-state system. The National Assembly, which previously had articulated and defended local and regional interests, became a docile institution, rarely taking the initiative to draw up legislation and automatically rubber-stamping bills introduced by the government with little debate.

Senghor's near absolute control over the party also meant that there was little debate within the party over doctrines and policies. Senghor imposed African Socialism and *Négritude* as the official doctrine of the party and the state. In UPS National Party Congresses, UPS militants dutifully listened to their secretary-general's long scholarly party reports and unanimously approved party resolutions drafted by the party executive while acclaiming the great qualities of their leader.

During the late 1960s, Senegal experienced an increase in overt resistance to the party-state's efforts to control all aspects of national life. Student and trade union unrest in the spring of 1968 led to a university strike followed by a general strike led by the leadership of the *Union National des Travailleurs Sénégalais* (UNTS). The Senghor government responded by closing down Dakar University, arresting student and trade union leaders, and using the President's special powers to declare a state of emergency. The government called upon the army and police to put down disturbances in Dakar's popular neighborhoods and the attempt to march on the presidential palace. Unrest in the countryside took the form of passive resistance when farmers decided to reduce the amount of peanuts produced for the market.

Responsive to growing hostility to the heavy-handed rule of the party-state, Senghor acquiesced to demands for greater Africanization and the transfer of more power and responsibility to the younger generation of technocrats in his government. In 1970, the constitution was revised to restore the office of the prime minister.

With the political opposition reduced to impotency, Senghor moved cautiously to liberalize the regime and to restore a semblance of multiparty democracy. The 1970s were marked by steady political liberalization that saw the reappearance of legal political parties, an independent though muted press, and trade unions not affiliated with the UPS. In 1974, Senghor released Mamadou Dia from prison and gave his blessings to Abdoulaye Wade, former head of the law faculty at Dakar University, to start a new political party, the *Parti Démocratique Sénégalais* (PDS) that was quickly recognized by the government. In 1975, he pardoned the leader of the outlawed PAI and permitted him to return to Senegal.

Constitutional revisions in 1976 provided for a three-party system in which each of the three competing parties would be identified with one of the ideological labels designated in the constitution. By this time, the UPS had changed its name to the *Parti Socialiste* (PS) as a prelude to joining the Socialist International and chose to represent the social democratic label.[8]

One of the ironies of the constitutional revisions was that the new constitution was more restrictive than the 1963 constitution, which guaranteed the right to organize political parties and placed no restrictions on their number. Mamadou Dia and Cheikh Anta Diop were not permitted to organize their own political parties. Nor were the spokesmen for diverse Marxist–Leninist currents permitted to do so. The return to a limited multi-party system was thus carefully controlled and regulated to insure that Senghor and his ruling party would continue to hold power.

Political liberalization in the 1970s was accompanied by a steady increase in the power of the state bureaucracy that corresponded with the growing economic role of the state and the expansion of parastatal enterprises. The BDS/BPS/UPS, which had been called the party of the schoolteachers in the 1950s, evolved steadily into the party of the bureaucrats with the expansion of the state. Senghor's technocratic vision of the state and his commitment to Jacobin centralizing traditions nurtured the emergence of a new class of technocrats and civil servants led by Abdou Diouf, his prime minister and protégé.[9] By the mid-1970s, civil servants controlled most of the ministries and had become major forces within the ruling party. In 1975, twenty-two of the twenty-four ministers were former state agents while only two came from the liberal professions.[10]

The Colonial Bureaucratic Legacy:
Centralization and Tutelage

Tocqueville maintained that centralization was an important bridge linking the Old Regime to the French Revolution. Centralization in Senegal also constituted a bridge between the colonial and the postcolonial regimes. With independence, the Senegalese replaced the French colonial government with a Senegalese one while keeping and expanding the highly centralized and hierarchical territorial administration inherited from the old colonial order.

Tocqueville distinguished between governmental centralization and administrative centralization.[11] Governmental centralization referred to the concentration of great social powers in a single hand or in a single place and the power and the force to compel obedience to them. Administrative centralization referred to the concentration in the same hand or in the same place of a power to regulate the ordinary affairs of the society, to dictate, and to direct the everyday details of its existence. While unchecked government centralization could lead to tyranny and the suppression of public liberties, administrative centralization led to the reduction of local liberties, the emasculation of local government institutions, and the stifling of local initiative and entrepreneurship. Administrative centralization perpetuated a paternalistic style of governance that kept the people dependent upon the state.

The leaders of Senegal's ruling party Africanized rather than dismantled bureaucratic structures inherited from the colonial regime. The 1960 administrative reform redrawing the old colonial administrative boundaries brought the state's territorial administration into closer contact with the rural populations. While replacing all the command posts with Senegalese right after independence, the government kept the old colonial titles of *gouverneur*, *commandant*, and *chef* for the officials who headed the new regions, *cercles*, and *arrondissements*. In April 1964, Senghor changed the nomenclature of the *commandants de cercle* to *préfets* and the *chefs d'arrondissement* to *sous-préfets* to mark a symbolic break between the old colonial and the new postcolonial administration. However, despite the name changes, the state expanded the powers of the *préfet* and *sous-préfet* and their tutelage over local government and the populations under their jurisdiction.

The New Administrative Elite

The new Senegalese administrative elite consisted of members of the corps of *administrateurs civils* who held the top positions in the state bureaucracy. Until independence, nearly all Africans who worked in higher levels of the French colonial civil service served as African auxiliary doctors, pharmacists, and veterinarians and had no connection to administration.[12] At the time of independence, Senegal had only a handful of *administrateurs civils* who had been trained in France. Shortly after independence, Senegal established the *École Nationale de l'Administration du Sénégal* (ENAS), modeled on the elite French *École Nationale d'Administration* (ENA), to train the civil servants who would be running the state apparatus in the future.

Like their French colonial predecessors, Senegalese *administrateurs civils* saw themselves as dedicated and honest public servants who represented the state and the country's national interest.[13] Trained primarily as generalists, the elite corps of state officials studied public law and some economics. Like their French counterparts, they believed in the efficacy of the legal-rational-Weberian-bureaucratic model based on hierarchy and a clearly defined chain of command and the unitary nation-state as the highest form of political organization. As the administrative elite, they were used to giving orders to those below them in the hierarchy and to carrying out the will of the president who "gave instructions" to the state bureaucracy through decrees and executive orders.

The elite corps of *administrateurs civils* came to dominate the higher echelons of the state bureaucracy. In addition to holding a near monopoly of the command posts in the territorial administration from governor down to the *sous-préfet*, they often ran the central offices of the technical ministries and regional development agencies based in Dakar. They also sat on the boards of many state and parastatal agencies and managed state enterprises such as the national railways, national lottery, and Cap Vert Public Housing Authority. Many rose to become ministers. President Abdou Diouf himself came from the ranks of the corps of *administrateurs civils*.

Tutelage over Local Government and Economic Development

After becoming head of the government in 1963, Senghor gave more power to the Ministry of the Interior and the territorial administration to supervise and manage municipal financial affairs. In the name of efficiency and depoliticization of communal affairs, state tutelage stripped the elected mayors of most of their prerogatives, limited their ability to provide jobs and other services to their clients and constituents as state officials, elaborated and approved municipal budgets, and controlled expenditures.[14] The state's direct intervention in communal affairs took much of the luster from the office of mayor, rendered municipal institutions dependent upon the largesse of the state for infrastructure investments and other services, and dampened the development of local civic pride and responsibility.

Senghor also delayed the setting up of rural communities and local rural councils, which had been alluded to in the early 1960s when Dia was heading the government.[15] The 1972 administrative reform laid the foundation for creating rural communities and councils throughout the country in the 1970s and early 1980s. In theory, rural councils were granted broad powers to regulate local markets, fairs, cattle walks, and residential zoning patterns; allocate uncultivated land and revise existing land tenure regimes in areas under their jurisdiction; and finance local development projects. However, in practice, the rural councils had even less autonomy than the urban municipal councils. In most instances, the *sous-préfets*, charged with supervising the state's *tutelle* over the rural councils effectively managed these institutions and imposed their will on locally elected officials.[16] The power of tutelage gave the central government the right to veto the deliberations of the rural councils, to suspend or dissolve individual Rural Councils, and to remove their presidents and other officers. The *sous-préfêts* elaborated the budgets, controlled expenditures, and presided over meetings of the Rural Councils. State tutelage was particularly heavy in financial matters and justified in official manuals related to local government finances in the name of the need for national unity and uniformity of rules.

The Senegalese state maintained the command functions of the old colonial territorial administration while adding an important new dimension—that of development administration. Although African Socialism was the official ideology of the postcolonial regime, Development became its main focus. The government counted on state officials and foreign experts to lead the way in planning and implementing development policies, especially in rural areas. In Senegal as throughout most of Francophone Africa, Western educated elites looked to the state to promote economic development in the newly independent African countries and to government service as their main career path.[17]

In the decade between 1966 and 1975, the state intensified its development activities in the countryside and its control over the country's economic life. With the financial support and technical assistance of the international donor community, the state created a vast network of rural credit, regional rural development, and agricultural extension agencies that covered the entire country and introduced new technologies designed to raise production and productivity.[18]

Centralization gave the government the power to draft national development plans and programs based on national rather than local priorities. Regional development programs initiated by the state and financed by external donors often failed to take into consideration local ecological and climatic conditions, production systems, and land tenure regimes. The imposition of the same uniform rules and technical packages and the neglect of local knowledge in areas with diverse and complex environmental and sociological conditions took its toll throughout the country. Programs designed to increase peanut production in the peanut basin by using animal traction, chemical fertilizers, and pesticides provoked the disappearance of the fallows, deforestation, and declining use of organic fertilizer and contributed to a sharp decline in productivity. In the Senegal River Valley, large-scale irrigation projects failed to produce enough rice to reduce Senegal's dependency on imported rice, disrupted traditional production systems, and aggravated Senegal's foreign debt.

The vocabulary of development administration employed by state officials reflected a top-down paternalistic approach. The role of state administrative and development officials was to supervise/train (*encadrer*), mobilize (*mobiliser*), and animate/inspire (*animer*) the masses to participate in the development programs of the government. Prefects affectionately referred to the people in their districts as "*mes administrés.*" State officials rather than the local populations generally initiated local development projects. State administrative officials also dominated the local and regional development committees in their districts and took the lead in elaborating local and regional development plans.

Government decrees and regulations stifled the initiative of Senegalese peasant farmers and African traders. State control over the cooperative movement and pressure on farmers to adopt new technologies and to buy fertilizer, seeds, insecticides, fungicides, and other inputs on credit soon led to increased indebtedness without any marked gains in productivity. By the end of the 1960s, farmers in the peanut basin were increasingly referring to themselves as "*captifs*/slaves" of the state administrative structures. Drought conditions exacerbated their situation and intensified what came to be known as the "*malaise paysanne*."

The monopoly granted by the state to rural cooperatives to market peanuts in 1966 prevented African traders from buying peanuts directly from the producers and meant that African transporters and other intermediaries involved in the peanut trade had to rely upon government contracts to continue their activities in the countryside. State decrees determined the price to be paid for peanuts and millet, the cost of inputs, and when and where producers could sell their peanut crops, which had to be marketed exclusively through government-sponsored cooperatives and sold to state agencies for transformation into peanut oil and export products.

In regions outside the peanut basin, Regional Development Agencies (RDAs) organized farmers into producers' groups under their supervision to grow rice, cotton, tomatoes, and other cash crops according to programs elaborated in Dakar by planners and technicians with little knowledge of the sociology and production systems of the regions they sought to develop. In the Sylvo-Pastoral Zone, the state attempted unsuccessfully to organize, settle, and transform traditional herders into commercial meat producers.

Tocqueville's comments concerning the perpetuation of dependency resulting from the efforts of the *ancien régime* in France to foster agricultural development from the top down, more than two centuries ago, could be applied with minor changes to what was happening in Senegal during the first decades of independence.[19] Ironically, Senegalese extension agents and administrators working in the interior often complained about the peasantry's "*mentalité d'assisté*" or dependency complex, which was greatest precisely in the areas where the state was most active.

Bureaucratic Versus Democratic Administration

Bureaucratic administration revolves around a monocratic structure where all civil servants are integrated into a hierarchy culminating in a single center of authority.[20] Democratic administration, on the other hand, is characterized by polycentricity, a belief that everyone is qualified to participate in the conduct of public affairs, participation and consideration of the community and its elected representatives in making important decisions affecting them, restriction of the power to command to a necessary minimum, and a shift in status and behavior of the civil servant from master to public servant.[21]

Although an advocate of national planning and a strong state, Mamadou Dia, while head of government, nevertheless, attempted to create administrative structures that were less hierarchical and more responsive to local communities than the bureaucratic structures inherited from the French colonial state. As part of the 1960 administrative reforms, Dia created multidisciplinary teams organized in *Centres d'Expansion Rurales* (CERs) at the *arrondissement* level. The CER teams consisted of agricultural extension agents, veterinarians, foresters, home economics specialists, and land-use planners working together to directly serve the local populations in their district. In principle, the technician designated to head an individual CER had no hierarchical authority over his colleagues. Moreover, the CERs were expected to act in response to specific requests by the local populations for technical assistance rather than to initiate and impose the government's development program. Unlike officials in the territorial administration who saw themselves as servants of the state and the national interest, CER officials regarded themselves, at least in theory, as public servants at the disposition of the local populations.

Another state agency imbued with egalitarian principles and eschewing hierarchy was the Rural Animation Service.[22] Officials in the Rural Animation Service went to the villages where they encouraged the people to select young men who would receive training in civic and technical education and then return to their villages where they would serve as unpaid agents for social change. Rural animation advocated participatory grassroots democracy and decentralized political and economic institutions. They saw the rural communes and rural councils envisaged by Mamadou Dia as the product of decisions taken by local communities to regroup according to common interests and mutual affinities. One of the most striking features of the Rural Animation Service during its formative years was the democratic and egalitarian structure of the organization. Unlike his counterparts in other agencies based in Dakar, Ben Mahdi Cissé, the head of the Rural Animation Service, spent most of his time in the interior, consulting with his staff and seeing to it that their logistical needs were met as quickly as possible.

Although Senghor continued to pay lip service to the importance of the CERs and Rural Animation Service in promoting rural development, in fact, these state agencies lost their momentum and went into decline after Dia's demise. Senghor chose to rely on large-scale and highly bureaucratized Regional Development Agencies to "*encadrer*" the rural populations and modernize the rural economy. The management style of the RDAs was top-down. Directors made policies in Dakar with a minimum of consultation with the technicians in the field. The elaboration of programs and projects by the RDAs depended heavily upon the recommendations of foreign experts and donor financing. Large-scale projects initiated from above often reflected lack of knowledge of local ecological and climatic conditions, production systems, and land tenure regimes and imposed uniform rules and technical packages ill suited to local realities. Although state officials and technicians often invoked the importance of participatory development, their notion of participation entailed the participation of the local populations in adopting economic objectives, technologies, and organizational modes defined and prescribed by the state and the donors financing the RDAs.

While concentrating extreme power in the hands of the presidency, Senghor deplored what he called the Ponce Pilatism of state and party officials who seldom accepted responsibility, made decisions, and took action on their own initiative. Yet, Senegal's centralized political and bureaucratic system encouraged this sort of behavior. Ministers wanted to be sure that the president approved of what they were doing before they would act even on the simplest matter. Below the presidency, ministers and state officials reluctantly delegated authority to state officials below them. The norm, a carryover from the colonial era, was that directors and heads of services made the decisions and gave the orders, which then had to be transmitted down the chain of command and executed. This centralized system of decision-making operated at every level of the chain of command and discouraged the upward flow of information and collective decision-making. The flow of funds and resources to the field were often subject to serious delays because a minister or agency director was out of the country and had not delegated authority to his colleagues to sign off on the simplest of decisions.

Corruption: Centralization, Party-State Bureaucrats, and Ceddo Ethics

Corruption was not a major political issue and apparently modest in Senegal during the early years of independence. The disappearance of the legal opposition, the absence of a dynamic and independent press, the consolidation of a party-state regime with weak law enforcement, and the rapid expansion of state control and regulation of the economy, however, created a favorable environment for corruption. By the end of the 1970s, corruption had become a major fact and political issue in Senegalese politics.

The Senghor régime was not insensitive to corruption.[23] Senghor himself repeatedly denounced ministers who took their 10 percent cut when awarding state contracts. In 1980, the government abolished the *Office National de Coopération et d'Assistance au Développement* (ONCAD) that had been created in 1966 to control all of the state's official market circuits and to manage the state's agricultural program.[24] Widespread mismanagement, the embezzlement of millions of dollars by high-ranking ONCAD officials, and ONCAD's milking of the rural economy through the low prices it paid farmers for their products had made ONCAD exceptionally unpopular, especially with the rural populations.

Shortly after becoming president in 1981, Abdou Diouf launched a major campaign against government corruption (*l'enrichissement illicite*) that led to the arrest and prosecution of some high-ranking officials. However, the campaign quickly ran out of steam. It soon became obvious that the government would not clamp down on or prosecute certain well-connected party and state officials, businessmen, and maraboutic authorities, the so-called Untouchables.

Although corruption affected and infected all levels of government, it was especially prevalent among ministers and other officials involved in awarding contracts, managing state budgets and payrolls, enforcing customs, marketing and other economic regulations, and levying fines for violations of the law. Government agents providing what were supposed to be free public services also expected to get money from their clients in exchange for delivering the services.[25]

The widespread disrespect of the law was, in part, due to the fact that many laws had no reference point in customary law and practice. Laws drafted in a foreign language and in imitation of little understood foreign practices had little legitimacy. However, because state officials like the policemen, customs agents, health officials, and others had the power to levy fines and other sanctions or to withhold services, citizens often engaged in negotiations with state officials to get around the law.[26] In Senegal's oral society, negotiations to circumvent the law took place through verbal discussions.[27]

While the emergence of a powerful centralized state apparatus in the 1960s and 1970s and the rise of the civil-servant class facilitated the expansion of corruption, the specific patterns of behavior associated with corruption in Senegalese society also had roots in the cultural and social norms of *ceddo* ethics in precolonial Senegalese society. Like the *ceddo* in precolonial Senegal, the political class and state officials running the party-state in Senegal often regarded themselves as above the law and having the right to tap the public till for private gain.[28] In the face of *ceddo* ethics, the absence of an independent judiciary to enforce the rule of law in Senegal deprived the country of an important check on corruption and the abuse of power by state officials.

Intellectuals, Ideological Models, and Centralization

Tocqueville criticized the French philosophers and intellectuals in eighteenth century prerevolutionary France, who ardently supported the use of state power to reform and transform society, as setting the stage for democratic despotism.[29] Thus, while denouncing inequality and seeking the abolition of all hereditary privileges, the Physiocrats and Economists advocated top-down state reforms to mold society according to their predetermined models.[30]

During the decolonization era and the early decades following independence, Francophone African intellectuals, for the most part, adopted models of governance that strikingly resembled those held by prerevolutionary French intellectuals. However, these ideas had little resonance among the African people.

While Western-educated Senegalese intellectuals adhered to different ideologies, nearly all agreed that the postcolonial state should be secular, highly centralized, and the main agent for economic development, modernization, and nation-building. Moreover, like many intellectuals they showed little interest in local politics and affairs and preferred to focus their attention on national and international issues.

Three distinct ideological models contended for the allegiance of Senegal's intelligentsia during the early years of independence.[31] The first model, which prevailed as Senegal's official ideology for two decades, was based on *Négritude* and African Socialism, eloquently articulated by Léopold Sédar Senghor. Although he often cited and praised Marx in his speeches, Senghor's African Socialism denied the validity of applying class analysis to Senegalese society. African Socialism proclaimed the virtues of traditional African values of dialogue, consensus, and tolerance while designating the state as the main agent of development and nation-building.[32]

The second ideology which drew the support of the majority of Senegalese intellectuals educated in France or at Dakar University reflected different variants of Marxism, denounced the evils of French neocolonialism and Western imperialism, and used the vocabulary of class analysis and class struggle to describe what was going on in Senegal. Marxist intellectuals, for example, described the maraboutic authorities supporting the regime as feudal elements aligned with a neocolonial state bourgeoisie.[33] During the 1960s, the majority of Senegalese students at Dakar University adhered to Marxist ideologies. The student revolts in 1968 and 1969 were led primarily by Marxists. Although he crushed the revolt, Senghor did not attempt to censor or suppress Marxism as an ideology. Instead, he successfully contained Marxism for many years within the narrow confines of the university. When different varieties of Marxist parties emerged as legal parties during the 1980s, it became clear that none of them could command any large following outside of university and trade union circles and the capital.

The third ideological model embraced by Senegalese intellectuals was based on cultural nationalism and closely associated with Cheikh Anta Diop, a Senegalese intellectual and scholar based at the *Institut Fondamental d'Afrique Noire* (IFAN) in Dakar.[34] Diop affirmed the cultural unity of Africa and rejected Africa's cultural inferiority vis-à-vis Europe. He argued that ancient Egypt was essentially a black African civilization and had been the cradle of European civilization and that Senegalese culture had much in common with that of ancient Egypt. Diop translated many literary and scientific texts into Wolof and advocated the adoption of Wolof to replace French as the country's official national language. Diop presented his "neo-pharaonic" model based on history and linguistic analysis as an alternative to Senghor's *Négritude* model based more on folklore and depicting Africans as attached to emotion and Europeans as guided by rationality.

Despite their differences, the three ideological models embraced by Senegal's Western-educated intellectuals saw the state as the main agent for transforming society. The intellectuals showed little interest in Islam and popular culture, a fact that kept them isolated and out of touch with the Senegalese people. Abdou Diouf, Senghor's successor, was more of a technocrat than an intellectual and could do little more than articulate a nebulous ideology based on national revitalization (*sursaut national*). *Négritude* and African Socialism more or less disappeared as an ideological model for Senegalese intellectuals after Senghor retired from the political scene. Many of the Senegalese intellectuals who rallied to Diouf in the 1980s abandoned their Marxist ideologies and vocabulary for a more technocratic language and worldview. By the end of the 1980s, Marxism became less attractive to university students and many looked toward Islam as an alternative model.

The participation of Marxist parties in government and the National Assembly in the 1990s was accompanied by a decline in Marxist fervor among party leaders. The collapse of the communist Soviet bloc and the discrediting of Marxism among intellectuals in the West also contributed to the decline of Marxist influence among Senegalese intellectuals. By the mid-1990s, the political leaders of the old Marxist parties had become social democrats who trumpeted the virtues of democracy, social justice, and fair elections rather than the need to overthrow a corrupt state bourgeoisie aligned with international capitalism. At the same time, they toned down their criticism of religion and Senegal's maraboutic authorities. The extension of democratic processes and the need to win the support of the electorate provided strong incentives to abandon the old ideologies and language of class struggle, which made little sense to most Senegalese.

The Decline of the Centralized State:
Decentralization from Above

In Senegal, decentralization was initiated from above. The institutions of local government reflected the rules and regulations elaborated by the central government of a unitary state that claimed that it alone had the authority to delegate its power. The central state delimited the boundaries of local government jurisdictions. Thus, the state determined which and how many villages would belong to the Rural Communities as well as the number, size, and boundaries of the regions. Local communities had no authority to organize their own units of local government.

During the last decade of the millennium, Senegal's rulers took several important initiatives to reduce the tutelage of the central government and administration over Senegalese society and local government institutions. In April 1990, several months before the November local elections, the Diouf regime passed legislation that gave urban mayors and presidents of Rural Councils the right to elaborate and manage local government budgets and expenditures, which previously had been managed by representatives of the central state. The so-called Second Administrative Reform turned over control of local finances to the local chief executives.[35]

Control over local government institutions provided little in the form of patronage and political spoils since local government expenditures accounted for only 5 percent of total public expenditures in Senegal. As in the past, the opposition parties decided to boycott the local elections on the grounds that the Ministry of the Interior and officials in the territorial administration responsible for overseeing the elections could not be trusted to remain neutral. Election rules that gave all seats to the majority party also discouraged opposition participation. Except for the PDS, opposition parties had no significant party organization outside of Dakar and the larger towns and were reluctant to reveal their lack of popular support. Most opposition party leaders lived and worked in Dakar and were out of touch with the rural populations. As centralizers, they also had little interest in local politics and saw control over the presidency and the National Assembly as the only significant stakes in Senegalese politics.

During the mid-1990s, Diouf continued to reaffirm his commitment to continue the process of decentralization and his intention to establish regional councils headed by popularly elected officials. In March 1996, a comprehensive series of laws revised the existing decentralization code and transferred broad powers to local government in addition to creating Regional Councils in each of Senegal's ten regions.[36]

The increased powers and resources of local government provided more incentives for politicians to become more involved in local politics and issues. The 1996 decentralization code increased the number of local body units by creating ten regional councils, ten new urban municipalities, and forty-three *communes d'arrondissement* in the Dakar region. It also placed more pressure on central party bodies to nominate people who were well known and popular in their local constituencies. The number of local government offices soared to nearly 24,000.

For the first time since independence, Senegal's opposition political parties decided to seriously contest local government elections and to organize in the countryside.[37] Changes in the electoral code provided for half of the seats in any given constituency to be allocated by proportional representation, thus assuring some opposition representation in nearly all of Senegal's local government bodies, and ending the monopoly of the PS over rural and urban councils.

The 1996 decentralization code marked a major setback for the centralizers. The authority of administrative officials in the interior began to decline. As a result of the reforms, the central government and its representatives in the territorial administration saw their prerogatives limited to a posteriori control over the legality of local government measures. The hitherto all-powerful regional governors saw their power wane as they had to cede to popularly elected regional council presidents who insisted upon their rights to run regional affairs. Local government units also received the authority to negotiate loans, grants, and other cooperative agreements directly with external donors, for example, international Non-Governmental Organizations (NGOs), private foundations, and local government bodies.

However, despite the decentralization measures undertaken during the late 1990s, the state retained many of its old prerogatives and its control over the decentralization process itself. The central government continued to hold extensive tutelage powers in financial matters. Thus, the state had to approve local budgets, aid agreements drawn up between Senegalese local government units and external donors, contracts signed between local government and private sector suppliers, and changes in local tax rates and categories before these could go into effect. Moreover, most local government units lacked sufficient funding to carry out their new functions because the central government had transferred only a tiny fraction of the financial resources needed.

While the decentralization reforms were very popular among the general public, they had been formulated by a relatively small group of technocrats and politicians in Dakar with little input from opposition parties, representatives of civil society, or the rural populations. State officials also dominated the various national advisory bodies created by the government to monitor and evaluate the progress of decentralization.[38]

Although decentralization had become a popular slogan in the 1990s, it had not become totally internalized by the Senegalese elites controlling the government and political parties. Many in the corps of *administrateurs civils*, who ran the state bureaucracy, saw the transfer of powers from the state to the local government as premature and argued that locally based politicians rarely had the skills needed to manage local government.

In transferring power to local government executives, the 1996 decentralization code concentrated power in the hands of the mayors and the presidents of regional and rural councils. In many instances, these officials continued to regard themselves as local monocrats. However, multiparty representation on the councils, factionalism within the majority party, and the growing assertiveness of diverse grassroots groups and associations made it more difficult for individuals to dominate the local councils than in the heyday of the party-state.

CHAPTER FIVE

Local Liberties

[T]he strength of free peoples resides in the local community.[1]

Unlike formal local government units established as legal entities by the state, for Tocqueville, local communities and institutions were not necessarily creations of the state, but rooted in nature and found among all peoples regardless of their customs and laws.[2] The self-governing institutions found in medieval Europe before the emergence of the centralized monarchies provided the prototype for Tocqueville's concept of local liberties stressing the freedom of local communities to manage their own affairs and solve common problems.

Self-governing urban communities thrived in France before the rise of the centralized monarchy. Many French towns won the right to govern themselves during The Middle Ages and continued to function as small democratic republics until the end of the seventeenth century. Village and municipal autonomy steadily declined with the expansion of the monarchy and the establishment of the *intendant* system begun by Louis XIV.

Tocqueville argued that in modern democratic societies, local institutions could not successfully defend themselves unless they reached full development, enjoyed a long-recognized legal existence, and had become part of national mores and habits.[3] Tocqueville saw these conditions met in the New England townships, which had a long history, legal status, enlightened leaders, and a relatively well-educated citizenry. These conditions were also met in Senegal's Four Communes.

Tocqueville described the local governments established by communities in America as "permanent associations" created by law to distinguish local government from other forms of community-based associations.[4] In Senegal, local governance institutions not formally sanctioned by law and rooted in what Tocqueville called "natural" communities emerged after independence alongside the Four Communes and the local government institutions created by the colonial and postcolonial state.

Self-Governing Communities and Local Liberties in
Precolonial Senegal

Unlike Western Europe, precolonial Senegal had no urban tradition of self-governing towns.[5] However, Senegal's village institutions bore a close resemblance to the self-governing villages in France during the Middle Ages described by Tocqueville.[6]

Most Senegalese lived in self-governing villages, many of which were loosely integrated into larger political units that rarely intervened except to collect tributes. Although subject to paying tribute and periodic raids, village communities enjoyed a great deal of autonomy in meting out justice and managing their own affairs.

Unlike feudal Europe where peasants were tied to the land, in Senegal individuals and rural communities enjoyed the freedom to move. Communities relocated their villages in response to a wide range of factors including deteriorating ecological conditions, overpopulation, efforts to gain more security, defeat in war, and dissatisfaction with rulers.

When Islam became the court religion in precolonial monarchies, rulers did not oblige their subjects to convert to Islam. Village communities retained the right to maintain their own religious practices. Non-Muslim rulers in the precolonial Wolof states often allocated land to marabouts to found their own villages, which followed Islamic law and practices. In maraboutic villages, the Muslim clerics assumed the same functions exercised by traditional village chiefs in allocating land to their followers and arbitrating disputes.

While the formal political structures of Sine and Saloum resembled those found in Wolof and Mandinka kingdoms, local Serer communities retained much of their autonomy and successfully prevented ruling dynasties and their allies from impinging on their rights.[7] Clusters of Serer villages, particularly those located within dense forests, successfully resisted attacks and invasions by external forces and often avoided conquest by Wolof armies from Cayor and Baol.[8]

Writing in the mid-1850s just before the French launched their conquest of the interior, Abbé Boilat, an Afro-European missionary, wrote glowingly about the small None "republic" and its independent spirit that preserved its people's liberties by resolutely closing its territory to all foreigners to protect itself from those engaging in the slave trade.[9]

Diola village republics in Lower Casamance staunchly defended their traditional religion and local liberties against efforts by nineteenth century Muslim-warrior marabouts in the Senegambia to incorporate them into Islamic states and afterward fiercely resisted the French colonial conquest. The last group in Senegal, to be "pacified" by the French and to submit to French rule, the freedom-loving Diola also constituted the heart of the separatist movement in the Casamance that began in the early 1980s.

Other communities also strove to preserve local liberties beyond the village level. Established at the end of the eighteenth century on the Cap Vert peninsula under the leadership of a small maraboutic party, the Lebu "Republic" was established by the Lebu to free themselves from the hegemony of the Wolof kingdom of Cayor after the ruler (*damel*) of Cayor signed treaties ceding Cap Vert to the French without informing the Lebu community.[10]

In Fouta Toro, the Halpulaar Torodo leaders who overthrew the ruling Denianké dynasty in the 1776 revolution established rules to preserve local liberties and prevent the emergence of a highly centralized theocratic state.[11] They did this by dividing the region into small "republics" controlled by the leading families of each locality and by frequently changing and rotating the person elected to serve as spiritual and political leader (*Almamy*) of Fouta Toro. Fouta Toro still remains organized largely within the spatial boundaries of the republics set up after 1776 revolution.[12]

The Four Communes as Schools for Democracy:
Local Liberties in a Colonial Context

The emergence of formal local government institutions in the Four Communes provided a new and different source for whetting the Senegalese people's taste for liberty and resistance to arbitrary rule.

During the height of the French Revolution, the inhabitants of Saint-Louis in 1791 presented a plan for establishing elective municipal institutions in Saint-Louis and Gorée, headed by a mayor living in the commune for at least one year. The plan excluded servants and slaves from voting, thus restricting the electorate to Frenchmen, Afro-Europeans, and a few assimilated Africans. According to the proposed plan, the mayor would represent local residents, have extensive police powers to maintain order and guarantee public safety, administer the civil register and census, and inspect weights and measures in the public markets.[13] Those presenting the petition also requested that the French Governor not interfere in the affairs of the local populace. Although the petition was buried in a committee and never acted upon, local municipal institutions continued to function without formal recognition from the *métropole*.

In 1823, when a senile mayor needed to be replaced, Saint-Louisians insisted on their prerogative to choose their own local-born mayor.[14] The French Governor at the time insisted upon his authority to name and depose the mayor. But in the end, he wound up choosing the man who would have won the elections if they had been held.

For the next half century, municipal government received no formal recognition from Paris since none of the regimes in power in France from the Restoration to the Second Empire, except for a brief interlude following the 1848 Revolution, were interested in extending political rights and devolving political power to local institutions. Local government in Senegal declined during the rule of Napoleon III who suppressed the *Conseil Général*, a territorial assembly that had been set up in 1840 under the Orleanist Monarchy (1830–1848) to debate local affairs.

In 1872, Saint-Louisians again took the initiative to petition Paris to restore the *Conseil Général* and revive the municipal councils. Although the Ministry responsible for colonial affairs rejected the restoration of the *Conseil Général* as premature, it recommended that Saint-Louis and Gorée be granted full communal status with the same rights as metropolitan municipalities. Efforts by French colonial business interests operating in Senegal to discredit the petitioners failed. As a result, Gorée and Saint-Louis became full communes in August 1872. Rufisque gained the status of full commune in 1880, while Dakar was granted this status in 1887 when it was administratively separated from the isle of Gorée. Throughout most of the French Third Republic, the Four Communes enjoyed the same privileges of self-government as their counterparts in the *métropole*.

While African citizens were allowed to vote and even to hold political office if they could read and write in French, few Africans before the end of the century served on the municipal councils then dominated by an oligarchy of French commercial agents and affluent Afro-Europeans.

Though marking the end of French and Afro-European domination of local politics, the December 1919 municipal elections, won by Blaise Diagne's Republican-Socialist Party, also reflected the tolerant and multiracial character of Senegalese urban politics where equal political status among the races was a reality rather than an abstract ideal.[15] Although race was evoked in election campaigns, race was not a criterion for participation. Unlike other parts of colonial Africa, which had representative institutions, no racial quotas restricted the African electorate in the Four Communes or insured a European majority.

The fact that the African citizens of the Four Communes had equal political status with Frenchmen and Afro-Europeans did not mean that all African citizens had equal access to political office. Rules requiring office-holders to be literate in French excluded the great majority of the African electorate. As a result, the African electorate had to rely on a small number of Western-educated Africans to represent them and to defend their interests.

While serving as a training ground for democratic politics, the Four Communes bore little resemblance to the New England townships described by Tocqueville in size, composition of the population, socioeconomic structures, degree of participation, organization of local government, and relationships with the state.

Tocqueville saw the rural New England townships as fitting somewhere between the French *commune* and the *canton* in size with a population from two to three thousand. When they obtained full commune status, Dakar, Saint-Louis, and Rufisque had larger populations than the New England townships described by Tocqueville.[16] Machine politics and patronage were also prominent features of local politics in the larger Senegalese communes and had more in common with municipal politics in America's larger cities than with the direct democracy found in the New England townships. Senegal's urban communes, especially Dakar and Saint-Louis, thus had little in common with the natural self-governing communities described so glowingly by Tocqueville.

On the other hand, the communal tradition in Senegal has had a profound influence in creating a strong taste for liberty among those living in the Four Communes and the basis for a democratic culture.

Another major difference between the New England Townships and the Senegalese communes was their relationship with the state. Townships and cities in America retained their autonomy while in Senegal, French colonial administrators exercised strict supervision over and surveillance of the communes.[17] Representing the central government in France, colonial administrative officials consistently sought to restrict the powers of the full communes.

After the French Revolution, conflicts between elected local government officials in Senegal and the colonial administration resulted from the efforts by Senegal's urban citizens to gain greater autonomy for local and territorial institutions vis-à-vis the officials of a highly centralized colonial state. Senegalese citizens steadfastly resisted encroachments by the colonial administration on the local liberties that they had won. The special prerogatives enjoyed by Senegalese residents living in the Four Communes gave urban Senegalese their first taste of modern democratic rights and the inclination to defend these rights when under attack by French colonial bureaucrats. Participation in Western-style local government institutions also provided a training ground for political leaders such as Galendou Diouf who served as mayor of Rufisque before succeeding Blaise Diagne as deputy and Lamine Guèye who was mayor of Saint-Louis.

After World War II, the French extended citizenship rights to their African subjects before they permitted full communes to be established in other overseas African territories that enabled Africans to run their own municipal councils. As a result, large African cities in other parts of French Black Africa did not gain the status of full communes until 1955.[18]

Urban Communes and the State in Postcolonial Senegal

Except for a brief period of rapid expansion of urban government institutions during the early 1960s, the history of Senegal's postindependence municipal institutions until the 1990s was characterized by the reinforcement of the state's tutelage.[19]

During the early years of independence, the scope of urban local government expanded rapidly. As part of his government's and administrative reorganization and decentralization program, Mamadou Dia in 1960 gave the urban capitals of the newly created *départements* the status of full communes and established a national fund to support communal investments. A strong advocate of state planning, Mamadou Dia echoed Tocqueville in asserting the value of local government and the commune as the basic framework of political life and a school where the conduct of public affairs was learned.[20]

Nearly all of the small urban centers transformed into full communes in 1960 had initially sprung up during the colonial era. Most had been administrative posts or commercial centers (*escales*) servicing the colonial peanut economy and historically dominated by French colonial administrators working closely with French and Afro-French traders. Creations of colonial trade and conquest, they had no precolonial traditions of local liberties.

Smaller towns in the interior had few sources of revenue and had to rely almost exclusively upon state subsidies to finance investments. Outside the Four Communes, most mayors had little experience in participating in the management of municipal affairs. The patron–client relationships, so characteristic of Senegalese politics, did little to foster self-governance practices. Patronage increased dependency on the state since the state controlled most of the resources. Mayors often squandered the resources provided by the state for infrastructure on popular but unproductive projects like the construction of municipal racetracks. They also padded payrolls with incompetent personnel recruited from their followers and diverted municipal funds to meet the immediate needs of their clients and constituents.

The reestablishment of the state's direct control over municipal finances dampened enthusiasm for participation in local-level politics and in competing for local political office. The Senghor government cited mismanagement of communal affairs by the mayors as the main reason for strengthening the state's tutelage.

In 1964, the state gave the governor of the region of Dakar extensive powers to administer Dakar's municipal affairs. The practice of relying on governors and high-ranking civil servants to assume control over the administration of municipal affairs was soon extended to the regional capitals. In 1965, the state took control over water and electricity services, which previously had been the domain of the municipalities. Again this was done in the name of efficiency. However, the increased involvement of the state in managing municipal affairs was not accompanied by any marked improvements in service delivery and performance. The same problems cited in government reports—padded payrolls, incompetent personnel, non-collection of fees for services, heavy debts, and few investments in infrastructure—persisted.

The implementation of the 1996 decentralization code led to an explosion in the number of Senegalese directly participating in urban local government and increased the opportunity for women and young men to serve as elected municipal officials representing their constituencies. It had its greatest impact in Cap Vert where forty-three *communes d'arrondissement* were created to bring urban government closer to the people and provided the opportunity for hundreds of urban citizens to become elected local government officials for the first time.

Outside of Dakar, however, these reforms had little impact as to how urban municipalities were managed. The majority of urban mayors in the smaller towns in the interior lived in Dakar. Most of them behaved much like government ministers and heads of government services in their reluctance to delegate decision-making authority to their deputies, thus delaying the taking of decisions and hindering the smooth functioning of local government. The Dakar-based mayors from the interior justified their reluctance to stay in their home towns on the grounds that they needed to be in Dakar to effectively lobby for their constituents, since local municipalities had so few resources that could be tapped and still relied primarily on state and donor resources—concentrated in Dakar—for public investments in their towns.

State Tutelage Traditions and
Formal Rural Government Institutions

Artifacts of the colonial state, the administrative structures—*cercle, sub-division,* and *canton*—had no roots in indigenous societies. The village was different. It was not an administrative creation but a living entity. Liberal French colonial administrators like Robert DeLavignette saw traditional village chiefs as the only real and legitimate authority in the countryside.[21]

Though the village persisted as the basic administrative unit at the grassroots level, the colonial system reduced the village chief to an auxiliary of the colonial administration whose main function was to collect taxes, identify young males for recruitment into forced labor gangs or military service, and to extend hospitality to visiting colonial officials. Village chiefs exhibiting a certain degree of independence in refusing to follow orders or not showing proper deference to French colonial officials faced imprisonment, public humiliation, and removal. The abolition of forced labor and the extension of full political and civil rights to the subject populations in the interior during the liberal postwar-decolonization era, though a major step toward democratization, however, were not accompanied by efforts to create representative local government institutions in the countryside.

At the time of independence, Senegal had approximately 13,000 villages. While village chiefs in 1960 had been integrated into the new administrative system and "elected" by the local populations, villages did not receive formal recognition as local government units. Moreover, village chiefs still needed the stamp of approval of the prefect and Minister of the Interior before they could assume office. The government considered most villages to be too small to be economically viable. Senegalese villages came under the jurisdiction of a larger administrative unit, the *arrondissement* run by a *sous-préfet* named by the central government.

Although adopting the French administrative system, independent Senegal, like most Francophone African countries, did not create the functional equivalent of the French rural commune established during the early days of the French Revolution largely within the boundaries of what had been parishes under the Old Regime.[22] In Senegal, communal status was accorded only to urban centers.

Rather than starting with villages as the basic grassroots unit of local government, Mamadou Dia established a nation-wide cooperative movement that would regroup several villages into multifunctional rural cooperatives to serve as dynamic development poles in the countryside.[23] Although organized and initiated by the state, the village-based cooperatives were eventually supposed to form self-governing rural communes, since state tutelage needed to get the movement started, would eventually wither away.

Following Dia's departure from the political scene, Senghor shelved the idea of transforming the rural cooperatives into self-governing rural communes or establishing other forms of rural local government units while encouraging the organization of functional rather than community-based peasant producer groups and cooperatives, which remained under the tight control of state rural development institutions.

In 1972, the Senghor regime cautiously introduced formal local government institutions in the rural areas, starting with the region of Thiès and gradually extending them to the rest of the country. By the end of the 1980s, Senegal had 317 Rural Communities, each with its own Rural Council.

The new Rural Communities did not reflect the voluntary joining together of natural communities; they were established by state fiat. The state determined the boundaries of the Rural Communities, the powers of the Rural Councils representing the populations, and the election rules.[24] Until the early 1990s, Rural Councils demonstrated little initiative and independence. Elective leadership positions tended to be regarded largely as honorary posts by the rural populations who frequently chose traditional and often illiterate notables to serve as president. In other instances, local party leaders intervened to impose their candidate. Tax collection proved difficult because of the reluctance of the people to pay taxes to an institution that provided very few public services and was deemed as unrepresentative by many of the constituent villages who saw the Rural Councils primarily as instruments of the state and the dominant party.

During the 1990s, the Rural Councils acquired greater autonomy as the state transferred control over the budget from the *sous-prefets* to the presidents. In transferring more responsibilities to the Rural Councils—for example, primary health care services, sanitation, education, natural resource management, etc.—the 1996 decentralization laws transformed the Rural Councils into more than just paper institutions.

Senegalese opposition political parties that previously boycotted local government elections responded by seriously contesting the 1996 Rural Council elections and participating in Rural Council deliberations after the elections. For the first time since the late 1970s, the ruling party no longer held all the seats on the Rural Councils. In the May 2002 local government elections, the new ruling party (PDS), led by President Abdoulaye Wade, other parties in the government coalition, the former ruling party (PS), and other political parties still in the opposition campaigned vigorously. As a result, the Rural Councils became increasingly more representative and open institutions.

Despite their growing importance and the diversity of the office holders, the Rural Councils are still far from becoming self-governing institutions.

Rural Councils don't represent natural communities. The Rural Communities set up by the government from the top-down were drawn up primarily to meet bureaucratic criteria that determined the size and number of Rural Communities to be established within an *arrondissement* and the number of villages to be attached to a particular Rural Community. Rural Communities often included villages that had no historic links to each other and villages with different traditional governance structures (herder villages versus farmer villages). Moreover, the village that was designated as the seat of the Rural Community tended to have a disproportionate number of public services and rural councilors while many villages had none.

Not having traditions of local liberties under colonialism, most Rural Councils in Senegal still look primarily to the state to solve their problems. Until recently, few Rural Communities showed much initiative in launching projects on their own or in mobilizing local resources. The 1996 decentralization code provided local government institutions with the power to conduct negotiations with local government institutions in other countries to obtain technical and financial assistance through the mechanism of *"coopération decentralisée."*[25] Enterprising Rural Councils have taken advantage of this possibility and have found alternative sources to those provided by the state.

Land tenure legislation gives the Rural Councils the formal authority to allocate new land or to take away land not being exploited in the areas under their jurisdiction. However, in most instances, the Rural Councils respect the wishes of traditional village authorities in these matters. When requested by an individual for a piece of land, the Rural Council's land tenure committee generally consults with the village chief and his council of sages before making a decision. The Rural Council's imposition of a decision contrary to the wishes of local village authorities often leads to serious conflict. On the other hand, the Rural Councils are emerging as increasingly important arbitrators of land use conflicts among different villages and groups in their jurisdictions.

Natural Communities and the Creation of
Informal Rural Governance Institutions

Since the beginning of the 1980s, three important developments have enhanced opportunities for village-based communities to establish self-governing institutions. The first has been a steady reduction in the formal tutelage of the state over local government. The second has been the disengagement of the state from the rural economy as a by-product of structural adjustment policies. The third has been the emergence of laws giving citizens greater freedom to establish groups and associations with a minimum of government supervision.

One of the major consequences of these developments has been the emergence of new forms of village-based self-governance institutions to provide public goods and services, partly in response to the state's failure to provide them. These institutions have been created by what Tocqueville referred to as "natural communities." Natural communities emerged from members of families, ethnic, and religious groups coming together on their own accord to found geographically based communities. Although usually based in the village, the new structures are not necessarily dominated by the village chief and the Council of Elders as in the past. Using indigenous and imported governance techniques, they reflect a successful adaptation to changing realities and new forms of social, economic, and spatial relationships.

Local Liberties in an Egalitarian Setting: Diola Village Associations

In the Lower Casamance, Diola village institutions have emerged that have close links with village associations consisting of migrants from the home village established in Dakar and Ziguinchor.[26] Each of the micro-associations organized by women, youth, adult males, religious groups, and fishermen in the village are consulted in decisions affecting the whole community. The micro-associations engage in human and financial investments in projects decided on by the village. The establishment of a day-care facility could have a village youth group construct the walls; an adult male association finance the purchasing of chairs; and a women's group buy the tin roof from dues and money earned through different activities.

The sections of village associations in the towns bring together members from all walks of life—civil servants, market women, street hawkers, mechanics, schoolteachers, and others, who meet on a monthly basis and choose a president. The association collects dues that are used to take care of the social and economic needs of its members namely medical care, burial expenses, marriage ceremonies, business loans, etc. Part of the dues and contributions collected by the association are sent back to the home village and used to invest in infrastructure such as schools, dispensaries, dikes, as well as to purchase medicines and pay for school expenses.

Many of the migrants return to the village during the rainy season to help with planting, weeding, and harvesting. During this period, the village convokes a general assembly, elects a bureau, and decides on projects that are to be organized for the coming year. Unlike the traditional village-governance institutions dominated by the Council of Elders, the annual village assembly bringing together migrants and villagers gives a much greater voice to young people from the towns because it is they who bring in more money and new ideas. The rise of influence of the young people often came at the expense of the power of the old gerontocracy.

The vibrancy of many Diola village associations reflects the capacity of local communities to adapt and to survive despite the loss of large numbers of its people to migration to the towns. The migrants retain their solidarity with their home village, which assumes the responsibility of raising their children, sending food and traditional medicines to the townsmen, and providing them with land after they retire.

Diola villages throughout the Lower Casamance have retained their taste for local liberties, revamped old community institutions, and organized new governance structures to produce and finance new kinds of public goods and services. These developments did not take place without tension and were not always successful.[27] Unfortunately, the rebellion in the Casamance has undermined the functioning of these institutions in rebel-controlled areas where rebel bands have raided villages and collected "taxes" to support their activities.

Local Liberties in a Hierarchical Society:
Halpulaar Village Associations

In the Halpulaar republics along the Senegal River, village-based governance institutions based on old and new patterns of authority have also emerged and developed to provide a wide range of public goods and services to the community.[28] The Halpulaar village associations resembled the Diola village associations in the way they functioned.[29] Both had village associations consisting of people born in the village, living in the towns, and those who stayed at home. Both provided social and economic support for the townspeople and funds to build infrastructure and social services back at home. Both elected its officials and set governance rules for making and enforcing decisions. Both stressed popular participation in decision-making, revenue generation, and project implementation.

While the traditional Halpulaar local power structures and leaders tended to capture the Rural Councils, leadership roles were more diversified in the various village associations that provided emergency assistance, constructed mosques, built schools and dispensaries, and offered equipment to women's groups starting vegetable gardens. In the village itself, governance structures more closely resembled traditional power relationships with the leaders of the different ethnic and functional groups—*torodo* (marabout/farmers), peulhs (herders), *ceddo* (warrior nobles), and *cubaalo* (fishermen)—holding the most important offices with ex-slaves and artisans still playing only marginal roles.

The Halpulaar hometown village associations in Dakar were somewhere in between those at home and those in France in its social composition and decision-making structures. Women and low-caste members remained on the periphery of decision-making. These associations provided accommodation for the newcomers, helped in getting work, and gave financial assistance for life-cycle events. They also mobilized financial and human resources to be sent back to their home villages.

In the hometown village associations set up in France by the *émigrés*, members of low-caste status—ex-slaves and artisans—had greater access to leadership roles than at home. Although continuing to show some deference to their social "superiors," lower caste representatives are now demanding a greater voice in decision-making and gradually finding greater acceptance in leadership roles. Representatives of the *émigré* hometown village associations based in France and Europe are gaining greater influence at the annual or bi-annual Congresses held in the home village, largely because of their ability to mobilize larger amounts of money and other resources.

One of the most striking characteristics of village-based associations in Senegal has been the general absence of partisan politics in the functioning of the association.[30] For example, in Fouta Toro, where partisan politics and factionalism within political parties is often fierce, members of different factions and political parties usually put aside their political differences and work together to promote the well-being of their community. There is a general awareness that village-based associations do not function very well if they are the objects of divisive partisan struggles, hence the effort to keep politics out.

The mix of rural and urban-based village associations and the forms of collaboration among them have been instrumental in raising the level of village infrastructure despite a sharp decline in the village-based economies at home. In 1960, few villages in Fouta Toro had a modern mosque, reliable sources of safe drinking water, schools, and dispensaries. Forty years later, thanks to the contributions of village associations abroad and in Dakar, many villages now enjoy these benefits.

Several lessons can be drawn from these examples. First, the village remains the focal point of community life in rural Senegal and is more salient to the rural populations than the Rural Communities. Second, the boundaries of what constitutes a village community have changed radically. The village community no longer consists exclusively of residents living within the spatial boundaries of the village. It now encompasses a network of people living inside the village, in the towns, and abroad who regard their village as their home, identify themselves as citizens of the village, and accept responsibility for participating in what Tocqueville called "*la chose publique*." Third, these villages are largely self-governing, performing rather successfully many of the governance functions generally associated with formal local government bodies. Thus, village-based associations tax their members, hold elections, deliberate in collective assemblies on allocation decisions, and sanction members who violate the rules and don't fulfill their obligations. Fourth, the rules affecting how these village associations are constituted and function reflect local traditions and mores and will vary accordingly. The village associations thus stand in marked contrast to the Rural Communities, rural cooperatives, and other formal village-based institutions initiated by the state that were required to follow uniform rules and regulations imposed by the state and subjected to close supervision by government officials.

In his work, Tocqueville tended to romanticize the notion of natural communities and perhaps exaggerate their innate capacity for democratic self-governance. In Senegal, the self-governing village development associations described above as emerging from the villages are not found everywhere.

Nor do they all function without serious tensions, rivalries, and conflicts among different social categories within village communities.

Local Liberties in a Religious Setting

Touba

The rise of Touba, the spiritual capital of the Mouride Brotherhood, provides the most spectacular example of the exercise of local liberties operating on the periphery of a highly centralized state system in Senegal.

In 1887, Cheikh Ahmadou Bamba decided to settle in an area in what was then a wilderness, away from the reach of the colonial authorities. He envisaged that Touba would eventually become a great spiritual center and elaborated plans for its development.[31]

After Bamba's death in 1927, Touba became a pilgrimage site for Mourides. Mamadou Moustapha Mbacké, the first Grand Khalife of the Mourides (1927–1945), began construction of a mosque on the site where his father was buried. After the war, under his successor, Falilou Mbacké (1945–1968), Touba became the joint property of all of the direct descendants of the founder. As a result, the Grand Khalife and other representatives of the Mbacké family administered and exercised collective control over Touba. When Senegal became independent in 1960, Touba had a population of 2,670.[32] After the completion of the Great Mosque in 1963, Touba expanded rapidly. By the beginning of the new millennium, Touba's population had soared to more than 300,000.

Unlike Senegal's urban communes and Rural Communities, Touba escaped the tutelage of the state. In Touba all administration is by Mourides, including education, health, water supply, public works, administration of markets, land tenure, and real estate development.[33] In 1976, Touba obtained legal recognition from the state as an autonomous Rural Community. However, Touba was never subjected to the tutelage of the *sous-préfet*. The Rural Council is essentially an emanation of the Khalife's authority and the president of the Rural Council is, invariably, the personal choice of the Grand Khalife. Despite its autonomous status, Touba has benefited from many urban amenities provided by the state—medical centers, telephones, electricity, and water—primarily because the government courts the support of the Brotherhood. However, many of Touba's urban services such as street lights, paved streets, sewage systems, laying out of new neighborhoods, Franco-Arab schools, a new hospital, and public buildings, Islamic library, Islamic University, and the expansion and renovation of the Great Mosque have been financed by members of the Brotherhood through voluntary contributions rather than through formal taxation. Contributions come from members of the Mouride community who can be found all over Senegal and Africa, and as far as Europe and North America.

Although Touba is in many ways a self-governing community, its leadership is not chosen in democratic elections. The office of Grand Khalife is hereditary and follows specific inheritance rules in which the office is handed down to the oldest survivor from the sons of the founder. The direct descendants of the founder constitute the Board of Directors of the city. While the spiritual leaders are tuned in to the needs of their followers, their followers have no direct and formal voice in decision-making. When the town is in need of money for some project, the Grand Khalife issues a directive (*Ndiguel*) asking the community for voluntary contributions in cash or human investments. The Mouride community usually responds rapidly and generously to such requests because they accept the legitimacy of the Mouride governance system. The rapid growth of Touba has also been fueled by the desire of the faithful living elsewhere to build a second home or a retirement home in the Holy City so that they can be closer to their spiritual sources. This has led to a huge demand for housing and for more social services to meet the needs of an exploding urban population.

The Mourides take pride in what they have accomplished and see Touba as a model of a self-governing and safe urban community without slums, juvenile delinquency, and crime.[34]

Touba's autonomy has been criticized by government officials and intellectuals who call it a state within a state. During the 1960s, Touba emerged as a major distribution center for contraband coming from the Gambia. Neither the government nor the Grand Khalife intervened to crack down on the smugglers operating freely in the Holy City. Critics complained that the massive smuggling cost the government billions of francs in revenue. Abdoul Lahat Mbacké (1968–1989), Falilou Mbacké's successor, however, took steps to reduce the smuggling that he felt was an embarrassment to the Mourides and their reputation as law-abiding citizens.

Others argued that Touba flouted the law in not collecting certain taxes mandated by law, and overstepped its powers in prohibiting smoking and drinking alcohol in Touba. During the 2000 presidential election campaign, the Grand Khalife took the decision to ban political rallies in Touba in the name of maintaining the sanctity of the Holy City, even though this decision violated the rights of political parties to campaign freely.

While insisting upon the Brotherhood's prerogatives in Touba, the Mouride leadership has also called upon its followers to be good citizens and to obey the law.[35] The Grand Khalife himself has become more sensitive to public opinion among his followers in Touba concerning the management of Touba.[36]

Médina Gounass

Touba is not the only example of a religious community that has declared itself to be largely beyond the pale of state control in Senegal. Médina Gounass founded in 1936 in what is now the region of Kolda by a Tijani Tukulor marabout, provides another example of a religious settlement that grew into an autonomous religious community with a population estimated to be 36,000.[37]

For over forty years, Médina Gounass maintained its autonomy in isolating the community from the state. For many years, the town was run by strict Islamic law and violators received severe punishments. Attendance at public prayers was obligatory, women had to wear their veils when leaving home, and men received 100 lashes if caught drinking alcohol.

The establishment of the Rural Community of Médina Gounass in the late 1970s and the declining health of the founder led to political and religious factionalism and the outbreak of violence between Tukulor and Peul inhabitants touched off by the holding of elections in 1978. Although the religious head of the community supported the PS, the opposition PDS won a narrow election. Since then, the politicization of the community has eroded community solidarity and provided an opening for greater state intervention in community affairs, notably to maintain the peace.

Decentralization and Local Liberties

Tocqueville regarded local liberty as embodied in the natural right of people to administer their own local affairs.[38] This best took place within the framework of natural communities whose members would constitute their own forms of local government.

While seeing autonomous local government as a school for democracy, Tocqueville did not regard it as a panacea. Local liberty could also engender a brand of local government that could be repressive and full of prejudices. Thus, the Puritan communities in seventeenth century America were intolerant and harshly treated dissenters. In Senegal, autonomous religious communities like Médina Gounass exhibited similar traits that caused considerable difficulties.

When local liberties persisted in aristocratic societies, the organization of successful community-based enterprises depended upon the initiative and leadership skills of the traditional hierarchy. In those parts of the peanut basin where the traditional rural hierarchy survived and remained in their villages, dynamic village-based associations were less likely to emerge. These areas tended to remain more dependent upon the state. Halpulaar village-based development and mutual aid associations tended to work better because the traditional aristocrats leading them were often well-educated, lived most of the time in the capital, and had strong ties to the government power structure.

Even when dominated by traditional notables, community-based development and mutual aid institutions provided opportunities for individuals to take part in deliberations and to contribute to community projects. These institutions grew up parallel to the formal institutions established by the government.

The 1996 decentralization reforms officially lifted the state's tutelage over formal local government institutions. Henceforth, state officials would no longer have the power to intervene to influence local government decisions. Central government and its representatives in the territorial administration were restricted to exercising a posteriori control over the legality of decisions taken by local government.

While formal local governments continued to remain weak institutions because of their lack of financial resources, financial dependency on the state and donors, and high degree of politicization due to electoral laws requiring candidates to be members of political parties, these institutions are nevertheless serving as schools for democracy and steadily becoming more representative of Senegalese society. In less than a decade, the composition of municipal and rural councils has changed considerably with greater participation of women and young men sitting on the councils. Representatives of different village and development associations at the local level are now more actively participating in monitoring the deliberations of local government councils and being solicited by political parties to run for office. In highly diverse settings within the country, Senegalese citizens have forged prototypes of Tocqueville's township-like style of government within the framework of village and community-based development and mutual aid associations. These associations involve active local engagement and the participation of citizens from a clearly defined geographic area in managing their own affairs and finding solutions to local community problems. In some rural areas, development associations are transcending the village level and organizing new associations that incorporate neighboring villages within the jurisdiction of the Rural Communities.[39] In the Greater Dakar metropolitan region, neighborhood associations have grown up that are addressing community problems like sanitation, garbage disposal, and security.

The exercise of local liberties in the form of dynamic community-based development associations coupled with the 1996 decentralization reforms giving more power to local government points to Senegal's moving to higher levels of self-governance. This trend is also evident in the evolution of Senegal's rich associational life that is also contributing to building Senegalese democracy from the ground up.[40]

CHAPTER SIX

Political Associations, Parties, and the Press

The press is, par excellence, the democratic weapon of freedom.[1]

Tocqueville asserted that democracy could not sustain liberty and flourish without political associations. Political associations served as "great free schools to which all citizens come to be taught the general theory of association."[2] Since political parties were not highly structured in his day, Tocqueville often used political parties and political associations interchangeably.

Tocqueville had little enthusiasm for political parties. He saw them as a necessary evil, which gave outlets to the expression of different interests. At their best, political parties might embrace broad principles and work for the common good. At their worst, they served simply as vehicles for individuals to pursue power for selfish interests.

Like European governments in Tocqueville's day, one-party and military regimes in postcolonial Africa considered political parties and associations not directly under their control primarily as adversaries seeking to overthrow them rather than organizations articulating and aggregating the interests of different individuals and groups in society.

The evolution of political associations, parties, and the press in colonial and postcolonial Senegal provides much evidence to validate Tocqueville's insights concerning the interrelationships between political associations and a free press in democratic societies and the centrality of freedom of association.

Political Associations, Parties, and the
Press in Colonial Senegal

Political Associations and Parties

Modern political associations in Senegal began under French colonial rule under the Third French Republic. For the last quarter of the nineteenth century, Senegalese politics in Senegal revolved around electoral clans dominated by Frenchmen and Afro-Europeans often aligned with colonial business interests.

In 1908, a group of young Western-educated Senegalese citizens founded *L'Aurore de Saint-Louis*, the first modern Senegalese political association. *L'Aurore* started out as a cultural group that met regularly in its members' homes to discuss various issues over tea and soon evolved into a political association that fought for freedom and racial equality.[3] In 1912, it changed its name to *Jeunes Sénégalais* (Young Senegalese), became involved in electoral politics, and enthusiastically supported Blaise Diagne in the 1914 elections for deputy. Their votes and support provided Diagne with his narrow margin of victory.[4] Several of the Young Senegalese, like Lamine Guèye, eventually became prominent Senegalese politicians in their own right.

In 1919, Blaise Diagne founded a political party, the *Parti Républicain Socialiste Indépendant* (PRSI), which organized neighborhood committees and branches in the four communes and sold party membership cards. Until then, Senegal had no formally structured political parties. Senegalese politics revolved primarily around personalities and material interests. Although more structured than the rival groups contesting the elections, the PRSI remained primarily a political clan linked to the fortunes of Blaise Diagne rather than a modern political party.[5]

After several years of independence, Diagne established an alliance with the Bordeaux companies dominating the Senegalese economy. This decision cost him the support of Lamine Guèye and the Young Senegalese. Diagne continued to dominate Senegal's political scene until his death in 1934. At that time Galandou Diouf emerged as the choice of the colonial establishment in Senegal to succeed him.

Lamine Guèye formed the *Parti Socialiste Sénégalais* (PSS) in 1934, which held its first party congress in 1935 and organized party branches outside the Four Communes. In 1936, Lamine Guèye and his allies organized a Popular Front committee that included the PSS, the League for the Rights of Man—a Communist Party cell—and the Senegalese branch of the French Radical Socialists to contest the election against Galandou Diouf who had taken over control of Blaise Diagne's PRSI.[6] Diouf won handily, a fact that Lamine Guèye attributed to electoral fraud and the hostility of the colonial administration.[7] In 1938, the PSS affiliated with the French *Section Française de l'Internationale Ouvrière* (SFIO), a metropolitan Marxist party. Although formally integrated with a metropolitan Marxist party, Guèye's party in Senegal retained its liberal democratic philosophy.

The interwar period saw a steady decline in the power and influence of the French and Afro-European communities in politics as the number of Senegalese African citizens expanded rapidly with the growth of the Four Communes. However, the limited size of the electorate, largely confined to citizens of the Four Communes continued to impede the development of mass-based political parties.

The Colonial Press

The liberal provisions of the July 29, 1881 metropolitan law concerning freedom of the press enabled French citizens to own and publish newspapers and protected them from prepublication censorship. French and Afro-European citizens in Senegal were thus able to invoke that law to establish newspapers espousing political views. *Le Reveil du Sénégal*, which became the first newspaper in Senegal to take political positions critical of the colonial state, began publishing in 1885.[8] *Le Réveil* soon aroused the ire of the governor and the French community. In 1887, its editor-in-chief, was sentenced to two months imprisonment and forced to pay a sizeable fine that led to the demise of the newspaper. A year later, *Le Petit Sénégalais* appeared to take its place.

Newspapers became increasingly involved in electoral politics. Blaise Diagne benefited from the political support he received from *La Démocratie du Sénégal*, a newspaper founded by a Senegalese Afro-European citizen. It was the only one of Senegal's three political newspapers to support Diagne during the 1914 election campaign. During the 1920s, newspapers like *Le Périscope* and *L'AOF* emerged that provided a forum for Senegalese to express their views concerning colonial economic policies favoring Dakar and the large-scale trading companies at the expense of Senegalese interests. In the 1934 election campaign for deputy, *Le Périscope* and *Le Sénegal* supported Galendou Diouf who had become the candidate of the administration following Blaise Diagne's death while *L'AOF* backed his main opponent, Lamine Guèye.

During the colonial period, newspapers had small circulations and were rarely read outside the Four Communes. However, they did reflect the views and debated issues of interest to educated Africans, Frenchmen, and Afro-Europeans participating in Senegal's embryonic political life.

Electoral and Ideological Politics and the Road to Independence

During the postwar period leading to independence, Senegalese political Party competition revolved primarily around Lamine Guèye's Socialist party and the BDS founded in 1948 by Léopold Sédar Senghor and Mamadou Dia. Political associations like the *Groupe d'Etudes Communistes* and the Senegalese branch of the *Ligue des Droits de l'Homme* became training grounds for organizing new Marxist and nationalist political parties. Smaller ideological political parties like the *Union Démocratique Sénégalaise* (UDS), affiliated with the French Communist Party in France, also emerged.

Senegal's two main political parties had their own weekly newspaper to present their views. The *Condition Humaine* became the official organ of the BDS while *L'AOF*, which had supported Guèye before the war, became the official organ of the Socialists. These newspapers articulated and defended their party's positions on the various issues of the day.

Other newspapers presented different political perspectives ranging from *Les Echos d'Afrique Noir*, the voice of the right wing of the French resident community in Senegal, to *Réveil* and *Réalités Africaines* that reflected the views of the UDS and left-wing Senegalese nationalist students respectively. *Le Prolétaire*, a newspaper founded by the Communist-dominated *Confédération Générale des Travailleurs* served as the official organ of the major trade union movement in Senegal and frequently attacked Senegal's two major political parties for collaborating with the colonial administration.

During the postwar era, Senegal's two main political parties were built around coalitions of different groups of leaders and their followers. This modern form of patron–client relationships in Senegal was widely referred to as clan politics and reflected the expansion of the more narrowly based patronage politics of the prewar era.[9] At the local level, clan politics incorporated large numbers of people into the game of electoral politics. Clan politics was highly personalized and depended largely upon the ability of the clan leader to reward followers with jobs, material resources, protection, and reflected glory. Clan leaders rarely appealed directly to individual voters. Instead, they solicited the backing of local notables and religious leaders who could deliver the votes of their followers. The spoils of power, however, were quite limited since winning elections did not gain control over the resources of the territorial government, which until 1957 continued to remain in the hands of the French colonial administration.

As independence approached, ideological politics became increasingly important. During the prewar period, Senegalese political parties had advocated the extension of the suffrage and other civil and political rights to the subjects in the interior in the name of equality. Seeking to woo the support of the younger generation of metropolitan educated Senegalese intellectuals, the BDS placed greater emphasis on African Socialism as an ideology, brought new blood into the party, and changed its name to the BPS in 1957 after fusing with the UDS and the *Mouvement Autonome de Casamance* (MAC). In April 1958, Lamine Guèye's Socialist Party merged with the BPS to constitute the UPS.

After the establishment of the UPS, the only other significant political party left in Senegal was the PAI, an orthodox Marxist-Leninist party founded in 1957 by Mahjemout Diop. In 1958, the left wing of the UPS favored a vote for immediate independence in the September 28, 1958 referendum.[10] Afraid of losing the support of the marabouts and their followers who provided the bulk of the party's electoral support, Senghor persuaded the UPS to opt for full self-government for Senegal within the framework of a French Community dominated by France. This decision prompted several prominent left-wing intellectuals who had recently rallied to the party to leave and organize the PRA-Senegal.

The political parties supporting immediate independence had no chance of winning with Senegal's largest political party, the country's leading religious authorities, and the French colonial administration all behind a yes vote. Only 3 percent of the electorate voted no. Shortly afterwards, Ibrahima Seydou Ndao, the leader of the conservative wing of the UPS and a group of rural notables and Muslim religious leaders nervous about the leftward drift of the UPS formed a new political association, the *Union pour la Vème République* that advocated maintaining close ties with France. After the Dia government dissolved the group in January 1959, Ndao resigned from the UPS and created the *Parti de la Solidarité Sénégalaise* (PSS). With the heads of Senegal's major Sufi Brotherhoods still behind them, the UPS won a smashing victory in the March 1959 national elections over the PSS and PRA-Senegal, which were the last national elections held before independence.

Political Parties, Associations, and the Press under One-party Rule

Since independence, the degree of dynamism, independence, and autonomy of Senegal's political associations, parties and newspapers have been closely linked with the extent to which the regime in power placed legal and informal limitations on freedom of association and the press.

Until 1966, the year that Senegal became a de facto one-party state, Senegal's association laws were based on the 1901 French law that authorized individuals to organize without prior approval by the state and to automatically receive formal recognition after depositing the statutes of the association and a list of its officers with the Ministry of the Interior. The Senghor regime placed restrictions on the freedom of association that required an association to submit its statutes *a priori* and gave the government the power to refuse recognition of new parties if it deemed the party or association to be a menace to public order, an instrument of a foreign power, or in violation of the law.[11] These rules gave considerable discretion to the government in determining which political parties and associations merited recognition. The government used the new rules to deny recognition to Marxist parties and parties organized by partisans of Cheikh Anta Diop and Mamadou Dia during the 1960s and 1970s. The application of these rules during the hiatus of the one-party state in Senegal forced opposition political parties to go underground and led to the arrest, imprisonment, and exile of many of their leaders. Sedition laws passed in 1965 gave the government the power to dissolve associations, by decree, that organized armed demonstrations or endangered the functioning of the country's constitutional regime.

Although Article 8 of the 1963 constitution guaranteed freedom of the press, independent political newspapers supporting opposition political parties went into eclipse during the 1960s. The disappearance of legally recognized opposition political parties in 1966 was accompanied by the disappearance of an opposition press. The governing party published *L'Unité Africaine*, the only partisan party newspaper in the country. During the 1960s, Senegal had only one daily newspaper, the apolitical, French-owned *Dakar-Matin*, which had begun in 1936 as *Paris-Dakar* before changing its name after independence. With the absence of political competition, *L'Unité Africaine* languished and appeared less regularly. During the 1960s, the government established its monopoly over the country's press services and radio stations and made sure that Senegal's national journalist association toed the party line. It also seized issues of foreign newspapers containing articles deemed to be too critical of the Senghor regime.

One of the main causes of the political and social explosion that precipitated the violent student and general strike that took place in Dakar in May–June 1968 was the absence of legal outlets—political parties and associations, and newspapers—to express political opinions hostile to the state.

Reacting to public opinion, Senghor in 1969 supported the creation of an organization of Senegalese intellectuals, civil servants, and profession-als called *Club Nation et Développement* to discuss and debate the political future of the country.[12] Although most of its leadership came from the UPS, *Club Nation et Développement* was not a mere appendage of the ruling party. Its membership represented a broad spectrum of Senegal's Western educated elite. After nearly a year of public debate widely reported in the press, *Club Nation et Développement* formulated a moderate reform program that called for restoration of the office of prime minister, Africanization of the administration, economy, and university, and greater political liberalization.

When Senghor authorized other political parties to function, political newspapers not sponsored by the ruling party appeared again.[13] Abdoulaye Wade and the PDS launched *Le Démocrate* in 1974 to present its views. A few years later, Cheikh Anta Diop (*Siggi/Taxaw*), Mamadou Dia (*Ande Sopi*), and leaders of diverse underground Marxist parties published their own newspapers despite the fact that the Senghor government refused to authorize them to create political parties. In 1977, *Le Politicien*, Senegal's first satirical newspaper appeared with the banner, "Democracy begins with freedom of the press," emblazoned on its masthead. Although tolerated, *Le Politicien* often ran into trouble with the government.[14]

In 1970, the government took over *Dakar-Matin*, Senegal's only daily newspaper, which became *Le Soleil*. Senghor's democratic opening in the mid-1970s also sparked the ruling party to resurrect *L'Unité Africaine* and to launch newspapers representing the party's youth and trade union wings.

Alarmed by the rise of a highly critical national press, the government elaborated a tough press code that tightened the state's control over the media and certification of journalists.[15] It also stepped up its prosecution of Senegalese editors and journalists for libeling public figures in government or for spreading false rumors.

At the end of the 1970s, Senegal had four legal political parties and an opposition press concentrated in Dakar. The government-controlled *Le Soleil* that had taken over *Dakar-Matin* in 1970 remained the only daily and the one with the greatest circulation. Most of the other political newspapers appeared weekly or sporadically, sold less than 3,000 copies, and circulated primarily among Dakar's Western-educated elite.

Electoral Reform, Multiparty Competition, and
the Proliferation of Political Parties

Senghor's resignation from the presidency in January, 1981 precipitated a sharp increase in the number of political parties when his successor changed the constitution to permit an unlimited multiparty system. Nearly all of the political groups that had been forced to remain underground during the 1970s transformed themselves into legal parties. By the 1983 presidential elections, Senegal had fifteen legal parties and more than twenty newspapers. Of the eleven new parties, Cheikh Anta Diop's *Rassemblement National Démocratique* (RND) was the only one not to espouse some form of Socialist or Marxist philosophy.[16] The establishment of party newspapers accompanied the legalization of several Marxist parties. By the end of the 1980s, independent weekly newspapers like *Sud-Hebdo* and *Wal Fadjri* appeared that were not tied to any single political party.

While liberalizing the written press, the government maintained its monopoly over radio and television broadcasting. Opposition parties complained bitterly that the ruling party used its control of radio and television and the country's only daily newspaper to deny them access to the media. As a result, the people were not well informed about the ideas, programs, and activities of the opposition parties. The state media served as mouthpieces for the ruling party while employment and promotion in the state-controlled media depended primarily on one's party connections rather than on merit.

During the 1990s, the Diouf regime yielded to many of the demands of the opposition for a more open and honest electoral system and greater access to the state-controlled media. The 1991 electoral code, which had the support of fourteen out of Senegal's seventeen political parties, created conditions for minimizing fraud and making elections more transparent. Henceforth, each voter would have to present a national identity card bearing his or her photo. All political parties would have the right to participate in the drawing up of registration lists, the distribution of voter registration cards, the supervision of balloting, and the counting of votes on election day. The reform also restored the secret ballot that had disappeared under Senghor. The 1991 electoral code marked an important improvement over the past when the administration controlled the entire electoral process, discouraged the secret ballot, and excluded representatives of opposition parties from verifying the vote tally.[17]

The government also agreed to give greater access to opposition political parties to state-controlled television and radio and created the *Haut Conseil de la Radio-Télévision* (HCRT) in 1992 to set guidelines and to monitor the government's compliance with access rules. During the official election campaign, opposition parties received more time on radio and television to present their views than in the past. At the same time, the state-controlled media provided greater coverage of political events organized by opposing political parties.

Diouf's acceptance of electoral and media reform also set the stage for the participation of other political parties in government in what became known as the Enlarged Presidential Majority.[18] Wade's party entered the government in 1992 and held several ministries. By this time, Senegal's Marxist parties had largely abandoned their old ideologies and revolutionary aspirations, jumped on the democracy bandwagon, and expressed their willingness to join the government.[19] With the ideological gaps among the major parties contending for power blurred, it became easier for opposition parties to justify entering the government in order to reform the system from within.

Thanks to the electoral reforms, the February 21, 1993 presidential elections reflected voter sentiment more accurately than previous elections. Although Diouf won the elections, official results gave Diouf 58.4 percent of the vote, the lowest score of any incumbent president since independence. Nevertheless, the opposition continued to cry fraud, refused to accredit the official results, and called for the establishment of an independent national election commission. Despite their charges of fraud and sharp attacks on the party in power, opposition leaders had no qualms about joining the government coalition after the May 9, 1993 legislative elections.

Throughout the 1990s, Wade and the PDS joined the government coalition on several occasions only to resign just before national elections. Smaller political parties like the *Parti de l'Indépendance et du Travail* (PIT), the *Ligue Démocratique-Mouvement pour le Parti du travail* (LD-MPT), and PDS-Rénovation, a breakaway party from the PDS also joined the expanded government coalition. The participation of non-PS ministers in the government aroused considerable grumbling in the ruling party who complained about other parties sharing in the spoils of power. Diouf tried to deal with this problem by expanding the number of cabinet level ranks to prevent a reduction in the number of PS ministers. When the demand and competition for high political offices dramatically increased within the ruling party during the 1990s, Diouf responded by increasing the number of political offices at all levels.

The government met the opposition half-way in its demands for an independent national elections commission by establishing a National Election Observatory/*Observatoire Nationale des Elections* (ONEL) in 1997. After the 1998 national legislative elections, most of the opposition parties, though maintaining their demands for an independent national election commission, expressed their satisfaction with ONEL.[20]

In the 1998 legislative elections, the ruling party obtained barely more than 50 percent of the total vote. Although the percentage of PS deputies declined, the actual number of PS deputies in the National Assembly didn't because the number of deputies in the National Assembly had increased from 120 to 140 members. To find more places for disgruntled PS party stalwarts, not nominated to run for deputy on the PS ticket and for those who lost their seats, the regime pushed through a law creating a Senate as a second legislative chamber, which was totally controlled by the PS, thus providing another sixty offices for PS politicians.

Between 1996 and 2000, the number of legally recognized political parties jumped from twenty-five to over forty. Many of the new parties were micro-parties with no real following. Most of them did not contest elections.

To contest the 2000 presidential elections, Wade and the PDS formed an alliance with former Marxist parties and other small parties who backed Wade in the first round rather than presenting their own leaders as candidates. Ideology was no longer an issue. The common goal held by the liberal PDS, their left-wing allies, and other small parties backing Wade was to bring down the Diouf regime and share the spoils of power. They called for *Sopi* or change and argued that it was time to usher in *alternance*.

In the first round, Diouf won 41 percent of the vote to Wade's 31 percent. However, in the second round, all the other opposition candidates and political parties but one rallied behind Wade who won 58 percent of the vote.

One of the major innovations in the 2000 presidential elections was the appearance of political parties whose candidates did not come from the older generation of political leaders and political parties.[21] For the first time in Senegal's political history, a trade union leader ran for president. Two Muslim religious leaders, both Mourides, also ran for president after setting up their own political parties while a third Muslim leader with a large following among Senegalese youth withdrew at the last minute.

Wade's victory in the 2000 presidential elections swelled the ranks of his party as several prominent politicians from the PS deserted their party to join the PDS. The number of political parties continued to grow after Wade's victory while the strength of the PS declined as many left to join the victorious Wade. Other former PS stalwarts quit and formed new political parties. By 2004, the number of legally recognized political parties had climbed to more than seventy.

The Rise of the Independent Media:
Informing the People

The emergence of a dynamic independent press and private independent radio stations in the 1990s provided a major impetus to the democratization of Senegalese politics by providing Senegalese citizens with nonpartisan information concerning political life and public affairs. The political liberalization measures of the 1990s that provided a more level playing field for opposition parties also provided opportunities for the expansion of independent newspapers and radio. Although nonpartisan, the independent dailies and radio stations offered details and discussions concerning Senegalese political life and a platform for different political parties and political associations to present their views.

During the 1990s, newspapers like *Sud-Hebdo* and *Wal Fadjri* that had started out in the mid-1980s as independent weekly newspapers highly critical of government policies and practices became daily newspapers. By the end of the millennium, Dakar had no less than five daily newspapers and two satirical weeklies (*Le Politicien* and *Le Cafard Liberé*) patterned on France's *Le Canard Enchaîné*.

Because of the centralization of political power and modern cultural life in Dakar, the Senegalese written press had much in common with the French press described by Tocqueville.[22] It was concentrated in the capital, controlled by a small group of people, and addressed a small audience of relatively well-educated people. By reviving an interest in public affairs and multiparty competition at the local level, the 1966 decentralization code also sparked the establishment of local and regional newspapers.[23]

Independent Senegalese newspapers offered their readers an alternative and regular source of general information about politics and public affairs to that provided by *Le Soleil*, the government-run daily or newspapers serving as organs of political parties and movements. Although not aligned with any opposition political party, the most prominent independent dailies like *Sud-Quotidien* and *Wal Fadjri*, and the satirical weeklies frequently criticized the government's policies while exposing corruption and mismanagement of public affairs. By the end of the millennium, the Senegalese press was exercising an enormous amount of influence in informing and shaping Senegalese public opinion in the capital. Meanwhile, the government was finding it increasingly difficult to censor the press or to take punitive action against journalists writing stories attacking state officials and party leaders.

In 1993, the Senegalese government authorized the establishment of independent radio stations for the first time. Until that time, the government held a tight monopoly over radio broadcasting in the country. The appearance of free radio stations was a major force contributing to the democratization of Senegalese politics. Newspapers reached only a relatively small number of people concentrated in Dakar and the larger cities that could read French and afford to buy them. The existence of independent radio stations provided the average Senegalese citizen with an alternative source of information to the state-controlled media. Radio stations offered information to a much wider audience than could be reached by the press. In addition to the urban areas, radio stations reached the rural populations in the interior. Independent radio stations also broadcast most of their programs in Wolof and other local languages, thus making political information accessible to those who didn't understand French. Radio stations like *Sud-FM* and *Wal Fadjri-FM* organized political debates and fora that gave listeners the chance to hear representatives of different political parties and discussions of national, regional, and local issues in the indigenous languages.

Independent radio stations differed considerably from that of the independent written press in their coverage and relationships with their audience. First of all, they presented a wider range of material to their public, offering music, religious teachings and commentary, coverage of sports events, political debates, and call-in shows that permitted listeners to express their views on the air and directly question prominent political personalities. Second, radio stations were more decentralized than the press. Regional radio stations based in

Saint-Louis, Kaolack, Ziguinchor, and other towns covered large areas of the country where newspapers could not be easily distributed and thus reached more people. Third, radio stations provided more immediate coverage of events. Cell phones enabled correspondents to report news as it occurred.

Sud-FM provided extensive coverage of the 1996 local government elections by using large numbers of regional and local correspondents. On Election Day, *Sud-FM* gave a blow-by-blow account of how the election went. Listeners were able to know where and why polling booths in different areas were or were not functioning properly. In one instance, a *Sud-FM* broadcaster vividly described a prominent local politician in Dakar carrying off a ballot box in his truck. The extensive radio election coverage vastly increased the transparency of Senegalese elections by making it far more difficult for the state media to cover up electoral fraud.

In addition to the private independent radio stations, Senegal also saw the emergence of dozens of community radio stations throughout the country. *Oxy-Jeunes*, based in Pikine in the Greater Dakar metropolitan region, was started in 1999 by a group of young men who wanted to "transform passive listeners into dynamic actors participating in the act of creating information and contributing to moving state authorities and local government officials to work for the interests of the community."[24] In its broadcasting, *Oxy-Jeunes* reflected the lives and daily concerns, problems, and aspirations of the people living in a sprawling urban area of more than a million people. It became actively involved in a campaign to encourage its listeners to register and vote in the 2000 presidential elections. Other community radio stations sprung up in the rural areas and provided information and discussions concerning public issues in the local languages.

The state, however, retained its monopoly over television broadcasting in the country and dragged its feet in authorizing independent national television stations to function. Although Wade promised to end the state monopoly over television broadcasting if elected, he did not do so. Instead, like his predecessors, he used the state television to puff up his image while providing little access to opposition political parties or critics.

The Political Class, Political Parties, and
Civic Advocacy Associations

Senegal's political history has been marked by a steady expansion in the size of its political class,[25] greater pluralism in its composition, and more recently the emergence of nonpartisan civic associations championing civil and human rights and good governance.

During the nineteenth century, Senegal's political class consisted of a small number of Frenchmen and Afro-Europeans. This class expanded with the incorporation of Black African citizens of the Four Communes who became the dominant force following Blaise Diagne's victory in the 1914 elections. After World War II, the French, for the most part, dropped out of politics. Although their relative weight in the political class declined, Afro-Europeans still held important leadership positions in Senegalese political parties.[26] The postwar era saw a rapid expansion of Senegal's political class as citizenship and suffrage were extended to the populations outside the Four Communes. Eligibility required literacy in French and membership in a political party. The higher ranks of the political class before independence consisted largely of schoolteachers, civil servants, traders, African doctors and veterinarians, and a few lawyers.

With demographic expansion and a sharp increase in the number of Senegalese having access to higher levels of Western education,[27] the number of Senegalese vying for membership in the political class aspiring to rule has grown considerably since independence while the composition of the political class has broadened to also include women, youth, trade unionists, university professors, computer scientists, marabouts, and peasant leaders. Although still skewed toward those with relatively high levels of Western education, the composition of Senegal's political class has become more representative of Senegalese society.

After more than four decades of independence, Senegal's political class still remains largely dominated by politicians and their protégés who came of age before independence and in the 1960s. However, the ideological disputes and cleavages that characterized political debates during the first three decades of independence have gradually faded away.

In Tocquevillian terms, Senegal's political parties no longer organize around broad principles. Instead, they have become "petty" political parties concerned primarily with gaining access to the halls of power and the perks that come with it. With the decline in importance of ideological cleavages has come greater acceptance of the rules of the game of democracy and the conquest of power through the ballot box. Although not a new phenomenon in Senegalese politics, co-optation rather than repression has become more widely prevalent as politicians change parties and enter governments that they had only recently violently attacked for incompetence, corruption, and antinational policies.

In the 1960s and 1970s, Marxist leaders went to jail or into exile and saw their parties banned. In the more liberal 1980s, Marxist parties contested elections but had little or no chance of winning elections or gaining seats in the National Assembly. In the 1990s, they won seats in the National Assembly as social democrats and some of their leaders even became ministers. Today, the radical opposition leaders of yesterday have become an integral part of Senegal's political class and are now part of the establishment. Most members of Senegal's political class are still committed to preserving the hegemony of the state and political parties.

Except for presidential elections, Senegal's election rules exclude independent candidates or slates from running for office. Senegal's political class has quietly opposed efforts to allow independents to run for office.[28] Few parties have come out in favor of allowing independent candidates and slates to run for office. The exclusion of independent candidates has facilitated the control of urban elites and national political parties over Senegal's representative political institutions and deprived many communities of effective representation. During the Senghor and Diouf eras, the executive committee of the ruling party often "parachuted" candidates into districts where they were not known to run on the party ticket. In other instances, urban party bosses, rather than rural communities, often had the last word in nominating candidates to run for the Rural Councils.

Political entrepreneurs in Senegal in recent years have been creating new political parties not to defend a new program or doctrine but to legitimize their claims to a share in the spoils, to increase their bargaining power with the larger political parties, and to enhance their chances of gaining political office and access to state resources. This phenomenon in a climate of political liberalization has led to a dramatic increase in the number of Senegalese political parties.

The opening up of the political system taking place since the 1980s also facilitated the rise of new forms of civic associations with political agendas focusing on strengthening democratic practices and institutions rather than the conquest of power.[29] Led by highly educated Senegalese men and women, these groups have generally declared themselves to be politically neutral while lobbying for electoral and legal reforms and women's rights and intervening to free political prisoners and stop human rights violations in the Casamance. Some of the older groups had affiliations with international human rights groups such as the *Ligue pour les Droits de l'Homme* and Amnesty International. Newer ones like the *Rencontre Africaine pour la Défense des Droits de l'Homme* (RADDHO) have protested the arrest of Senegalese trade union leaders by the government and launched voter registration drives. The *Forum Civil* with ties to Transparency International, an international organization tracking the degree of government corruption in the world has campaigned to legalize independent candidates, promote good governance practices, and strengthen the independence of the judicial branch of government. Women's organizations like the *Conseil Sénégalais des Femmes* and *Yewwu Yewwi pour la Libération des Femmes* have lobbied to increase the number of women candidates and worked to defend women's rights. Many of these new civic associations have received funding from the international donor community.

Since the mid-1980s, winning the support of key "civil society" leaders has become an increasingly important part of the electoral strategies of Senegal's major political parties. Senegalese usage broadly refers to civil society as encompassing well-educated members of the urban elite not affiliated with a political party. The term includes civil servants, doctors, educators, and jurists who work for the state.

While the leaders of most civic society associations involved in promoting civil and human rights, rule of law, and good governance remained unaffiliated with a political party, some maintained close ties with political leaders and used their associations as vehicles for entering the government as "representatives" of civil society. The growing disaffection of Senegalese public opinion with Senegal's aging political class and political parties has reinforced the position of Senegal's urban civil society. During the 1970s and 1980s, Senghor and Diouf bypassed the party and increased the number of technocrats in the government. During the 1980s and 1990s, Diouf encouraged the creation of various nonparty associations to support him in presidential elections.[30] Recognizing the declining popularity of the PS, Diouf sought to present himself as above the political fray and the representative of the people rather than a single political party. Leaders of these support movements were often rewarded with high government posts after the elections.

In the early years of his presidency, Wade bypassed his own party and coalition allies by naming civic and civil society leaders to hold key ministries in the government, such as the Interior, Foreign Affairs, and Justice. After the 2001 national legislative elections, Wade selected nine of the twenty-four cabinet ministers in his government from the ranks of civil society. His own party only received eleven posts and the other four posts were divided between two parties of the Left who had backed him during the first round of the 2000 presidential elections. However, in 2002, Wade reversed himself and decreased the number of civil society ministers in the government, often replacing them with members from his own party and coalition. By the middle of 2004, several of the prominent political parties that had backed him in the 2000 presidential elections had left or been forced out of the government.

It remains to be seen whether the younger generation of Senegalese civil society leaders will be co-opted by those in power, join existing political parties and attempt to reform them from within, or form new political parties to challenge the older parties and leaders.

Multiparty Competition Versus a Free Press as Indicators of Democracy and Self-Governance

During the 1980s and 1990s, Senegal's political parties fought hard to pressure the government to change its electoral rules and behavior and set the stage for ending one-party rule in the country. This period also saw a rapid expansion in the number of political parties and a steady movement toward greater multiparty competition. The 2000 presidential elections demonstrated that regime change—*alternance*—could be achieved peacefully through the ballot box. These developments permitted Senegalese to change their political leadership in open and fair elections, thereby satisfying the basic criteria for a democratic system established by Huntington and others choosing a minimal definition of democracy.

Tocqueville would agree that political parties, multiparty competition, and free elections are essential elements in democratic systems; however, he would also argue that these elements are not sufficient. The right to choose and change leaders does not necessarily contribute to enhancing the capacity of citizens to participate in public affairs or to prevent those in power from abusing their authority. Nor does it insure the preservation of basic freedoms.

Although an indicator of multiparty competition, it is not evident that the proliferation of political parties has contributed to improving the quality of Senegalese democracy.[31] The number of political parties is not a very good indicator of the state of democracy in a country. During the last years of the Mobutu regime, Zaire had more than 200 registered political parties.

While political parties may effectively serve as an instrument for articulating and aggregating their supporters' concerns and interests, they do not always do this. Their main purpose and function is to contest and win elections and take power. Once in power, elected officials may be tempted to break their campaign promises, abuse their authority, and govern without consulting and informing the people.

Despite the high hopes raised by Wade's victory, Senegal's political parties and political class continued to practice politics as usual once Wade and his coalition took power. Those in power continued to sing their own praises, favor their friends and clients, and work to use the system to make sure that they would stay in power. Those out of power complained about the undemocratic and authoritarian nature of the Wade regime, corruption and nepotism, and manipulation of election rules and processes to rig the elections.

Tocqueville's analysis of the motivation underlying debates between supporters of the government and those in the opposition during the last days of the July Monarchy seemed quite applicable to the situation in Senegal today.[32] Tocqueville wryly observed that those who supported the government did so only to keep their salaries and positions, while the opposition attacked only to gain them.[33]

While in the opposition, Wade demanded more freedom of the press, fair elections, a stronger role for Parliament, an independent judiciary that would insure application of the rule of law, and greater transparency in government operations. Once in power, Wade broke many of his campaign promises and adopted a personal style of governance that tarnished his image as one of Africa's greatest fighters for democracy.

In 2003, a prominent Senegalese journalist published a book that argued that Wade was a much better democrat while in the opposition than while in power.[34] The book provided a detailed and scathing critique of Wade's personalization of presidential power. It also documented Wade's sensitivity and hostility to criticism from the press. The book quickly sold out, served as a catalyst for mobilizing public criticism of Wade's regime, and put Wade on the defensive. The success of the book underscored the growing power of the press in informing and shaping Senegalese public opinion and defender of freedom and democratic principles.

Tocqueville regarded freedom of the press as the principal constituent element in freedom.[35] A free press provided citizens with facts and ideas needed to make informed and rational choices between the different opinions debated by their contemporaries.

A free press subjected political figures and government officials to public scrutiny. Tocqueville's eloquent description of the immense power of the free press in the United States could arguably also be applied to Senegal.

It makes political life circulate in every corner of that vast land. Its eyes are never shut, and it lays bare the secret shifts of politics, forcing public figures to appear before the tribunal of opinion . . . through the press, the parties without actually meeting, listen and argue with one another.[36]

Independent radio stations rather than the written press have brought political information to nearly every corner of Senegal. As a result, political issues once confined to discussion among the Senegalese urban elite are now being discussed openly and widely in the towns and the countryside. The free press—newspapers and radio—in Senegal has provided a vehicle for politicians to express their views and debate issues and to appeal directly to public opinion.

During the Senghor era, Senghor and the ruling party did not have to worry about the press because the Senegalese free press was too small and muzzled to influence public opinion. Moreover, public opinion itself was largely restricted to Western-educated urban elites, religious authorities, and rural notables. During this period, those in power showed more concern with criticism of the regime in the foreign press and media. In Senegal, as in many other francophone African countries, the elites read French newspapers or listened to French language international radio stations to get a different perspective on what was happening in the country than that presented by the state media.

The situation changed dramatically during the 1980s and 1990s with political liberalization and the rapid development of independent media. As elections became increasingly more competitive, the ruling party and opposition parties realized the importance of using the media to appeal to public opinion. With the introduction of independent radio stations, public opinion itself expanded to include ordinary citizens who now had greater access to political information and a diversity of political opinions.

Over the past two decades, those in power as well as those in the opposition have been courting the free press and using the media to reach the electorate.[37] During the 1990s, the Diouf government reduced its pressure on the press to tone down its criticism of the regime. Diouf himself began to hold public press conferences and engage in dialogue with prominent media leaders to discuss the role of a free press in a democracy.

While in the opposition, Wade himself relied more on the independent media to reach the public than *Sopi*, his own party newspaper, which appeared irregularly. Opposition leaders acknowledged the contribution made by the free press in making a peaceful regime transfer through the ballot box possible.

The independent media have favored the emergence of a growing sense of citizenship. Senegalese, especially those in the urban areas are becoming increasingly more aware of the rights and responsibilities of citizenship and

demanding greater transparency and accountability on the part of politicians and government officials.[38] The media has provided citizens with
information about the functioning of government institutions and civic
education concerning the importance of voting and participating in public
affairs. Thanks to the independent media, ordinary citizens, women, youth,
professional organizations, and other associations are generating information
concerning their concerns, priorities and evaluation of government policies,
articulating their aspirations to participate in the life of the nation, and
demonstrating their capacity to make political leaders and government
more responsive and accountable to public opinion.

CHAPTER SEVEN

The Art of Association

> If men are to remain civilized or to become civilized, the art of asso-
> ciation must develop and improve among them at the same speed as
> equality of conditions.[1]

Tocqueville maintained that civil associations—associations without political
objectives—were essential to a vibrant democratic society where individuals sharing common concerns, interests, and views had the freedom to
organize civil associations to make their opinions heard and to influence
government policy.[2] In democratic societies, civil associations engaged in a
myriad of religious, moral, economic, commercial, social, cultural, intellectual, and recreational activities and provided public goods and services outside
the realm of the state. By instilling in their members habits of cooperation,
solidarity, and concern for the public interest, civil associations contributed
to the effectiveness and stability of democratic government.[3]

Tocqueville asserted that the absence of political associations adversely
affected the number and quality of civil associations.[4] When government
banned political associations and restricted political life, they also discouraged
citizens from organizing civil associations. In Senegal, as throughout much
of Africa, the development of associational life was highly correlated with
the expansion of political associations and the freedom to associate.

Associational Life in Colonial Senegal (1885–1945)

Because of its long history of freedom of political association for the "citizens"
during the colonial era, Senegal had more modern voluntary associations
than in other French colonies where the subject status of the indigenous
populations and autocratic nature of colonial rule restricted their rights.

Even in the *métropole*, the French were slow to recognize the rights of
their citizens to form their own associations.[5] It took until 1884 before
France authorized the establishment of trade unions and until 1901 before
associations could be formed without needing the prior consent of the
government.

In Senegal, civil associations, like political associations and parties, were largely concentrated within the Four Communes. Senegalese involvement in modern associational life intensified during the interwar period (1920–1939).

When the Popular Front government in France, in 1936, passed legislation recognizing the legality of trade unions in French West Africa, the legislation restricted membership to Frenchmen and Senegalese citizens literate in French. Despite these constraints, Senegal had forty-two registered trade unions and sixteen professional workers associations by the end of 1937.[6] Civil servants, railway workers, sailors, and employees working for French trading companies were the most active elements in the trade union movement.

Western-educated Senegalese also formed a variety of cultural, student, and alumni associations like the *Association des Anciens Elèves de l'Ecole William Ponty*, organized by the graduates of the elite teacher training school, which produced many of Senegal's and French West Africa's political leaders.[7]

In contrast to the relative dynamism of associational life in the Four Communes, the rural populations in the interior had little freedom to create their own forms of voluntary associations. The few modern associations that functioned in the countryside were creations of the colonial state. The Native Provident Societies (*Societés Indigènes de Prévoyance*) first created by a *commandant de cercle* in Sine-Saloum in 1907, reflected both the paternalism of the French colonial administration and the stereotype of the African as lazy and lacking foresight.[8] The state thus needed to provide an organization to protect the peasants from themselves and to insure that they had enough seeds to cultivate the next year's peanut crop. The Native Provident Societies were clearly not voluntary associations. Membership was compulsory for all adult males living within the *cercle* while all the meetings were run by the *commandant de cercle*.

Upon taking power after the fall of France in 1940, the Vichy government abolished Senegalese trade unions and employer associations and established sports and cultural associations closely watched and indoctrinated by a reactionary colonial administration. Vichy proposed to replace Senegal's civil associations with corporate structures guided by the state. The ousting of the Vichy administration in November 1942 set the stage for a revival of associational life, which did not take place until the restoration and expansion of political life after the end of the war.

Civil Associations in the
Postwar Era (1945–1960)

The elimination of distinctions between citizens and subjects after the war created a favorable environment for the rapid expansion of civil associations. New associations emerged that adopted the language and organizational structures of their metropolitan counterparts while other associations built on indigenous institutions and values.

Modern Advocacy and Interest-Based Associations

Western modes of organization and ideologies highly influenced African trade unions and student organizations during the postwar era. Civil servants, government employees, municipal workers and teachers joined trade unions along with factory workers and employees in the commercial and construction sectors. Most Senegalese trade unions[9] affiliated with metropolitan trade union movements such as the communist-dominated *Confédération Générale des Travailleurs*, the SFIO-dominated CGT-*Force Ouvrière and the Confédération Française des Travailleurs Croyants* linked with the French Catholic Left. The Railway Workers Union, that launched the famous Dakar–Niger strike in 1947, remained one of the few major trade unions in Senegal to remain independent. The fact that their principal employers were the French colonial state and French-controlled private firms reinforced the militancy of Senegalese trade unionists affiliated with the French Left.

The rise and expansion of radical student associations coincided with a sharp increase in the number of scholarships for African students to study in French universities. Senegalese and students from other French colonies went to France to study because there were no post-secondary institutions in the African colonies before the establishment of the *Institut des Hautes Etudes de Dakar* in 1950, which eventually evolved into French West Africa's only university. Their stay in France put them in contact with other African students as well as students from North Africa and Indo-China and other parts of the French Union. Senegalese students played a major role in establishing the *Fédération des Etudiants d'Afrique Noire en France* (FEANF) in 1950 that brought together students from all over Africa.[10] FEANF became politically active and made pronouncements on a wide range of political issues, which included demands for independence and support of national liberation movements in North Africa and Indo-China. Many Senegalese student activists in France became prominent political figures after independence, including Majhemout Diop, founder of the PAI, Cheikh Anta Diop, and Abdoulaye Wade.

Community-Based Urban Associations

Urbanization sparked a sharp rise in associational life in Dakar and other towns that reflected an effort on the part of individuals to retain traditional communitarian values in a changing world. Generally small in size and localized in neighborhoods, these associations emphasized social and recreational activities, the provision of mutual assistance and credit to finance important life-cycle events, and a social safety net to help the needy. These urban associations were not organized as interest groups to lobby or fight the government. Instead they had more in common with the civil associations described by Tocqueville whose members came together to work for common purposes and community needs.

Many of these associations had originated during the interwar period but expanded rapidly after World War II when Dakar's population jumped from 132,000 in 1945 to over 350,000 by 1960.[11] Dakar had many informal voluntary associations, which organized dancing, drumming, and other recreational activities for youth; groups (*mbotaay*) that brought women together to socialize; rotating credit associations (*tontines*) for men and women; and hometown (*ressortisant*) and regional associations that provided advice on how to get employment, housing, and financial assistance for life-cycle events—marriages, baptisms, and burials. The Catholic church sponsored a wide range of cultural, sports, and recreational associations while different branches of Muslim brotherhoods established various urban neighborhood-based associations (*dahiras*) that brought the faithful together to sing and pray and to provide mutual assistance and charity.

Griots and casted artisans formed their own associations as did migrants from different regions and ethnic groups. Social, cultural, and sports associations flourished at the neighborhood level. Youth associations involved in social, cultural, and sports activities proliferated, as did a wide range of women's groups engaged in diverse social and economic activities.

The myriad of urban voluntary associations that emerged in Dakar could also be found in other major towns in colonial Africa during the postwar era.[12] These included tribal associations, sports clubs, old boys networks, cultural societies, market women's associations, burial societies, and groups organized by prostitutes.[13] Participation in these groups often gave its members training in modern forms of administration and skills that could be used in the political arena.

In Senegal's major towns outside of Dakar, the number and density of associations were not as great as in the federal capital because of smaller populations and less differentiated social structures and economic activities. In the towns of the interior, new forms of associational life developed after the war. For example, after the elimination of restrictions on subjects to form associations, urban-based Senegalese traders and transporters in the interior became increasingly active in the peanut trade and created their own associations in defense of their interests.

Associational Life in the Countryside

After the passage of a cooperative law in the métropole in 1947, influential religious and political leaders with close ties to the Senegalese Socialists created the first modern agricultural cooperatives in Senegal.[14] These cooperatives did not respect the spirit of the cooperative law, which called for internal democracy based on one man, one vote rules and the open election of officers. Marabouts, politicians, and merchants controlled the new cooperatives which were set up primarily in the peanut basin to market peanuts. By the mid-1950s, it was clear that the cooperative movement was not working very well.

The tutelage of the French colonial administration in the countryside continued to stifle the development of new forms of autonomous associations.

As a result, the countryside had few modern voluntary associations. In 1955, the *Sociétés Mutuelles de Développement Rural* (SMDRs) replaced the old Native Provident Societies. Although the SMDRs were more democratic than their predecessors in having two-thirds of the officers elected by the members, dues and membership remained compulsory.

The acceleration of the rural exodus contributed to the creation and expansion of community-based associations with links to hometown associations in the cities. In villages that had schools, youth groups took on modern trappings as young people organized soccer teams. Work groups based on age-sets continued to function and provide labor where needed. The *daras* set up by the marabouts to provide religious education for their followers and to produce food crops and peanuts for the market expanded while the number of seasonal agricultural workers (*navétanes*) coming to the peanut basin declined as uncultivated land became scarcer.

State Tutelage and Associational Life in Independent Senegal

Unlike one-party regimes in Mali and Guinea, where membership in the party and in state-sponsored associations was compulsory, the de facto party-state in Senegal did not impose compulsory membership in the ruling party and its affiliated associations. Instead it chose to closely regulate, supervise, and domesticate associational life rather than eliminate it. Like the colonial administration, the regime insisted that voluntary associations had to remain apolitical and not get involved in political action, or more accurately, political activities hostile to the party and government in power. As a result, one saw the repression and banning of trade unions and student associations hostile to the government.

After dissolving the radical *Union Générale des Travailleurs d'Afrique Noire*, the country's strongest union, in 1960, the emerging Senegalese party-state promoted the creation of a UPS-dominated trade union movement, the UNTS, which by the end of 1963 had absorbed most of Senegal's trade unions.[15] In May 1968 the UNTS launched a national strike to protest government austerity policies that had frozen wages and depressed the living standards of public and private sector employees. The government reacted by arresting union leaders behind the strike and instigating the formation of a new trade union in 1969, the *Conféderation Nationale des Travailleurs Sénégalais* (CNTS) led by UPS loyalists that could be counted on to not openly oppose the government's economic policies. The CNTS soon became formally integrated into the structures of the party-state. Seats were set aside for CNTS leaders in party councils, the National Assembly, and the government. With the dissolution of the UNTS in 1969, the CNTS became Senegal's only comprehensive national trade union. In 1971, the government changed the Labor Code and placed more restrictions on public sector employees' right to strike to insure that government would have the last word in arbitrating disputes between employers and workers.

Although the Senghor regime suppressed all national-level confederations of trade unions with the exception of the progovernmental CNTS, it permitted sectoral trade unions to function. During the 1970s, teachers unions like the *Syndicat des Enseignants du Sénégal* (SES) and its successor, the *Syndicat Unique et Démocratique des Enseignants* (SUDES) remained hotbeds of antigovernment agitation. The return to a multiparty system in the mid-1970s sparked the reemergence of independent trade union activity. In 1975, the government recognized the *Union des Travailleurs Libres de Sénégal* (UTLS), which had close links with the PDS as a national trade union confederation. Other autonomous trade unions emerged during the last years of the Senghor regime, often controlled by leaders from political movements that were still underground.

The radicalism of student associations continued after independence. Efforts to domesticate university and secondary school student associations and to restrict their political activism failed. Despite laws banning students from participating in political activities, students played a major role in the political and social crisis that shook the stability of the regime in May 1968. The government invoked antisedition laws and laws defining associations as apolitical to justify its crackdown on dissident student groups. The rapid expansion of the number of university and secondary school students studying in Senegal after independence increased the relative importance of this group in politics while the absence of legal political parties reflecting their views stoked their militancy expressed by strikes, demonstrations, and destruction of university property. To counteract the influence of opposition student groups on the campus, the regime encouraged the establishment of UPS/PS university student associations that became a training ground for future PS leaders like Moustapha Niasse and Djibo Ka.

The Senghor regime also contested the establishment of autonomous national employers' associations critical of government economic policies. In 1968, a group of Senegalese businessmen created the *Union des Groupements Économiques du Sénégal*, which bitterly criticized the government's economic policies and French and Lebanese domination of the economy. Senghor responded by backing the creation of a rival organization that supported the government. After much coaxing by the government, the two groups merged and formed the *Groupements Économiques du Sénégal*, a highly politicized organization whose leadership was closely allied with the ruling party. After the state began nationalizing and Africanizing various sectors of the economy, Senegalese firms and entrepreneurs benefited from their ties with the party in power to obtain government contracts and loans, thus reinforcing the postindependence Senegalese business class' dependence upon the state.

The UPS had its own youth wing that recruited young males between the ages of eighteen and thirty-five. However, unlike integral party-states like those in Guinea and Mali, the government in Senegal did not require all young people to join the party youth group.[16] Although the Senghor regime permitted various non-party youth groups to organize, it sought to control them and carefully regulate their activities. When schoolteachers, students, and youth groups took the lead in organizing soccer and other sports activities, the government introduced legislation in 1969 to regulate and supervise sports activities that placed sports associations under the tutelage of regional and departmental inspectors from the Youth and Sports Ministry. The state did not simply regulate sports and cultural associations organized by youth; it also sought to become their patron and sponsor by providing financial and material support.

Sports activities were not the only area in which the state exercised its tutelage during the Senghor era. Different state ministries regulated associational life in their respective spheres of competence. Thus, the Ministry of Labor supervised trade union activities; the Ministry of Commerce, Industry, and crafts regulated the activities of employer, merchant, and artisan associations; the Ministry of Agriculture/Rural Development regulated associations organized around farming, herding, and natural resource management; and Ministry of Women's Affairs promoted the establishment of village-level adult women's associations *Groupements Féminins* to participate in development projects and economic activities as members of a national federation of women's groups under its tutelage.

Most of the rural producer associations initiated by the state in the first two decades of independence failed to achieve the ambitious objectives laid down by the state. These associations had few of the characteristics of self-governing voluntary associations consisting of people who came together to solve common problems. State tutelage exercised by regional development agencies imposed unsuitable organizational modes, governance rules, and regulations on largely unwilling or passive populations. Rural producers became increasingly dependent upon the state and the international donor community during the drought years of the late 1960s and early 1970s.

Resilience and Adaptation of Indigenous Associations

With the growing commercialization of the rural economy, traditional age-grades organized themselves into work parties to earn money. These work groups eventually transformed themselves into more formal organizations with numerous officers and a wider membership when they formed village-level youth associations that incorporated all members of the same age-grade or several age-grades.[17] Many of these village-level youth groups evolved into the most dynamic and effective associations in the country and constituted the base for a strong peasant movement in many parts of the country.[18]

The history of one youth group in Ronkh, a village in the Senegal River Delta where the government promoted irrigated agriculture, illustrates the resiliency and adaptive capacity of precolonial Senegalese institutions.[19] In 1963, a group of 200 young people encompassing five age-grades decided to create a cultural, educational, and sports association and registered with the Ministry of Youth as the *Foyer des Jeunes de Ronkh*. Led by a young schoolteacher, the *Foyer* eventually won the support of the village elders by contributing labor to build a mosque, a high priority of the community for many years. During its early years, the association engaged primarily in noneconomic activities financed by revenues generated by collective fields.

By the end of the 1960s, the *Foyer* was openly criticizing the policies of the state water and irrigation agency (SAED) that allocated land on the irrigated perimeters for its heavy-handed tactics in organizing agricultural activities. The *Foyer* refused to join the state cooperatives in order to gain access to land. Eventually, its members acquired land during the early 1970s with the support of the area's traditional landholders.

The example of the *Foyer des Jeunes de Ronkh* sparked the creation, in 1976, of a broader-based association—the *Association Socio-Educative Sportive et Culturelle, L'Amicale du Walo* (ASESCAW)—which represented scores of youth groups organized on the Ronkh model. By the mid-1980s, ASESCAW had access to over 3,000 hectares of land, much of which had been acquired from the Rural Councils that had denied them access to land during the early 1980s.

As an association, ASESCAW brought together young men and women and gave village elders and other traditional decision-makers an important role in decision-making. Unlike the rural cooperative and producer groups initiated by the state, ASESCAW was a grassroots movement, which first emerged to meet the needs of young people for land. And unlike the farmer groups organized under the tutelage of the central government as instruments of national economic policies, ASESCAW engaged in a wide range of economic, social, and cultural activities of interest to its members and to the community at large.

When left alone by the state, rural Senegalese with little fanfare successfully adapted and expanded precolonial institutions like the rotating weekly rural market. Weekly rural markets sprung up throughout the country in response to the need to provide rural producers with markets to sell various local products and a place to purchase basic consumer goods because of the vacuum left by the departure of the French trading companies and Lebanese merchants from the countryside after independence.[20] This remarkably successful institution received relatively little attention from government decisionmakers and donors largely because they were not part of national programs and donor projects.

Bowling Together: The Explosion of
Autonomous Associational Life

In *Bowling Alone*, Robert Putnam noted how an explosion in associational life reflecting the creation of an unprecedented number of voluntary associations during the last decades of the nineteenth century revitalized American democracy and civic life as new types of associations multiplied, chapters of preexisting associations proliferated, and associations increasingly federated into national and state organizations.[21]

During the last two decades of the twentieth century and the early years of the new millennium, Senegal experienced a similar explosion in the number, density, and variety of voluntary associations. Besides the political liberalization policies begun in the mid-1970s that revitalized and expanded political life and created the space for the development of a wide variety and range of modern civil associations and the loosening of the state's tutelage over the economy and associational life that provided more opportunities for Senegalese to organize a wide range of autonomous economic enterprises and associations, several other factors contributed to the boom in associational life. The decline of the rural economy, the negative effects of structural adjustment programs on the urban populations and the impact of globalization prodded and inspired Senegalese to create new kinds of organizations and to adapt old ones in order to survive. At the same time, rapid urbanization, improvements in communications, and the rising number of literate Senegalese shook up old social, cultural, and economic structures and created an environment that made possible new forms and modes of associational life not possible in the past.

Democracy From Above: National Level Urban-Based Civil Associations

In discussing the relationships between associations and democracy, most of the attention of contemporary analyses of democracy in Africa has been placed on predominantly urban-based associations organized around professional, functional, and civic concerns led by individuals with relatively high educational levels. These associations generally operated as (1) interest groups—trade unions, employers' associations, student associations, professional associations, etc.—striving to advance the corporate interests of their members; (2) advocacy groups seeking to promote human, civil and women's rights, good government, and democracy; and (3) civic minded economic, social, and cultural associations—development NGOs, Rotary, Lions, and Soroptimist Clubs, Red Cross, etc.—involved in projects to address the needs of the poor, improve their city or region, or support major cultural events. These associations usually operated at the national level and frequently sought to influence government policy. Although not necessarily run by aristocrats, they were essentially elitist organizations working primarily in French and using Western-inspired concepts and rules of operation. These kinds of associations boomed during the 1980s and 1990s and made an important contribution to accelerating the processes of democratization that took place during the 1990s by challenging the government's efforts to control associational life and asserting their own autonomy.

During this period, autonomous business associations and trade unions emerged that articulated the interests of their members and showed a willingness to oppose and lobby against the government's economic programs and policies.[22] Thus, Senegalese employers' associations like the *Conseil National des Employeurs Sénégalais*, representing newer Senegalese-controlled formal sector firms and the *Union des Commerçants et Industriels du Sénégal* (UNACOIS), which represented the burgeoning "informal sector," criticized

the government's preferential treatment to older firms and monopoly privileges and tax benefits granted to companies and businessmen tied to the
regime. Founded in 1989, UNACOIS marked the rise of a new class of self-
made Senegalese businessmen, less educated, more traditional and attached
to Islamic values, and outside the select group of Senegalese businessmen
closely tied to the state. At its peak, UNACOIS had close to 100,000 members
representing thousands of small-scale enterprises concentrated in trade,
transport, and services throughout the country.

During the 1990s, independent trade unions like the *Union Nationale des
Syndicats Autonomes de Sénégal* (UNSAS) conducted strikes to protest government austerity measures and privatization of state-owned utilities companies. Despite its affiliation with the PS, the CNTS increasingly showed
more initiative and militancy in articulating the grievances of state and private
sector workers concerning unpopular economic measures imposed by the
government's structural adjustment programs.

Teachers' unions like SUDES continued to criticize government educational policies and to press for more teachers, higher salaries, and increased
resources allocated to primary, secondary, and university education. Although
the teachers' unions maintained a high degree of militancy, they became less
radical and ideological following liberalization of the political system in
the 1980s and the entry of former opposition parties into the government
in the 1990s.

Expansion of the numbers of Senegal's Western-educated elite was accompanied by the growth and strengthening of professional associations of
administrateurs civils, lawyers, magistrates, engineers, accountants, doctors,
pharmacists, journalists, communications specialists, and musicians. These
associations established guidelines for their professions and defended the
corporate interests of their members.

Human rights and civic minded associations like the *Organization National
des Droits de l'Homme* (ONDH), RADDHO, *Forum Civil* and *Aide Transparence*
led by lawyers and intellectuals criticized the government's violation of
human rights in the Casamance, the jailing of political leaders, corruption,
and the state-controlled media's failure to provide more access to opposition
leaders and critics of the regime. These associations also took the lead in
lobbying for fair and open elections, good government practices, and reform
of the legal system.

Western-educated women in Dakar formed associations like the *Conseil
Sénégalais des Femmes* (COSEF) to promote the status of women in general
while others formed groups specifically to fight violence against women,
female genital mutilation, and AIDS. Other women's groups reflected specific
professional, economic, and intellectual concerns, which led to the creation of
women's associations for judges, entrepreneurs, and development researchers.

Civic and charitable organizations like the *Convention des Saint-Louisiens*
and the *Convention des Thièssois* emerged in the 1990s to promote their city.
Older civic associations like the Senegalese Red Cross, Rotary Club,
Masons, and Soropimists continued as Senegalese versions of Western-style

institutions that brought Senegalese elites together socially to organize various civic and charitable events.

Senegalese development-oriented NGOs also expanded their scope of activities during the last two decades of the century. The NGO movement in Senegal began in the 1960s when international faith-based organizations like Catholic Relief, CARITAS, and Protestant missions came to Senegal to provide technical assistance to Senegal's rural populations. NGO activities expanded during the 1970s following the severe drought that hit Senegal and other Sahelian countries. NGOs became increasingly important after donors began to direct more of their aid away from government agencies and look more to international and national NGOs to implement development projects during the 1980s and 1990s. As late as 1988, Senegal had more international (sixty-nine) than Senegalese NGOs (fifty-seven). However, by the end of the millennium, Senegalese NGOS numbered in the hundreds.

The legal status and organizational structure of Senegalese development NGOs differed markedly from community-based development associations. NGOs registered as private nonprofit apolitical associations working in various sectors including agriculture, natural resource management, education, health, marketing, and credit and savings and were heavily dependent upon external financing.

Created in 1982, The *Conseil des Organisations Non-Gouvernementales d'Appui au Développement* (CONGAD) sought to coordinate the activities of the diverse international and national NGOs working in Senegal. CONGAD regarded itself as the voice of the national NGO movement and had close links with many of the peasant-based associations that had emerged during the 1970s and 1980s. At first, the government regarded the development NGOs as competitors for donor funds as well as hotbeds of political opposition.[23] Tensions between the government and the NGO movement declined considerably in the 1990s as the government reduced its tutelage over associational life. Although primarily oriented toward social and economic development activities, CONGAD articulated a participatory development ideology as an alternative discourse to the top-down development approach adopted by the party-state and lobbied for greater democratization in Senegal.

While many of the national-level urban-based civil associations disseminated democratic norms and values, most are still dominated by Senegal's Western-educated elite. Located primarily in metropolitan Dakar, they directly touched only a small fraction of the population. Although advocating democracy and development and claiming to be the voice of the Senegalese people, these elite based organizations did not emanate from local grassroots communities.

Democracy From Below: GrassRoots

Community-Based Associations

In looking at the processes of democratization in Africa, relatively little attention has been paid to popular grassroots community-based associations organized on the basis of gender, age, ethnic, and religious affiliations. Members of these associations generally had lower levels of Western education and operated on a smaller scale. These associations engaged in a wide range of social, cultural, and economic activities and frequently produced public goods and services not provided by the state or the so-called formal sectors of the economy. Working within the framework of the larger-scale community-based village and neighborhood associations and based on indigenous modes of social organization, many of these associations successfully adapted to changing social and economic conditions.

Top-down efforts to revitalize and democratize the cooperative movement by revising the Cooperative Law in 1983 failed despite measures to grant legal status and financial autonomy to village-level cooperative groups (*sections villageoises*), and give more voice to youth and women in cooperative decision-making.[24] The 4,200 village sections organized by the Cooperative Service to "decentralize" the movement were initiated by the state, indicating that cooperative structures continued to be shaped by government fiat rather than emanating from the grassroots. The revival of the cooperative movement also suffered from an innovative law passed in 1984 that permitted small groups of farmers to have access to credit without being members of a cooperative.

The new law permitted two or more individuals to establish a *Groupement d'Intérêt Économique* (GIE) to pursue a common economic activity during a determinate period. GIEs had legal status, access to credit, and freedom to organize without interference from the state. The GIEs contributed to the further decline of the various producer groups directly linked to the Regional Development Agencies (RDAs)[25] as farmers, herders, and fishermen opted to set up their own autonomous groups made up of friends, family, and age-sets rather than to stay in producer groups closely supervised by the state. Their smaller size generally made the GIEs more manageable. Two-thirds of the GIEs had less than fifty members. By 1990, Senegal had 4,745 registered GIES with a third of them concentrated in the Senegal River Delta and Valley where producer groups formerly affiliated with SAED transformed themselves into GIEs.

Associational life in the countryside also flourished in other areas. Young people organized their own sports and cultural associations and soccer leagues. Participation in local soccer leagues helped to promote village civic pride and brought youngsters into contact with young people from other villages. Women's associations previously involved primarily in social activities carried on a wide range of economic activities—growing vegetables, marketing local food and artisan products, and raising sheep and goats.

Another major development in associational life during the 1980s and the 1990s was the regrouping of autonomous village-based peasant and grassroots rural youth associations that that had sprung up during the 1970s into regional and national federations. The rise of autonomous federations in rural Senegal coincided with the government's disengagement from the rural economy and the decline of associations initiated and organized by the RDAs and other state agencies.

Founded in 1978, the *Fédération des Organisations Non-Gouvernementales du Sénégal* (FONGS) acted as an umbrella group that brought together a wide variety of peasant associations operating throughout the country.[26] By the early 1990s, twenty-three peasant associations with 100,000 members in 850 villages had affiliated with FONGS.

FONGS worked to increase the autonomy of rural associations and the bargaining power of rural producers vis-à-vis the state. Groups like FONGS and its member organizations consciously sought to reverse the top-down approach to development and authoritarian modes of governance that characterized government intervention in the countryside during the first two decades after independence. In 1993, FONGS brought together the leaders of seven national organizations and cooperatives representing farmers, women, herders, fishermen, and horticulturalists to discuss the possibility of creating a national federation that would articulate and defend the interests of rural producers. The result was the creation of the *Conseil National de Concertation des Ruraux* (CNCR).

The 1993 Thiès Declaration acknowledged that political transformations over the past decade in the direction of greater democratization had facilitated the rise of the associative movement in Senegal and "provided opportunities for all segments of society to express themselves, to organize themselves, and to act so that the State would take into consideration their concerns and interests."[27] Recognizing the great diversity of the groups it represented, the rules relating to the organization of the CNCR affirmed the autonomy and independence of its member organizations that were not obliged to apply any decision taken by the CNCR contrary to their statutes and principles.

The return of hundreds of rural development extension agents to their home villages, due to the government's downsizing and elimination of the regional development agencies provided expertise that strengthened community-based peasants' associations and the CNCR. In a relatively short period of time, the CNCR became an authentic representative of the concerns and priorities of rural producers throughout the country and met regularly with the president to discuss the government's agricultural policy.

During the early years of the new millennium, the CNCR emerged as an ardent defender of the Senegalese family farmer and opposed efforts by the Wade government to pass a land tenure law giving the Senegalese government sweeping powers to transfer large tracts of community land for development by large-scale agribusinesses.[28]

Although hierarchical associational structures still persist in the countryside run by rural notables or heavily dependent upon the state, one can see a clear trend toward more and more self-governing horizontally based grass-roots associations propelled by the growing importance of youth and women's groups and the spread of Western education. These groups are complemented by a growing number of health committees, parent–student associations, water management committees, and rural producers' organizations. These associations constitute the basic building blocks of village and extra-local development associations and demonstrate the desire of different groups within the community to work together to resolve their problems.

As in the countryside, some of the most dynamic grassroots associations that have emerged in Dakar and other large towns have been organized by Senegalese youth and women. The more successful *Associations Sportives et Culturelles* (ASCs) offer excellent examples of democratic self-governing institutions. The ASCs are pluralistic horizontally based organizations bringing together young men and women living in the same neighborhood. Leaders are generally democratically elected and chosen on the basis of competence. ASCs generate civic pride at the neighborhood level. In addition to their sports and cultural activities, neighborhood ASCs have mobilized their members to provide security, garbage removal services, and other public goods and services for their neighborhood and have played a key role in urban antipoverty campaigns.[29]

The *Set Setal* cleanup campaign that took place in the capital in 1990 demonstrated the mobilizing capacity of urban youth and their potential to work for their community.[30] Unlike previous clean-up campaigns organized by the state or the ruling party, the *Set Setal* movement was initiated by youth groups throughout the city. Inspired by a song written by Youssou Ndour, one of Senegal's most popular musical artists, the movement reflected the aspirations of Dakar's urban youth to take matters into their own hands to change the capital's dirty and run-down environment and improve sanitation conditions. Although the *Set Setal* movement lasted only a short time, it set an important precedent for implicating urban youth in civic affairs and offering an alternative to drugs, street crime, violence, and vandalism. This idealism was mobilized again during the 2000 presidential campaign when record numbers of young people voted for the first time.

Many informal urban women's rotating credit associations (*tontines*) over the past two decades have evolved into savings and credit associations. These groups developed because of the failure of formal large-scale banking and state credit institutions to accommodate the needs of people of modest means to accumulate and mobilize capital. Dakar now has hundreds of mutual savings and credit associations that finance small-scale economic enterprises, access to housing, and the pilgrimage to Mecca.

Members of diverse neighborhood social, cultural, and recreational groups have set up GIEs that engage in a wide range of economic activities. Most neighborhoods in Greater Dakar now have a dense network of grassroots associations. These include sections of hometown associations, *dahiras*, church groups, parent–teachers associations, health and sanitation committees, market women's groups, neighborhood security associations, sports and cultural clubs, GIES, *tontines*, tea groups, and rap groups. Since the creation of the *communes d'arrondissement* in 1996, these groups have come together to establish their own local development committees to evaluate their neighborhood's needs and to develop plans to improve the level of public goods and services. Neighborhood development committees have become more directly involved in the functioning of local government; some have provided candidates for public office.

The rising participation of grassroots organizations in local governance has been accompanied by a heightened sense of citizenship on the part of their members. These developments are slowly changing the nature of local politics by undermining patron–client relationships and party control of associational life and making local government officials increasingly account-able to their constituents rather than to their party.

Self-Interest Properly Understood and
Grassroots Associational Life:
The Foundation of Senegalese Demokarassi

Tocqueville underscored the importance of the concept of *self-interest properly understood* as a key factor explaining the vigor and dynamism of associational life in America. For Tocqueville, the doctrine of self-interest properly under-stood avoided the dangers of unbridled individualism and contributed to the sacrifice of private interests for the common good.[31] The application of the concept of self-interest properly understood built and strengthened social capital, that is, trust, mutual reciprocity, and networks, thus facilitating cooperation and the establishment of voluntary associations.[32]

Tocqueville's concepts of self-interest properly understood and how it fostered the creation of voluntary associations had much in common with Senegalese communitarian values. Old attachments to the values of mutual reciprocity and solidarity became an integral part of the notion of *Demokarassi*, the newly coined Wolof word for democracy. An unschooled Wolof rural household head asserted that Demokarassi was important because

> What one person can do, two can do better. Twenty people can do more than five. That's how it is here in Thiourour. We have several associations. In each one the money is managed by all the members. We deliberate and make common decisions. *Demokarassi* means that the group is united in wanting good and refusing bad.[33]

In Western societies undergoing democratic transformation, Tocqueville argued, individuals had to learn the art of association in order to prosper and retain their liberty. The situation was somewhat different in Senegal where the art of association was not new. The huge stock of social capital inherent in Senegalese precolonial institutions had remained underutilized because of the stifling of associational life under the centralized and authoritarian colo-nial state and the postcolonial party-state. Greater freedom has permitted the Senegalese people to reactivate and build on their old stock of social capital.

In Senegal, the problem is not how to foster the art of association among Senegalese,[34] but how the Senegalese can use and adapt their already considerable skills in the art of association to cope with economic scarcity and move forward.

While self-interest properly understood was the main concept underlying the proliferation of voluntary associations in America, a somewhat different version of this concept prevailed in Senegal where the drive for participating in voluntary associations, especially in urban settings, was based on the belief that strengthening one's social relationships and networks was the key to individual security in a new environment. While some associations had primarily economic objectives, all associations had social objectives. Senegalese did not define poverty in terms of material assets but in terms of social relationships. Thus, the poor person was not someone without money or assets but someone without social relationships, that is, people in his life.[35] Membership in associations widened the potential resources that individuals could tap when in need by expanding one's social network beyond friends, family, and neighbors.[36] At the same time, reciprocity and solidarity norms obliged individuals to be prepared to contribute when others in their social networks expressed the need for assistance.

Rotation of resources, rather than accumulation of resources, was a major organizational principle of Senegalese social networks and organizations like the rotating credit associations (*tontines*). Mutual trust and reciprocity were important ingredients needed to insure the integrity and success of the *tontines*. Members trusted that everyone would make their contributions on time, wait their turn in making a claim on *tontine* resources, and not abandon the *tontine* after they received their sum of money. The rapid circulation of scarce resources enabled individuals to tap for them relatively large sums of money on a one-time basis to help them solve their immediate problems. While providing its members with a lump of money to pay for a life-cycle event or to start a small business, membership in a *tontine* and other associations and networks reinforced social relationships which could also be used in case of emergency. Women who joined *tontines* often participated in other associations such as such as *mbootays* whose members gathered on a regular basis to share meals, local religious associations (*dahiras*), market women's groups, and ethnic and hometown associations.

Because of the Senegalese version of self-interest properly understood, the specter of the dangers of unbridled individualism in American and European societies evoked by Tocqueville does not appear to be as dangerous in Senegal. Massive rural exodus, rapid urbanization, and widespread poverty have not been accompanied by the atomization of Senegalese society. Most Senegalese still retain strong ties of solidarity with their villages and regions of origins regardless of where they live and work. Urbanized Senegalese have established new neighborhoods and community organizations. Rather than withdrawing into the nuclear family, Senegalese seem to be reaching out and broadening their membership in social networks and associations. While it is true that crime, prostitution, drug use, and mendacity have increased markedly since independence, few homeless people haunt the streets of Dakar.

CHAPTER EIGHT

Spirit of Religion

Each sect worships God in its own fashion, but all preach the same morality in the name of God.[1]

For Tocqueville, religious faith was an inherent part of human nature and not about to disappear. Religion would survive in democratic times because religious beliefs were deeply rooted in the heart of man, especially the common man. Rather than experiencing greater secularization and decline in religious sentiments with the advance of urbanization and Western education, postcolonial Senegal underwent a period of intense Islamization of society.

Tocqueville's experiences in America reinforced his belief that religion was compatible with democracy. There, the spirit of religion supported the spirit of liberty and religious values reinforced democratic politics.[2] Tocqueville had little confidence in Islam's potential for fostering social equality and democracy. He regarded Islam as too detailed in its prescriptions and a rigid unbending fundamentalist religion where all the rules were clearly laid down and enforced by a theocratic state.[3] However, this was not the case in Senegal where Islam was tolerant, flexible, and not formally part of the political power structure.

Hierarchy and Equality within the Sufi Brotherhoods

The Muslim clerics who founded new branches and dynasties of Sufi Brotherhoods in Senegal had some traditions in common with the dissenting Protestants who came to colonial America. Like the Puritans, they opposed the monarchy and aristocracy, asserted that God alone was sovereign, and preached the virtues of work, religious education, and leading sober and austere lifestyles.

However, the Sufi Brotherhoods in Senegal also differed from the Protestant sects in America in significant ways. For Protestants, the minister was an official of the church and not an intermediary between the individual congregant and God. Protestant communities elected their ministers. In the Sufi Brotherhoods, the spiritual guide was the undisputed leader.

The most hierarchical and centralized of all the Sufi orders in Senegal in its organization, the Mouride Brotherhood also demonstrated the most egalitarian spirit toward its followers. Every *talibé* had the possibility of becoming a *cheikh* in the religious hierarchy regardless of their previous social rank or economic status.[4] Ahmadou Bamba, founder of the Mourides, designated former slaves, artisans, and griots to become *cheikhs* while also recruiting *cheikhs* from traditional maraboutic families of noble origin. More than other Sufi leaders, Bamba consciously sought to break down the aristocratic mores and lifestyles of the nobles and warriors who had flocked to his banner as well as caste prejudices. He did this through the sanctification of work and by ordering his followers to shift traditional roles. Thus, haughty nobles were consigned to drawing water to teach them humility while former *ceddo* warriors who previously had earned their living by pillaging peasant villages, found themselves working in the fields. In a similar manner, freemen were often asked to sew clothes and weave cloth, tasks usually restricted for the artisan castes.

While Bamba himself came from a prominent maraboutic family well-connected to the court in Cayor, his critique of the monarchy, *ceddo* society, and the court marabouts reflected his adherence to egalitarian principles in Islam and his ambitions to build an alternative society based on Muslim values. He proposed to do this by going beyond classical modes of Muslim education focusing on studying the Koran and the *hadiths* of the Prophet. Bamba maintained that only a small minority who had the talent and the vocation could or should devote themselves to becoming learned Muslim scholars. On the other hand, he believed that even the most illiterate person could become a good Muslim by practicing the basic precepts of the religion. In addition to providing high levels of religious education for the talented elite, Bamba thought it crucial to provide a different form of instruction to the illiterate masses to build character. This form of instruction emphasized work as essential to salvation and traditional Wolof values such as the capacity to support difficulties, courage based on confidence in God, endurance, moderation in eating food, humility, and solidarity.

Unlike the Anglo-American Protestants who came from societies where individualism was already prevalent, the Senegalese who belonged to the Sufi Brotherhoods came from societies with strong communitarian values that stressed the subordination of individual preferences to community norms. Unlike the relatively homogenous and often middle-class membership of the Anglo-American Protestant sects described by Tocqueville, the faithful in Sufi Brotherhoods consisted of a wide range of social categories—former slaves, artisans, peasants, and nobles—whose status had been determined by birth.

In reconstituting new communities previously shattered by the colonial conquest, the establishment of *daras* and new villages by the Sufi orders contributed to a decline in the importance of kinship relations.[5] The people who flocked to the *daras* and new maraboutic villages often came as individuals. In swearing allegiance to a marabout, they cut off or reduced their ties to their home villages and family. New patterns in which marabouts allocated land to their followers replaced old patterns of land allocation whereby fathers transmitted usufruct rights to their sons. While traditional patterns of solidarity based on kinship and community identity persisted, these forms of solidarity often became secondary to solidarity with one's marabout and fellow congregants, especially among the Mourides.

While the Sufi Brotherhoods did much to break down old social prejudices by espousing the equality of all believers, the assymetrical relationships between marabout and *talibés* perpetuated patterns of patron–client relationships and dependency that had been embedded in the old aristocratic order. In the spiritual arena, the *talibés* depended upon their marabout for salvation. In the material sphere, the *talibés* often depended upon their spiritual leader for material support. The large tracts of land granted to the leaders of the Sufi orders, the contributions of their disciples, and the extent of their influence vis-à-vis the political authorities transformed marabouts into patrons. As patrons with considerable resources at their disposal, marabouts could provide their followers with all kinds of advantages, for example, access to land, money to start a new business, protection against the administrative authorities, and preferential treatment for those applying for a government job or seeking political office. Their capacity and willingness to redistribute resources also enhanced the prestige of the marabouts among their followers.

Marabouts and Talibés: Submission and Autonomy

Much of the literature on Senegal's Sufi orders focuses on the top leadership rather than how the Brotherhoods function at the local level. This focus gives the impression that the Brotherhoods are monocratic in their organization and exaggerates the power of the Grand Khalife to impose his will within the order. In fact, marabouts with large followings were not accountable to the nominal leader of the order as to the manner in which they dealt with their followers or with the resources collected and distributed to them. Rather than being tightly organized along hierarchical lines, the Sufi orders consist of largely autonomous networks of marabouts loosely joined together under the leadership of a brother or son of the founder.

While there are marabouts of different standings at different levels of society, there exists no preestablished hierarchy or chain of command within the orders.[6] The leading maraboutic families within the Brotherhoods enjoyed a remarkable degree of autonomy in pursuing their own ways, administering to their own constituencies, and in developing political alliances with politicians. Some marabouts preferred to stay away from politics entirely while others used their influence to obtain favors from those in power. Some marabouts pursued careers in business while others led a reclusive life of prayer.

Within the Tijani and Mouride orders, the *sheikh*'s prestige and influence depended upon the number of the disciples rather than his right to confer the special litanies of the Brotherhood, which had been traditionally the most important attribute of the *sheikh*.[7] The marabout's need for *talibés* to enhance his standing led to competition among the marabouts for followers.

Although disciples tended to stay with the same marabout for long periods of time because of the high costs involved in developing a relationship with a new marabout, *talibés* were free to change marabouts and often did, especially when a marabout could not help his disciple get a job, garner capital for a business venture, or finance an important family event. To keep and expand their following, marabouts thus had to compete in the marketplace much like American Protestant churches.[8] The neutrality of the state toward the different Brotherhoods lessened potential sectarian conflicts among the Brotherhoods. With dogma less important, people felt freer to change Brotherhoods and marabouts in the much the same way that many Protestants in America felt free to change denominations and churches.

Urban-based Islamic associations (*dahiras*) reinforced allegiances and ties between the marabouts and their followers. In the towns, members of the *dahiras* met to sing together, collect money for their marabout, and to organize charity for the needy. Most *dahiras* were largely self-governing grassroots religious associations. The *talibés* did the basic organizing, ran the meetings, and democratically elected their own officers.

Marabouts avoided openly asking their followers to organize a *dahira* for them because they feared that this might be interpreted as self-seeking. Because some marabouts frowned upon mixed meetings, women often had their own *dahira* or a women's section within the male one. The *dahiras* usually had close ties with local and prominent marabouts or as was in the case of many Mouride *dahiras* with the Grand Khalife himself.

Marabouts at the local level could themselves be *talibés* of other marabouts, represent a higher placed marabout in a locality, or operate on their own providing various services for their own followers. Local marabouts derived their status from three sources: their personal piety, learning, and charisma; inherited status; and their association with more prominent marabouts.[9] Marabouts often inherited their status from their fathers while families of followers often "inherited" their marabouts.

Urbanization and higher levels of education are leading followers to become less submissive in following the orders of their marabouts in secular matters. More and more followers now see their marabouts as primarily spiritual guides and don't feel obligated to follow their advice or orders in political and economic matters. As a consequence marabouts have become more reluctant to issue directives to their followers to vote for a particular political party.

The Spirit of Religion

Tolerance and Coexistence

Despite differences in leadership styles, philosophy, and constituencies, the emergence of the new Sufi orders in Senegal was not accompanied by major religious cleavages.[10]

The Sufi orders in Senegal placed more emphasis on the unity of the Muslim community than on differences in dogma or practices. The doctrines of the Tijani order followed the traditional Sufi path of tolerance.[11] All spiritual roads followed by different Muslim Brotherhoods led to the same end. In His wisdom God had given individuals freedom of belief. As a result there was great diversity of religious beliefs. Malick Sy preached to his followers the necessity to venerate all authentic spiritual masters and to respect all believers.[12] All religions and believers merited to be treated with respect as long as they did not attack Islam. Islam was never to be imposed on others.

These attitudes, held by Tijani and Mouride marabouts, led to a high degree of religious tolerance toward the different Sufi orders and even toward the Christian minority. Members of different Sufi orders attended each other's religious ceremonies and celebrations. Their children went to Koranic schools run by another Sufi order rather than the one with which they were affiliated. In Dakar, pious Muslims had no qualms about sending their children to Catholic private schools.[13] Some people had more than one marabout and maintained good relationships with marabouts from different orders. The belief that all marabouts were good, regardless of affiliation, was widespread throughout Senegal.[14]

For the most part, the leaders of the Brotherhoods also maintained cordial relationships with Senegal's Christian minority and had little problem accepting the political leadership of Léopold Sédar Senghor, a Catholic, or objections to Abdou Diouf, his successor, because he had a Catholic wife who actively participated in public affairs. Representatives of the Catholic Church shared the same place of honor on the dais in official state ceremonies as representatives of the Sufi Brotherhoods. Most leaders of the Brotherhoods and their congregants warmly welcomed the Pope during his visit to Senegal in 1992.[15]

Catholics in Senegal have staunchly embraced democratic values and principles of religious freedom and tolerance for various reasons. As a minority, it was particularly important for Catholics that political and religious liberty be respected so that they could enjoy their own beliefs in freedom and not be excluded from participation in public affairs.[16] Staunch supporters of the secular state, Catholic Church leaders have pointedly avoided intervening in politics to publicly endorse political parties or candidates. At the same time, Catholics have stressed that Catholics have a duty to participate in public affairs and to exercise their rights as citizens.[17]

One of the most interesting phenomena has been the growing tolerance of religion on the part of Senegal's Western-educated intelligentsia who had embraced antireligious Marxist ideologies in their youth. Over the years, antireligious sentiments have waned among the small group of avowed Marxist intellectuals who had organized Marxist parties and underground movements in Senegal during the first two decades of independence. By the end of the century, it was increasingly difficult to find Senegalese intellectuals and politicians willing to express antireligious views in public.

Senegal's traditions of religious tolerance contrasted sharply with the situation in northern Nigeria and the Sudan where the imposition of the Sharia or Muslim law on minority Christian populations has resulted in widespread violence and bloodshed.[18] In Nigeria, orthodox Muslim clerics have fiercely condemned and attacked the Sufi orders as un-Islamic and Sufi doctrines and practices like marabout veneration, praying at the tombs of the marabouts, and regarding marabouts as intermediaries between the believer and God as heretical evil innovations.[19]

Charity and Social Welfare

One of the most obvious manifestations of the penetration of the spirit of religion in Senegalese society has been the people's strong attachment to charity and almsgiving to sustain those in need. Charity is one of the five pillars of Islam. In Dakar, the mosques dispense money, food, and clothing to the needy every Friday; taxi drivers give small coins to the beggars and handicapped[20] when stopping for a red light; and ordinary Senegalese dig into their pockets and purses to meet their religious obligations.

The heads of the Sufi orders are expected to be very generous in handing out charity to the needy, the handicapped, and the poor. The needy may also include those who need money to finance a family life-cycle event and wealthy men who desperately need money to repay their debts to avoid insolvency and public humiliation. By extension, politicians, especially those in high government positions that control large sums of money, are also expected to be generous in giving charity to the needy.

After independence, religious leaders began to organize voluntary associations to provide a wide range of social services and help for the needy. During the 1970s, and 1980s, modernizers within the Sufi orders and Muslim fundamentalists established their own associations while more than a dozen international Islamic NGOs offered social services and assistance to the needy.[21]

In Senegal, the religious networks and associations set up by Muslims and Christians offered an alternative to the state in providing social services for the needy, especially the blind, physically handicapped, and lepers. The state often took a harsh formal position toward beggars. Senghor referred to them as "*les encombrements humains*" (human obstructions) and he and his successor periodically conducted campaigns to round them up and expel them from the city, especially during periods when Dakar was hosting a major international conference.[22]

The failure of the state to deliver more social services for the poor and its hostility to beggars coupled with religion's growing involvement in issues of social welfare reinforced the prestige of religious institutions and undermined the claims of the state to be the incarnation of national unity and solidarity.

Religious Education and Outreach: Making Good Muslims

Since the establishment of colonial rule, the Sufi orders have placed a high emphasis on the importance of Koranic schools and Islamic education. During the early decades of colonial rule, the marabouts resisted efforts by the French to put their children in French public schools and to limit the establishment of Koranic schools.

As an institution, the *daras* provided the rudiments of an Islamic education and also served as Koranic schools. In addition to memorizing the Koran and learning basic prayers, *talibés* learned the importance of discipline, austerity, self-sacrifice, and work while serving their marabouts.

During the early years of independence, marabouts in the rural areas, especially among the Mourides continued to discourage their followers from attending the public schools while encouraging Muslim children to attend Koranic schools. In the mid-1960s, the younger generation of marabouts associated with the Tijani order in Tivouane set up Islamic cultural associations like the *Féderation des Associations Islamiques au Sénégal* (FAIS) and the *Union pour le Progrés Islamique au Sénégal* (UPIS) to promote Islamic education and the teaching of Arabic.[23]

Starting in the mid-1970s, leaders of the Sufi orders began to change their attitude towards secular and religious education. On the one hand, they sought to increase the level of Islamic learning by expanding the number of Koranic schools, establishing Islamic secondary schools, and sending advanced students abroad to study in Islamic universities in North Africa and Egypt. On the other hand, they no longer discouraged their children from attending French public schools and universities and created several Franco-Arabic secondary schools that offered a mixture of religious and secular education. This trend reflected efforts by the Sufi orders to establish their credentials as being within the mainstream of Islam and to counteract the influence of outside reformist and orthodox groups.

Abdoul Lahat Mbacké (1968–1979) also supported the organization of Mouride student associations at the University of Dakar and in France to propagate the teachings of Ahmadou Bamba. A student in urbanism and architecture in France, Abdoulaye Dièye founded the *Association des Etudiants et Stagiaires Mourides d'Europe* in 1977.[24] Dièye presented Islam and Amadou Bamba's teachings as the alternative to cultural alienation. He attacked the left-wing ideologies still prevalent among many African students studying in Europe and castigated Arab Muslims for their racism and denigration of African Islam, accusing them of being the worst kind of Muslims. Unlike some of the Tijani reformers, who wanted to modernize and Arabize the Brotherhoods, the Mourides saw the teachings of Ahmadou Bamba as closer to the message of the Prophet and providing the basis for a model Islamic society.

In the towns, fundamentalist Muslim intellectuals established new learning centers and received support from the Arab world. Influenced by Wahabi Islamist principles, fundamentalists accused the leaders of the Sufi Brotherhoods of not being orthodox Muslims and perpetuating the ignorance of their followers.[25] The anti-Western Wahabi brand of Islamic fundamentalism appealed more to Senegalese intellectuals than to the common people who remained loyal to the Sufi Brotherhoods and their more personal and tolerant forms of Islamic practice.

By the end of the 1980s, the new and more radical orthodox Islamic associations had toned down their criticism of the popular Sufi Brotherhoods, which continued to retain the loyalty of most Senegalese Muslims. Fundamentalist Islamist associations made little headway in Senegal because their ideologies were foreign to Senegalese Islamic traditions. In the end, the fundamentalists failed to discredit the Sufi Brotherhoods or to win large numbers of new adherents to Islamic orthodoxy. During the 1980s and 1990s, the Sufi Brotherhoods increased their efforts at outreach. They sent marabouts to work with students at the university, encouraged the formation of Mouride and Tijani student associations, and provided more religious instruction for Muslim girls and women. Although accepting modern secular education, the marabouts insisted on the truths of Islam and maintained that Islamic values created righteous people and good citizens.

Some of the younger maraboutic leaders also strove to create a mass youth movement in the urban areas to combat drugs, prostitution, and criminality and to teach Islamic principles. Moustapha Sy, the son of Cheikh Tidjiane Sy, became the effective leader of the Tijani-based *Moustarchadine* movement (loosely translated as the "Movement of Those who Seek the Straight Path") founded by his father in 1980.[26] Sy organized seminars on Islamic themes, which drew thousands of young people. His movement also created women's auxiliary associations and stressed the importance of educating women in Islamic values.

The Mouride counterpart of the *Moustarchadines* was the *Mouvement Mondial pour l'Unicité de Dieu* (MMUD) founded in 1995 by a prominent young marabout from the Mbacké family. Like Moustapha Sy, Kara Mbacké also had a large following among urban youth. He organized his movement along paramilitary lines and often referred to himself as general of the Mourides and members of his group as his soldiers. Sy and Mbacké frequently attended each other's events and ceremonies. Both men eventually sought to capitalize on the discontent of urban youth and to use their movements to position themselves in the political arena and to make their respective movements a force in Senegalese politics.

The Mouride Work Ethic and Entrepreneurship

Sanctification of work was an important religious value for rural Senegalese Muslims who attended *daras* and Koranic schools and provided labor for the marabout's collective fields. The Mourides in particular used the *daras* to instill a strong work ethic among their followers and to sanctify work as a way of life.

Mourides prided themselves on their economic independence and solidarity. They boasted that a Mouride does not die of hunger.[27] Mourides were able to work under harsh conditions, forego current consumption for future gains, and to help fellow Mourides get started in business enterprises by offering them advice and capital.

During the 1970s the Mourides began to migrate to towns throughout the country and became involved in the so-called informal sectors of the economy as artisans, peddlers, and petty traders. By the end of the 1980s, they could be found throughout West Africa, Europe, France, and North America while in Senegal, they constituted the heart of the informal economy. By the end of the millennium, they had successfully established international trading networks and had replaced the Lebanese and Moors as the dominant force in retail trade in Dakar. Mouride shops and businesses could easily be identified because most had references to Touba or various forms of the name and title of the founder.

Over the years, people with little or no formal education, and often from low traditional status backgrounds—the *móodu-móodu*—amassed considerable wealth and offered a new model of success for the average Senegalese to follow.[28] Self-made men and women, these people generally had some Islamic religious education, started from humble beginnings, lived simply, reinvested their profits, and contributed to the well-being of their communities through charity and the support of social projects. Although they constituted a disproportionate percentage of this new group of entrepreneurs, Mourides were not the only *móodu-móodu* in Senegalese society. Wolof and Halpulaar Tijani businessmen and diamond dealers also rose from humble beginnings to make their fortunes.

The emergence of the *móodu-móodu* strongly influenced by Islamic values and the rapid development of the informal sector also offered an alternative to the government bureaucrat and the state as the main motors of economic development.[29] The values held by the *móodu-móodu* provided the basis for criticism of the state's role in the economy, its inefficiency, and its predatory behavior. The members of groups like UNACOIS shared these values and were in the forefront of those demanding the liberalization of the Senegalese economy.

After his election as president in 2000, Abdoulaye Wade frequently gave speeches echoing the Mouride's work ethic in exhorting Senegalese to work more and harder.[30]

Religion and Politics

The Postcolonial State and Religion

Senghor's ideology of African Socialism explicitly rejected the atheism implicit in classical Marxist theory and urged Senegalese to turn to the basic tenets found in the Gospels and the Koran.[31] In embracing rather than discarding religious values, Senghor's African Socialism was far less threatening to Senegal's religious leaders than the antireligious Marxist ideologies then espoused by the younger generation of Senegalese nationalists. This position coupled with the decision not to choose immediate independence in the September 28, 1958 referendum assured Senghor's party of the support of most of the country's leading religious authorities and enabled the UPS to retain its status as Senegal's dominant party in the years immediately preceding independence.

With independence, those controlling the new Senegalese state made an effort to domesticate the religious authorities and to bring them under the authority of the state. Shortly after independence, Prime Minister Mamadou Dia's support for reform programs to create a modern Islamic education system and an Islamic Council to oversee the organization of religious holidays and the pilgrimage to Mecca alarmed the heads of the Sufi orders and was a major factor explaining why the marabouts supported Senghor rather than Dia during the political crisis which led to his downfall in December 1962.

When Senghor assumed full power in 1963, he put a halt to Dia's attempts to reform the Sufi Brotherhoods and sought to stifle the development of radical reformist Islamic movements. At the same time, Senghor inaugurated a policy of co-opting moderate Islamic associations and encouraging the organization of Islamic associations led by government loyalists.

During his twenty-year tenure as President of Senegal (1960–1980), the Catholic Senghor used government resources to court the leaders of the Sufi Brotherhoods in an effort to transform them into clients of the state by following the French colonial practice of offering state services, favors, and honors. Senghor had a special relationship with Falilou Mbacké, the Grand Khalife of the Mourides (1945–1968) who helped Senghor's rise to power during the postwar era. His successor, Abdoul Lahat Mbacké (1968–1989) began to distance himself from the state soon after he assumed office and became an increasingly vocal advocate of rural interests.

While soliciting the backing of the marabouts, Senghor worked hard to reinforce the authority of the secular state and to make the legal system more in line with Western norms. One of the few areas in which the Sufi Brotherhoods publicly criticized the secular state concerned the Family Code, which became law in 1972 despite the opposition of the marabouts, which was publicly expressed in a letter addressed to the National Assembly in 1971 in the name of the *Conseil Supérieur Islamique*.[32] From the perspective of the state, then led by a Catholic president, the Family Code reflected an effort to unify the law, strengthen the secular nature of society, acknowledge individual rights, and insure the equality of all citizens, notably women in society.[33] Because the Family Code discouraged polygamy, gave equal inheritance rights to women, and made it more difficult for husbands to divorce their wives, critics disparaged it as the *Code des Femmes*. Sufi religious leaders attacked the Family Code because it contradicted Islamic law, especially in the domains of marriage, divorce, and inheritance issues. Though proclaiming that they had no intention to intervene in the conduct of the affairs of the nation, they declared that it was their duty as religious guides to reject the legislation as violating the Koran and Sunna.

Despite the united opposition of the Sufi Brotherhoods, Senghor did not back down in this matter. On the other hand, neither did the Sufi Brotherhoods. The result was that the law was more or less enforced in the larger urban areas when individuals brought their case to the courts and ignored in the rural areas. The nonenforcement of the law avoided a direct confrontation between the state and the Brotherhoods.

Following its break with Israel during the 1973 Yom Kippur War, Senegal intensified its ties with the Muslim world and benefited from large amounts of financial aid and scholarships for Senegalese students to study the Arab language and to pursue more advanced Islamic studies in Arab countries. With the expansion of aid from the Muslim world to the government, the Senghor regime adopted a more tolerant position towards orthodox Islamic associations.

After Senghor retired, the growing strength and popularity of Islam in Senegal compelled Senegalese politicians to adopt a more overtly visible Islamic life style and to make frequent references to God in their speeches. The emergence of Abdou Diouf as Senegal's first Muslim president in 1981 marked a new era in Senegalese politics as the "spirit of Islam" became increasingly integrated into Senegal's public life. Shortly after taking power, Diouf went on pilgrimage to Mecca where he asserted Senegal's identity as an Islamic country.[34] At the same time, Diouf continued to retain good relationships with the Catholic community who were well represented in Senegalese governments.

Abdou Diouf continued Senghor's policy of soliciting the backing of the heads of the Sufi brotherhoods while supporting moderate Islamic associations. However, unlike Senghor, Diouf also used government resources to support and co-opt orthodox Islamic associations to counterbalance the power of the Sufi Brotherhoods and to attract financial support from the Arab world. In 1991, Senegal became the first Black African nation to host a meeting of the World Islamic Conference.

Although continuously courted by the state and politicians, the heads of the Sufi Brotherhoods distanced themselves from politics during the 1990s. The 1988 national presidential elections was the last presidential election in which the Grand Khalife of the Mourides issued a directive to his followers to vote for his candidate. Despite his affiliation as a Mouride, Abdolulaye Wade never received an official endorsement from of the Mouride religious community.

With Wade in power, the state has taken a more positive stance toward religion in general. References to God and quoting of verses from the Koran have become more frequent while religious education has been formally introduced into the school curriculum.

Marabouts as Politicians

Despite constitutional restrictions banning religiously based political parties, the younger generation of marabouts have became increasingly involved in Senegalese politics.

The 1979 Iranian Revolution inspired the creation of an illegal Islamic political party (*Hizboulahi*) founded by Khalifa Niasse, a marabout related to the Niassene dynasty in Kaolack who called for the overthrow of the regime and the immediate establishment of an Islamic state. Relishing the title of "Ayatollah of Kaolack" and the attention of the press, Niasse found little support in the country for his views.[35]

While a handful of marabouts had occasionally run for political office, usually under the banner of the ruling party or the PDS, Cheikh Abdoulaye Dièye became the first marabout since independence to establish a formal political party. Dièye created the *Front pour le Socialisme et la Démocratie* (FSD) as a platform to advocate Islamic values and the moralization of public life. In the 1996 municipal elections he headed his party's list as candidate for mayor of Saint-Louis and won a seat in the municipal council. Dièye gave political speeches in the mosques arguing that a good Muslim had to be involved in politics to fight against corruption and injustice. Although often quoting the words of Ahmadou Bamba, he peppered his speeches with references to the founders of the other Sufi Brotherhoods, preached mutual respect and tolerance for religious differences, and called for social peace. Dièye criticized the government for not respecting Islamic law and advocated political and social reforms based on religious values.

During the 1993 presidential election campaign, Moustapha Sy sharply criticized Diouf, attacked the West, and warned that violence would erupt if Diouf won the elections. On the day after Diouf's victory, Sy's followers rioted and killed several policemen sent in to quell the disturbances. The regime responded by arresting Sy, putting him in jail, and banning the movement's activities. After spending time in prison, Sy was released. For the rest of the 1990s, Moustapha Sy and his movement oscillated between supporting the regime and opposing it.

The 2000 presidential elections marked a new direction in Senegalese politics as Senegalese marabouts for the first time presented themselves as candidates for president of a secular republic. Cheikh Abdoulaye Dièye[36] and Ousseynou Fall, a grandson of Ibra Guèye, the founder of the Baye-Fall branch of the Mouride Brotherhood decided to run against Diouf. Moustapha Sy formed a new political party, the *Parti de l'Unité Républicain* (PUR) and was on the point of contesting the presidential elections as the candidate of his party when his father, who publicly supported Abdou Diouf, asked him to withdraw from the race. Kara Mbacké, who had drawn thousands of alienated youth to his banner through his criticism of the Diouf regime, also changed course late in the game and decided to support Diouf in the 2000 presidential elections, much to the chagrin of his followers.

The political engagement of representatives of the younger generation of more worldly marabouts contrasted markedly with the positions of the leaders of the Sufi orders who opted not to publicly support any of the candidates. Thus, Saliou Mbacké, the Grand Khalife of the Mourides, remained neutral in the elections and refused to endorse any of the Mouride candidates, including Abdoulaye Wade. Senegalese public opinion seems to support the position that the heads of the Sufi Brotherhoods should maintain their political neutrality and not get involved in politics. The leaders of the Brotherhoods also fear that the endorsement of one candidate would undermine unity and make it more difficult to exert their role as spiritual leaders. At the same time, Senegalese public opinion also accepts the right of individual marabouts as citizens to run for public office and form their own political parties.

The entry of marabouts into the political arena as candidates for public office continued after Wade's victory. In the 2002 national elections, several marabouts ran for office. The younger generation of religious leaders are capitalizing on their religious authority and a profound belief among many Senegalese Muslims that only Islam can save Senegal and end the political, economic, and moral crises confronting the country.

The Sufi orders in Senegal will soon be entering a new phase as the older generation of leaders directly descended from the founders of the Brotherhoods die off. The Grand Khalifes of the Umarian and Tivouane Tijanis are in their eighties as is the Grand Khalife of the Mourides.[37] When the older leaders die, it may be difficult to find replacements for them among the large pool of grandsons of the founders positioning themselves for the succession. It remains to be seen whether the politicization and direct entry into politics of the "generation of grandsons" will contribute to the discrediting of the Sufi Brotherhoods and religion or simply reflect the Islamization of political institutions and public life and the secularization of those Muslim religious leaders entering politics as citizens in pursuit of power.

Islam and the Future of the Secular State

The Islamization of Senegalese society has raised questions concerning the future of the secular state in Senegal. Since independence, Senegal's Western-educated intelligentsia has been the staunchest proponents of a secular state and separation of church and state. At the other extreme, the Islamists, have called for the establishment of an Islamic Republic based on the Sharia. The postindependence Islamic revival in Senegal has been accompanied by increased pressure by Muslim religious leaders on the state to support religious education in public schools and to eliminate contradictions between the law of the land and Islamic law, especially in the domain of family law.

Two concepts of the secular state predominate in the modern world. The first insists that the state must be totally secular in orientation and the supreme law of the land in all matters. It stresses complete separation of church and state, prohibits using public funds to support religious institutions and religious education, and enforces the law of the land without making any concessions to religious beliefs.[38] A second concept of the secular state, potentially more favorable to religion, places greater emphasis on the non-denominational nature of the state and its equal treatment of all religions rather than separation of church and state. Separation of church and state in this context means that the state will not establish any one religion as the state religion or favor one religious group over another. This concept leaves room for the state to adopt a positive stance towards religion, support religious institutions and religious education, and establish a pluralist legal system that does not force individuals to violate their religious precepts.

Following the French Constitution of 1958, all of Senegal's constitutions have declared that Senegal is "a secular, democratic and social Republic." The Senegalese Constitution guarantees all individuals equal treatment before the law regardless of race, religion, and origin, and the right to profess any religion. It also provides protection against religious discrimination. Senegal's penal code sanctions those who promote intolerance against people from different religions and sects, insult and assault clergymen in the exercise of their functions, and desecrate churches, mosques, holy places, and religious objects.

In recognizing religious institutions and communities as equally valid instruments as the state for providing education, the 2001 Senegalese Constitution moved away from the more secular approach embedded in the French Constitution. Under the Senegalese Constitution, religious institutions and communities have the right to develop without restrictions, are free from the tutelage of the state, and free to regulate and manage their own affairs in an autonomous manner. The banning of political parties based on religion, race, ethnicity, region, language, and gender was one of the few areas in which activities related to religion were restricted.

Following the restoration of multiparty democracy in the mid-1970s, Senegalese political leaders began to call for greater state support for Islamic institutions.[39] Boubacar Guèye, leader of the conservative *Mouvement Republicain Sénégalais* in underscoring the centrality of religion for the Senegalese people called on the state to take responsibility for providing religious values in the public schools and supporting private religious schools. While rejecting the Islamization of political institutions, Abdoulaye Wade argued that the state should free itself from antireligious notions and pursue a positive form of secularism. After his release from prison, Mamadou Dia wrote several works on Islam asserting that Islam was compatible with democracy and industrialization. Though still critical of the political influence of the Sufi Brotherhoods, and declaring his support for the secular state as treating all religions equally, Dia recommended that the secular state in predominantly Islamic societies should work together with progressive Islamic forces in society to modernize Islam through education.

During his tenure as president, Abdou Diouf successfully balanced different Islamic forces in Senegalese society, particularly during his first decade in that office. However, following the death of his close ally, Abdoul Lahat Mbacké, the Mouride Grand Khalife, Diouf began to lose his influence and standing as a Muslim leader with the Mouride community, which gravitated toward Abdoulaye Wade. During the 1990s, the rise of the Moustarchadine movement, the expansion of Muslim education and the Islamist press, the establishment of the FSD in 1996, and the entry of marabouts as candidates for the presidency in 2000 marked the growing importance of Islam as a force in Senegalese politics willing to openly contest the secular nature of the Senegalese state in a society where 95 percent of the population was Muslim.

Senegalese Islamists in Senegal have attacked Western-style democracy based on the principles of government of the people, by the people, and for the people and insist that democracy in Islam is based on "a government of God, by the people, and for God."[40] According to this view, the sovereignty of God is above that of the people and is exercised through application of the Sharia.

Islamists have sharply attacked the concept of the secular state. For the Islamists, the secular state stands for a godless state and therefore is not tolerable. The secular state, they assert, is more than godless; it is also antireligious. The Islamists have argued that most of the ills of society—drugs, prostitution, crime, sexual promiscuity, corruption, poverty, and economic injustice—stem from the consequences of having a secular government and propose Islam and an Islamic Republic as the only solution.

During the 2000 presidential campaign, Cheikh Abdoulaye Dièye presented himself as a reformist candidate championing the ideas of Ahmadou Bamba and preaching religious tolerance. At the same time, he injected religious issues into the 2000 presidential election campaign that echoed some of the major demands of the Islamists, for example, elimination of the word secular from the constitution and revision of the Family Code to conform to Islamic law.

In the months preceding the elaboration of constitutional revisions following Wade's election, rumors abounded that the word "secular" would be eliminated from the constitution and Senegal would become a "democratic and social republic" rather than a secular, democratic, and social republic as in the past. But in the end, the term secular was retained.

The separation of church and state has become more problematic since Wade came to power. One of Wade's first acts as president was to go to Touba to ask for the blessing of the Grand Khalife and to reconfirm his submission to his spiritual guide. Wade's frequent visits to Touba created the impression that he was favoring the Mourides over the other Sufi orders and violating the principle of the neutrality of the state vis-à-vis different religious groups. In 2003, Wade also violently attacked the Catholic hierarchy for criticizing his government's inability or unwillingness to take more vigorous measures to stop a wave of threats against journalists and assaults against political leaders critical of the regime. Critics maintain that Wade may be playing with fire in his efforts to court Mouride support. Tijanis and

Catholics have reacted strongly and Senegalese public opinion is concerned that that Wade's practices pose a threat to Senegal's long-standing traditions of religious tolerance and coexistence.

Given the limited influence of the Islamists, Senegal is not likely to become an Islamic Republic unless the heads of the leading Sufi Brotherhoods throw their support behind such a project. At the present time, the current leaders of the Sufi Brotherhoods, though pressing for the injection of Islamic values in the schools and revisions of the Family Code, are not challenging the authority of the secular state. However, some elements from the younger generation of marabouts—the so-called generation of the grandsons of the founders—may be tempted to use Islamist slogans and popular discontent to ride to power.[41]

CHAPTER NINE

Language

Language is perhaps the most enduring link which unites man.[1]

Deeming language to be "the chief tool of thought,"[2] Tocqueville regarded the sharing of a common language as an instrument for bringing people together and cementing their group identity. In *Democracy in America*, he observed that the Anglo-American identity of the immigrants coming to America from Great Britain was reinforced by the fact that they all spoke English. This sharing of a common language permitted them to communicate easily and to understand the rules governing their political institutions.[3]

For Tocqueville, the sovereignty of the people consisted in the right of the people to make their own laws and rules of governance. This was particularly true at the township, neighborhood, or village level where speech communities used language to create common knowledge, shared communities of understanding, patterns of social accountability, and mutual trust.[4] Communities sharing a common language and culture that made their own rules were more likely to be self-governing than communities forced to submit to political laws established outside the community and using a different language as was the case in Senegal and other French colonies in Africa.

Tocqueville observed that in aristocratic societies language separated the aristocrats from the masses. Class differences led to differences in the language of the nobility and the language of the common people. Aristocratic societies coined few new words and placed great emphasis on style and themes that reflected the values and worldview of the aristocrats.[5] On the other hand, democratic societies constantly added new words to the mother language, gave new meanings to old words, and put words together in different ways.[6] With equality, Tocqueville argued, the language gap among classes would narrow as language became less bound by convention.

Language, Communication, and
Group Identity in Precolonial Senegal

Language was a major factor determining ethnic identity among the different groups inhabiting precolonial Senegal.[7] In Senegal, each ethnic group had its own language.[8] The main languages spoken north of the Gambia River were Wolof, Pulaar, Serer, and Soninké. The major languages in the south and east of the Gambia River, were Diola, Mandinka, Pulaar, and Bambara.

Nearly all of Senegal's languages fall into two major linguistic groups—West Atlantic and Mande. Ninety-two percent of Senegalese speak west Atlantic languages—Wolof, Pulaar, Serer, Diola—a factor that facilitated interethnic communication and the ability to speak and understand more than one's own maternal language. Senegalese generally spoke the dominant language in their region as well as their own maternal language if they were an ethnic minority.[9] Learning another language was made easier by the fact that different languages spoken in a particular region often had common roots.[10]

The relatively high degree of linguistic unity facilitated the development of a common cultural identity and contributed to the absence of major conflict along ethnic lines in Senegal.[11] Cheikh Anta Diop has argued that Pharaonic Egyptian provided a common linguistic foundation for West African languages and a culture that reflected similar patterns of precolonial family and state structures, philosophical concepts, and moral values.[12] The spread of Mande languages under the Ghana and Mali Empires throughout most of west Africa further reinforced cultural and linguistic unity.

Senegal's major ethnic groups intermingled freely through migrations and intermarriage.[13] Few taboos existed against marrying outside one's ethnic group. Individuals from ethnic groups migrating to areas dominated by another ethnic group often adopted the patronymics prevalent among the host community. The adoption of new patronymics and languages made it easier for newcomers from another ethnic group to become integrated into the majority culture.

Precolonial African societies in Senegal were primarily oral civilizations. Speech, rather than the written word, was the main vehicle for communicating, governing, preserving records of historical events, and transmitting values from generation to generation. Proverbs incorporated the popular wisdom, philosophical concepts, and moral values of society. Individuals injected popular proverbs to make points in debates and in community discussions. The use of proverbs depersonalized debate because proverbs had the weight of tradition behind it and reflected the collective wisdom of society rather than the personal views of an individual.

Different ethnic groups had different sets of proverbs that reflected their specific history, social organization, and value systems. Pulaar and Wolof proverbs, for example, often had negative things to say about rulers and their entourages.

Pulaar proverbs reflected popular mistrust of rulers who were portrayed as unreliable, seizing the property of others and abusing their power.[14] The good ruler was generous and brought prosperity. The bad ruler who pillaged his people would see his realm shrink. The best master was one who you didn't see and was far away. Pulaar proverbs also contained frequent admonitions to ally with the powerful. Individuals thus needed to show submission and respect for the strong, find a protector to succeed in life, go with the winners even if one had to suffer some humiliation, and wait until the battle was over to see who the winner was before joining sides. Some Pulaar proverbs pointed to the corrupting effects of power on religious leaders. Marabouts begat kings and kings heathens.

Wolof proverbs often portrayed rulers as uncaring and greedy.[15] A ruler was not a kinsman and thus had no obligations to his subjects. Rulers, however, were rarely attacked directly. Thus, rulers were not evil; they simply had evil entourages. Wolof proverbs also placed a high premium on generosity and loyalty. Rulers were expected to be generous and their followers loyal.

Tales, fables, epics, and genealogies were also transmitted orally. In Senegal's oral civilization, written literature in the indigenous languages was rare. The griot, or Master of the Word, assumed the main responsibility for transmitting the genealogies of rulers and the collective memory of their society. As Masters of the Word, griots served as the guardians of ethnic linguistic traditions and spoke the "purest" version of the language. Oral traditions and genealogies were handed down from father to son for many generations. Hampaté Ba, the Malian philosopher, likened the death of a griot as the repository of popular traditions to the burning down of a library.

During the precolonial era, Arabic was the language of the literate and confined largely to Muslim clerics and their students. Literacy in Arabic was highest among the Halpulaar living in Fouta Toro. The marabouts serving in the courts of pagan rulers often produced and sold amulets containing verses from the Koran to protect those who wear them. Rulers would also use those literate in Arabic to compose letters for them. These letters used the Arabic alphabet to transcribe indigenous languages. Wolof Muslim leaders like Ahmadou Bamba also composed religious poetry in Wolof using Arabic letters. Although relatively rare, a small body of written literature took root in precolonial Senegal using the Arabic alphabet. During the nineteenth century the Koran was translated into Wolof.[16]

European languages were not unknown to the peoples of precolonial Senegal. Some Senegalese learned French, Portuguese, and English as commercial languages. The Afro-European population, in particular, became important intermediaries in trade during the precolonial era precisely because they spoke both European and indigenous languages and thus could serve as interpreters and intermediaries for European trading companies seeking to do business with the rulers who controlled Senegal's internal trade.

Colonial Language Policies: The Primacy of French

French colonial language policy was based on presumptions of superiority and ignorance and denigration of indigenous languages, promoting French as the language best suited to "civilize" the indigenous populations, excluding those who did not speak French from participating in public life and access to elite status, and conducting public affairs and administering justice exclusively in French. The French colonial authorities systematically sought to create a new indigenous elite in their image based on mastery of the French language and loyalty to French institutions to help them administer their colonies. These language policies created a wide gulf between the colonial administration and the colonized populations, especially the rural populations living in the interior where French schools were rare.

France's colonial policy of imposing French as the only official language and suppressing other indigenous languages also reflected national language policies in the métropole. During the French Revolution, only three million of the country's 25 million inhabitants spoke French fluently while only 9 percent of the population was literate in French.[17] The Constituent Assembly's decision to translate decrees into local languages in 1789 was vigorously opposed by those supporting a unitary state.[18] With the defeat of the Federalists by the Jacobins, the views of those advocating French as the only official language prevailed. Between 1792 and 1794, a series of decrees imposed French on all schools and required all official documents to be in French. Other languages spoken in the country like Breton were denigrated as *patois*, labeled counter-revolutionary, and suppressed in the name of national unity. For the French-speaking elites concentrated in Paris, national unity required that the army, schools, and administration use French and French only. France also applied this policy to her Black African colonies.

French colonial administrators had little or no knowledge of indigenous African languages.[19] Training programs for colonial administrators at the *École Coloniale* in Paris focused primarily on French administrative law and paid little attention to linguistic training.

The ignorance of French colonial officials of African languages made them heavily dependent upon French-speaking interpreters for transmitting directives and getting feedback concerning the thinking of the local populations on various issues. French colonial administrators rarely made the rounds of their districts without an interpreter at their side. Pursuing their own interests, interpreters often misled and misinformed their superiors as well as the local populations by deliberately failing to translate accurately.[20]

Since French was the official language of governance, literacy in French became a prerequisite for Senegalese to become part of the French colonial administration. In choosing canton chiefs to serve as their intermediaries, the French colonial administration stressed literacy, knowledge of French, and familiarity with French administrative procedures over hereditary status.[21] Interpreters and office clerks were sometimes chosen to be canton chiefs despite having lowly social origins.

After launching the conquest of the Senegalese interior, Governor Louis Faidherbe founded what became known as the School for the Sons of Chiefs and Interpreters in 1856 to improve the quality of those serving as intermediaries between the French and the conquered indigenous populations. Located in Saint-Louis, the School for the Sons of Chiefs and Interpreters became the main training ground for Senegal's auxiliary elites serving in the French colonial administration.

Those attending the School for the Sons of Chiefs spent no time studying indigenous history, institutions, and languages. By the 1920s, students were required to have a primary school certificate from a French school in order to enter. Much of the curriculum was devoted to the study of French metropolitan institutions and colonial administrative texts, procedures, and organization. Arabic and the study of Muslim law related to marriage and inheritance were also part of the curriculum.

In addition to the School for the Sons of Chiefs, the French established the William Ponty School in Senegal to train the most promising African primary school graduates from all over French West Africa as teachers, interpreters, doctors, and veterinarians. Graduates of William Ponty became an important part of the new colonial elite based on their mastery of French and frequently championed assimilationist policies.

While a privileged few having subject status had access to William Ponty and the School for the Sons of Chiefs, few subjects in rural Senegal had access to French primary schools. Shortages of teachers and resources coupled with the reluctance of rural Senegalese to send their children away to French schools resulted in a tiny percentage of young children attending school in rural areas. Few villages had their own schools. The people who sent their children to school often had to send them to regional schools far from their home villages. During the mid-1930s, less than 20,000 Senegalese attended public and private primary schools, which were heavily concentrated in the Four Communes.[22]

Senegalese conscripts who had not been to school learned some French during their years of military service. Thousands of Senegalese conscripts sent to Europe to fight in World War I learned the rudiments of French. When they returned home, their knowledge of French and service to France slightly elevated their social status with the colonial administration. War veterans received preferential treatment in getting jobs in the lower echelons of the colonial administration.

Subjects in the interior had to work hard to obtain the same status, as citizens, as their compatriots in the Four Communes. Few Senegalese subjects made the effort to become naturalized citizens, which required a high level of French education and/or exceptional service to France.[23] Léopold Sédar Senghor became one of the few exceptions to this rule. Senghor won considerable fame and prestige by becoming the first African to obtain an advanced French teaching degree. He was the first African to teach at the *École Coloniale* where he taught courses on African civilization and African languages.[24]

Although a poet and one of the founders of the Négritude literary movement, which praised the virtues of traditional African culture, Senghor firmly believed in the superiority of French over indigenous languages as an instrument for modernization. Senghor's attachment to the French

language and French culture influenced his policies when be became
president after Senegal's independence.

The imposition of French as the language of government and law stifled
popular participation and understanding of Senegal's colonial, political, and
legal institutions. Orders from the governor were issued in French. When
directives reached the grassroots level, the local populations were expected
to obey them, not discuss them. Only those educated in French had the
language skills needed to fully understand the rules and regulations of the
colonial regime.

Language and cultural barriers made it extremely difficult for European
administrators to render justice fairly. These problems were evident to
French observers of the administration of justice in the French colonies
who underscored the European magistrate's ignorance of the character,
customs, and language of the people he was judging.[25]

To communicate with the French colonial officials, Senegalese often had
to use public letter writers who would write down and translate their
complaints and requests into French and send them on to the proper
authorities. The presence of a literate class of public letter writers served as
a check on the authority of local colonial officials who often saw the letter
writers as troublemakers.[26] The most effective letter writers were citizens
who could not be arbitrarily thrown in jail under the *indigénat* and be easily
intimidated by local French colonial officials.

The spread of Islam during the colonial period was also accompanied
by a sharp rise in the number of Senegalese who attended Koranic schools,
learned the Arabic alphabet, and obtained a modicum of literacy. Attendance
in Koranic schools increased the number of Senegalese who could write
letters in their local language using Arabic script. In the rural areas, far
more Senegalese were literate in Arabic than in French, especially in areas
where the marabouts discouraged their followers from attending French
schools. Regions with the largest concentration of Mourides also had the
lowest percentage of school-age children in French schools.

Even in the large towns where colonial public schools were more accessible,
more people attended Koranic schools than the French schools and had
attained some level of literacy in Arabic.

Under colonial rule, Wolof became increasingly important as a lingua
franca.[27] By 1900, Wolof was already the commercial lingua franca in the
Senegambia region. During the nineteenth and early twentieth century,
Wolof emerged as the lingua franca of Senegal's major urban towns, most of
which were located in predominantly Wolof-speaking areas. However,
Wolof became the dominant language even in cities like Ziguinchor, the
regional capital of the Casamance, where 80 percent of the population
could understand Wolof at the time of independence. Wolof served as the
common language of the migrants from other ethnic groups who came to
the cities because they needed to learn some Wolof in order to communicate with their fellow townsmen. Wolof had less success in making headway
among Senegal's rural populations in Fouta Toro, the Casamance, and

eastern Senegal where relatively few Wolof lived. In rural areas, the Wolof language advanced the most amongst the Serer, especially those living in close proximity to the Mourides where Islamization and Wolofization went hand in hand.

During the post-World War II, period, Senegalese nationalists studying in metropolitan universities protested against the denigration of indigenous African languages and insisted on the importance of indigenous languages. Cheikh Anta Diop translated Shakespeare and scientific treatises into Wolof to demonstrate that Wolof could adapt to the modern world and recommended that Wolof, Senegal's lingua franca, be adopted as Senegal's national language. Others called for the teaching of African languages in the primary schools.

At the end of the colonial period, French still remained entrenched as the only official language of the schools, the administration, the legal system, the army, and commerce. Under colonialism, the French made little effort to teach other European languages and discouraged Senegalese from studying abroad in non-French universities. France expected educated Senegalese to share the same degree of linguistic patriotism as metropolitan Frenchmen.

Senghor's Language Policy (1960–1980): Reasserting the Primacy of French

Article 1 of the 1960 Senegalese Constitution established French as the official language of the Senegalese Republic. The fact that less than one-fifth of the Senegalese population was literate in French or spoke French fluently at independence made it highly unlikely that the people would be active participants in government. At independence, Senegal's political leaders asserted that universal primary school education in French would resolve this problem. Four decades later, this goal was still far from being obtained with less than 70 percent of the school age population attending French language schools.

Senghor and Mamadou Dia both shared the view that French was needed to unify the country as part of the nation-building process. Senghor believed that French was the language of choice for developing the country and nation-building. A specialist in African languages, Senghor argued that Senegal's indigenous languages and Arabic lacked the logic and rationality needed to transform and modernize the country.[28] Senghor's educational policies reiterated the primacy of French as the language of instruction at all levels of the educational system and favored the expansion of higher education at the expense of primary school education. In 1976, the percentage of school-age children in school was just under 30 percent, a percentage not much higher than the rate in 1960, despite the fact that the number of children in school had nearly tripled.

After independence, proficiency in French remained a prerequisite for government employment and for working for the French trading companies dominating the modern sectors of the Senegalese economy. As French was the only official language used by the government, one had to be literate in French to enter government services. This fact motivated many Senegalese families to send at least some of their children to school in order to be eligible for employment. After independence, the public sector expanded rapidly and provided employment for school graduates at all levels. Between 1960 and 1981, the number of civil servants multiplied more than ten-fold from 6,000 to 67,000.[29] French-speaking primary school graduates entered the lower levels of the government bureaucracy while Senegalese high school and university graduates filled its upper echelons.

The preference for French as the only official language continued the policy of elite closure begun by the colonial regime. Although part of the elite, French-speaking intellectuals in the opposition during the 1960s denounced Senghor's language policies as neocolonialist and demanded that the national languages enjoy the same status as French.

In response to demands for recognition of indigenous languages, the Senegalese government in 1971 extended official recognition of six languages as national languages—Wolof, Pulaar, Serer, Diola, Mandinka, and Soninke. Recognition, however, did not mean that these languages would supersede French as the official language, require that all official documents be translated into the local languages, or that primary school instruction would be given in these languages. The equal status accorded to all six indigenous languages also made it clear that Wolof, which was spoken or understood by more than 80 percent of the population, would not receive official recognition as Senegal's lingua franca.

Despite their nominal commitment to national languages, political debate among the Senegalese elite was conducted in French and was disconnected from the overwhelming majority of the Senegalese people who communicated with each other primarily in Wolof and other indigenous languages. Moreover, the content of the vocabulary was based on largely unfamiliar European concepts. Senghor would give long and learned talks about African Socialism in his reports to the UPS Party Congresses punctuated by frequent references to Marx, Engel, Lenin, Prudhomme, Teilhard de Chardin, and other European philosophers and thinkers. These speeches addressed the Senegalese intellectual elite rather than the party faithful. For their part, Marxists in the opposition couched their critique of the régime in unfamiliar Marxist categories of little relevance to the general population.

Senghor was one of the founders and major proponents of the *francophonie* movement, which affirmed that all French-speaking countries shared a common cultural patrimony and should join together to preserve it.[30] Senegalese nationalists saw the Francophone community as an instrument of French neocolonialism and an effort to thwart the development of indigenous African languages.[31] France used the Francophone community as an instrument for preserving its political and cultural influence in its former colonies and to bolster the status of French as a world language in the face of the growing dominance of English.

Language Policy and Linguistic Developments
in the Post-Senghor Era

Abdou Diouf proved to be more sensitive to Senegal's historical traditions than his mentor Senghor who saw national languages as relics of the past and ill suited for the tasks of nation-building and development. Diouf accepted much of the critique leveled at Senghor's language policy by the *États Généraux de l'éducation et de la formation* that met in January 1981, shortly after he became president.[32] The *États Généraux*, a forum of representatives of the government, teachers' unions, parent associations, and other groups concerned with the future of Senegal's educational system, criticized Senghor's favoring of French over the national languages and the adoption of a curriculum based on that of the métropole. The forum also criticized the presence of more than a thousand French teachers in the school system after two decades of independence as a form of neocolonialism. Their recommendations included making universal primary school a reality by 1990, accelerating the use of national languages as a medium of instruction, recognizing the importance of promoting the Arab language in the schools, and sharply reducing the number of French teachers in the Senegalese school system.[33] When Diouf left office in March 2000, the only one among the above recommendations to be implemented was the radical reduction of the number of metropolitan French teachers in the school system.

Whereas Senghor regarded Senegal's precolonial culture primarily as folklore and to be preserved in museums, Diouf asserted that oral traditions and the collective memory of the people transmitted through the national languages, especially Wolof, had to be resurrected and revitalized.

Although French remained the official language of the Senegalese administration and all official documentation, Senegalese administrators and politicians increasingly communicated with each other and their constituencies in Wolof.[34] While French was the language defining the rules, Wolof was the language used to negotiate and to resolve conflicts between government officials and the public.

While French prevailed in the formal classroom, Wolof prevailed in the schoolyard and in the home. In Dakar, it was particularly difficult for non-Wolof speakers to retain their maternal language over the course of time. Thus, Serer brought up in Dakar often lost fluency in their maternal language after one or two generations while Halpulaar traditionalists, much to their regret, saw their children adopt Wolof as their first language.

With the democratization of the school system and increasing number of primary school, secondary school, and university graduates, literacy in French no longer guaranteed access to elite status and a government job as it did during the colonial era and the early days of independence. The downsizing of the state bureaucracy, the rapid expansion of the informal sector as the main source of urban employment, the intensification of the Islamization of Senegalese society during the 1980s and 1990s, and globalization also contributed to a relative decline in the prestige and importance of French as the language of modernity.

Before independence, primary-school graduates had access to the lower echelons of the colonial administration. With the upgrading of educational requirements to enter government service, few government jobs were available for primary school graduates. More and more primary-school leavers and graduates now looked for employment in the rapidly expanding informal sector where Wolof was the lingua franca. Decentralization and pressures imposed by structural adjustment programs to keep down the numbers and salaries of government officials also made government employment less attractive and less accessible to secondary school and university graduates. Low salaries, overcrowded classrooms and poor working conditions made primary-school teaching a less attractive profession than in the past. Overcrowding led to doubling sessions, hiring a corps of "volunteer" teachers with less professional qualifications to meet the growing demand for education, and a decline in the standard of French language education. Poor performance in exams led many to demand that primary school instruction be in Wolof and in the indigenous languages. In the fall of 2002, the Wade régime finally introduced the study of national languages in the primary schools in the fall of 2002.

As Tocqueville might have predicted, democratization reduced the language gap between the elites and the masses as French-speaking government officials and politicians felt more comfortable discussing public affairs and dealing with the general public in Wolof; and as more people could understand French in urban Senegal. In the rural areas, the decentralization laws of the 1990s reduced the authority and power of the French-speaking *préfêts* and *sous-préfêts*, which was transferred to local politicians who communicated primarily in the dominant local language of their districts.

During the 1980s and 1990s, the government and international donor community placed greater emphasis on translating basic government texts into the national languages and organizing functional literacy and numeracy classes in the rural areas. The 1996 decentralization laws providing for the election of more than 24,000 local government officials, accelerated the demand for translation of local government texts in the national languages since many of the newly elected officials, especially in the rural areas, were not literate in French. By the end of the century, most local government officials throughout the country had participated in training programs presented in the national languages. These programs sought to increase their understanding of local government mechanisms and issues and their responsibilities as local government officials.

The introduction of democratic themes and governance techniques into adult literacy programs in the national languages contributed to changes in political behavior. Thus, after participating in a functional literacy module focusing on democracy and human rights, a women's group in the village of Malicounda in the Thiès region decided to end the practice of female genital mutilation in their village. After discussing the issue with the community, they succeeded in convincing the village to end the practice. The idea spread with women in hundreds of Senegalese villages abandoning this practice. In this case, unschooled Senegalese women and their communities were ahead of the Senegalese National Assembly, which did not adopt a law banning female genital mutilation until several years after the women of Malicounda had set a precedent in their village.

By the 1980s, use of the recently coined Wolof word *demokarassi* had become an increasingly important part of Senegalese speech-making and used interchangeably with the French *démocratie*. However, the meaning of these apparently similar words differed because of different historical reference points, allusions, and contents. A popular 1991 hit song in Wolof entitled *Démocratie* praised Diouf for making Senegal into an exemplary *demokarassi* because of his willingness to share the benefits of his office with others and his efforts to make everyone comfortable (*nguuru*).[35] This interpretation of *démocratie/demokarassi* placed the emphasis on clientelist and solidarity traditions and values. Diouf's political speeches in Wolof stressed words that identified him as a leader (*njiit*) and above the rough and tumble of partisan politics.[36] Diouf stayed away from portraying himself as a *buur*, the traditional Wolof ruler because of the negative images associated with these rulers among the Wolofone masses.

The language of politics reflected greater use of Wolof as politicians mixed French and Wolof in delivering their speeches, especially in urban areas where Wolof was the lingua franca. Abdoulaye Wade's use of the Wolof word for change, *Sopi*[37] eventually became the battle cry of the political opposition and caught on with Senegal's disenchanted urban youth. At the same time, opposition politicians continued to use the French word, *alternance* in calling for fair elections that would oust the Diouf régime and bring them to power.[38]

Opposition leaders used the Wolof terms *fal* and *folli* as synonyms for "to vote in" and "to vote out" of office. However, in precolonial Senegalese political traditions and language, *fal* referred to the process of selecting a ruler through consensus while *folli* referred to the process of deposing a ruler. For the opposition, the concepts of *fal* and *folli* were the key to real *demokarassi*. They, thus, translated the French concept of *alternance* or the people's right to change governments and leaders through the ballot box in a manner that favored their interests.

In the 2000 presidential elections, the opposition coalition that rallied behind Abdoulaye Wade called itself the *Front pour l'Alternance* (FAL) whose initials reflected a play on the Wolof term while also continuing to use *sopi* as its rallying cry. Responding to the demand of the public for change and the advice of a French political campaign consultant, Abdou Diouf in the 2000 presidential election campaign adopted the slogan, "Change in Continuity" but used the French term, *Le Changement dans la Continuité* in election posters. In his campaign speeches, Wade used *sopi* even when speaking in French to refer to the need for change. The fact that Wade was an excellent orator in Wolof and could more easily move back and forth from French to Wolof gave him a distinct advantage over Diouf, who felt more comfortable speaking in French when campaigning in urban areas.[39]

The intermingling of French and Wolof in political discourse created a blend of concepts related to Western-style democracy and precolonial Wolof concepts of good governance adapted to the modern political scene.[40] The establishment of independent private radio stations, broadcasting primarily in Wolof, provided the people with greater and immediate access to information about political and governance issues and enhanced their ability to participate in informed political debate and to evaluate the performance of their political leaders and government.

Linguistic Pluralism and Multiple Identities

The strong linguistic connection and identity that the French-speaking Senegalese elite had with France and the Francophone community has steadily declined since independence. The elite that took power at independence owed much of their elite status to the fact that they had mastered and assimilated the language and culture governing the political, economic, and legal institutions inherited from the colonial regime.

By establishing French as the official language of government, giving priority to French language institutions of higher education, and championing the Francophone community, Senghor attempted to preserve French as the primary language of the country's elite. His successor, Abdou Diouf, also had a strong attachment to the French language and to the Francophone-linguistic community.[41] Diouf was part of the French-speaking technocratic elite composed largely of *administrateurs civils* who rose to prominence in the 1970s and 1980s. By the 1990s, French had lost some of its mystique as the ticket to modernity and upward mobility. Senegalese increasingly studied English and other European languages and pursued higher education outside the Francophone community.

The higher echelons of the French-speaking Senegalese elite began to send their children to American universities. Although French has remained the official language of the country and its mastery essential for holding high posts in government, English has become increasingly important among the educated elite. As president, Abdoulaye Wade recognized this trend and appointed many more English-speaking ministers with degrees from American and Canadian universities than his predecessor.

The learning of other European languages has also been accompanied by changes in approaches toward governance practices and the economy. Government officials, politicians, and journalists trained in American universities in business, political science, and telecommunications have a markedly different approach toward government than the *administrateurs civils* who dominated government and administrative institutions under Diouf and Senghor.

Other factors have also contributed to the relative decline of the prestige of French among Senegalese: the hostile treatment of Senegalese workers in France; pilgrimages to Saudi Arabia and studying in Islamic universities in the Arab world; the growing influence of Afro-American music and American popular culture among Senegalese youth; and more frequent contacts of Senegalese with other cultures in Africa, Europe, and North America.

Senegalese national identity has become more and more associated with speaking Wolof while an Islamo-Wolof cultural model has become the dominant one in the country.[42] Without being imposed, Wolof is becoming Senegal's national language. Rapid urbanization and the diffusion of much of radio broadcasting in Wolof have accelerated this process. Wolof has become the primary language of most young Senegalese in urban areas, regardless of ethnic background. Wolof will become even stronger in the future as Wolof-speaking youth marry and use Wolof in the home as the primary language of discourse.

Wolof also dominates popular culture. Urban Wolof has emerged as the language of Senegal's urban youth. The disengagement of the state from the cultural sphere reduced the cultural gap between the government and the people and opened more space for the development of an autonomous urban culture and new language idioms.[43] Urban youth in the 1980s and 1990s repudiated the intellectual foundations of the Senghor era—African Socialism, Négritude, Francophonie—and the administrative culture of the Diouf era.[44] They also rejected the top-down approaches of democratization imposed by the Diouf régime and have insisted upon the right to manage their own neighborhoods. Their distaste with and revolt against Senegal's political establishment eventually led to the demise of the Diouf régime and helped bring Abdoulaye Wade to power.

The stance of urban youth reflected their defiance of Senegal's political, economic, social and cultural institutions, and a tendency to organize autonomous organizations free from the control of the government and political parties. Their music incorporated a critique of the injustices of the present system and a yearning for cleaning up Senegalese society. The *Set Setal* movement was inspired by a popular song in Wolof sung by Youssou Ndour.[45] *Set Setal* can be translated as "cleaning for purity," or "be clean and clean up."

Frustrated at the inability of the opposition to bring down the Diouf regime, Senegal's urban youth culture and the optimism and reformism embodied in the *Set Setal* movement gave way to a more aggressive and pessimistic musical and linguistic style based on Afro-American rap influences.[46] The number one Senegalese popular rap group, formed during the late 1980s, took the name of Positive Black Soul (PBS). Their first album, entitled *Boule Falé* (Don't Care!) became the rallying cry of what came to be called the New Generation Boule Falé of disillusioned youth. Rap music spread rapidly. By the beginning of the new millennium, the greater Dakar region alone had 3,000 rap groups. Wolof dominated as the language of Senegalese rap with some French and English phrases thrown in.

A resurgence of interest in local languages and local culture, particularly among the Halpulaar and the Diola, accompanied the rise of urban-Wolof as the dominant indigenous language in Senegal. During the 1990s, cultural days celebrating traditional culture and languages were organized in various towns throughout the country. Baaba Maal who sang in pulaar shared the stage with the Wolof-speaking Youssou Ndour as Senegal's two main World Music superstars. Halpulaar intellectuals from Fouta Toro also organized a movement for the Renaissance of Pulaar[47] to revitalize the language and to resurrect knowledge of literary traditions that went back to precolonial times.

Language also played an important role in defining the identity of the predominantly Diola speaking rebels seeking Casamance's independence from Senegal. Much of the resentment, which resulted in the outbreak of violence in the Casamance during the early 1980s, reflected Diola resistance to the imposition of an Islamo-Wolof cultural model coming from the North. Senegalese from the North have tended to regard the Diola and their language as backward and provincial. In contrast to the image of the Diola as a primitive savage, the Diola, in fact, had the highest percentage of their school-age children attending French schools.[48] Moreover, the Diola have also had the highest rates of migration to Dakar where Wolof is the lingua franca.[49] The older Diola in Dakar prefer to speak French with non-Diola rather than Wolof and resent the fact that their children, like most of the younger generation in Dakar, prefer Wolof to their maternal language.

The Diola language became a rallying point for the emergence of nationalist sentiments among the Diola. In 1979, Diola migrants working in France established a cultural association called *Esukolal* in Paris, which published a magazine having articles concerning how to promote literacy in the Diola language, poetry in French and Diola, and other articles referring to Diola religious traditions, stories of Diola heroes, sports, and present day grievances.[50] The organizers of *Esukolal* eventually became important leaders in the *Mouvement des Forces Démocratique de la Casamance* (MFDC) that spearheaded the movement for independence. Ironically, the movement's emphasis on traditional values and customs was the product of a Western-educated elite who reinforced the notion that the "authentic" Diola was attached to the land, sacred forests, traditional religious practices, and historically separate from Senegal at a time when young Diola men and women were abandoning agriculture to find employment in Dakar and other towns, settling in Dakar, and learning to speak Wolof. The emphasis that the predominantly Diola leadership of the MFDC place on the Diola language and Diola traditions, undermines their claims to speak for all the populations of the Casamance. The resolution of the conflict in the Casamance between the government and the rebels may well depend upon mutual recognition of and respect for plurilingual identities by all parties.

Although the largest single ethnic group, the Diola represent only a third of the urban population in Ziguinchor, the regional capital where Diola, Wolof, Mandinka, French, and Portuguese Creole are spoken.[51] In the secondary schools, the Diola prefer to speak French rather than Wolof in communicating with students from other ethnic groups. For the Diola, their language remains a primary component of their ethnic and group identity. The Diola often mix French and Diola together just as the Wolofones mix Wolof and French together. Wolof is the language of the immigrants from the North. But it is also increasingly becoming accepted by young people of all ethnic groups in Ziguinchor as a national language and the one in which Senegalese can best communicate with one another. The linguistic trends in Ziguinchor reflect linguistic trends developing throughout urban Senegal and suggest that non-Wolof Senegalese are acquiring multilingual identities as reflected in their use of language. While maternal languages—Diola, Wolof, Serer, Mandinka—constitute a primary component of non-Wolof ethnic identity, Wolof has evolved into something more than a lingua franca and is becoming more recognized as the national Senegalese language because it enables all Senegalese to communicate with one another. This is particularly true in a country where more than half of the adult population is still not literate in French.

The strengthening of attachments to Islam has also reinforced the importance of the Arabic language as an important component of Senegalese religious identity for the Muslim majority. Religious leaders are injecting more Arabic words in their sermons and lectures. More and more Muslims are attending Koranic schools and learning Arabic. One of the major developments in the past few decades has been a sharp increase in the number of Senegalese girls attending Koranic schools. Arabic has become part of the curriculum in Senegalese high schools and universities while the number of Franco-Arab schools has steadily expanded. Radio stations like *Wal Fadjiri-FM* have regular broadcasts in Arabic. Senegalese also have greater access to Arabic language programs through satellite television stations broadcasting from North Africa and the Middle East. The younger generation of marabouts is more conversant in French and even English, attuned to Senegal's urban youth culture, and in touch with Muslim currents outside of Senegal.

Linguistic Pluralism and Democracy

Linguistic pluralism in Senegal has blossomed in Senegal in tandem with the development of a pluralistic political system. Rather than becoming a divisive factor, linguistic pluralism has fostered greater communication, brought people together, and enriched Senegalese culture. Greater access to learning different languages and the freedom to choose which language to use in which context—at home, in the market, in mosques and churches, and in political debate—is reducing the communication gap and contributing to the spread of a democratic culture. French, Wolof, other Senegalese vernacular and European languages, and Arabic are now being used to enable Senegalese to discuss and participate more effectively in the country's political, economic, cultural, and religious life at all levels of social interaction.

The French language no longer monopolizes and defines the boundaries of political debate. National political debates are now being conducted in Wolof and more accessible to the people. At the same time, more people are learning French and expanding the pool of future political leaders and government officials. The spread of Islamic education means that marabouts no longer have the monopoly of access to holy texts because of their knowledge of Arabic.

Thanks to their multiple linguistic skills and talent for communication, the Senegalese people are using these as tools to build the foundations for a democratic culture based on respect for political, cultural, and religious diversity within the framework of a predominantly Islamic-Wolof culture.

CHAPTER TEN

Equality

[T]he gradual progress of equality is something fated.[1]

The breakdown of the old aristocratic order in Senegal following colonial conquest reduced the social gap between the nobility and the lower orders and castes. Tocqueville's comments about the steady march toward social equality in France could also be applied to Senegal:

> The noble has gone down in the social scale, and the commoner gone up; as the one falls, the other rises. Each half century brings them closer, and soon they will touch.[2]

After Senegal obtained its independence in 1960, the movement toward greater social and political equality accelerated and affected all levels of Senegalese society.

Toward Social Equality under Colonial Rule

Nobles and Commoners

The destruction of the old order by colonialism undermined the political and economic foundations of the ruling nobility. Under colonialism, nobles no longer could collect taxes and pillage. The French colonial state's control over "vacant" and "ownerless" lands deprived them of potential rents while the emancipation of slaves deprived nobles of labor to work their lands on their behalf.

Notwithstanding the political and economic decline of the nobility under colonialism and the rise of a new political elite based on French education, their social prestige persisted for many years, especial in the interior. Outside the Four Communes, social prejudices and old patterns of clientelist relationships changed slowly despite the rapid expansion of a market economy based on peanut production.

The situation was somewhat different in the Four Communes that were overseas extensions of France and not integrated into the precolonial

Senegambian aristocratic order. The Lebu community that inhabited Dakar
and Rufisque before these areas were annexed by the French in the second
half of the nineteenth century had social structures that were less hierarchical
than the aristocratic orders found in the Wolof, Mandinka, Halpulaar, and
Soninke states in the interior. Although traditional biases against candidates of
slave and caste origin persisted in electoral politics in the Four Communes,
few Senegalese of noble origin rose to prominence in modern politics.

In the Four Communes where Frenchmen, Afro-French, and Senegalese
citizens enjoyed equal rights and where the level of Western education was
a more salient criterion of elite status, noble status did not count as much as
it did in the interior. The status of commoners in the Four Communes also
differed from that of commoners in the interior because citizens enjoyed a
degree of security and civil and political rights that remained largely
unknown to rural subject commoners. In the Four Communes, Western-
educated commoners from modest social backgrounds could aspire to the
highest political office. Blaise Diagne was the son of a male cook and a
housemaid.[3]

Notwithstanding the persistence of respect for descendants of noble origin in Senegalese society, Senegal's most prominent national political leaders during the colonial era from Blaise Diagne to Léopold Sédar Senghor
were commoners as were most local party leaders and elected officials.
During the postwar era, commoners constituted more than 90 percent of
the members of Senegal's Territorial Assembly.[4] The election of commoners
was more widespread in Senegal than in other French West African territories like Guinea, French Soudan, and Mali where chiefs and descendants of
the old nobility outnumbered commoners in the territorial assemblies

Although commoners in the aristocratic order shared the status of freemen
with nobles, most had little power during the heyday of the precolonial
monarchies. Commoners had to pay a wide range of taxes and rents to the
nobility and contribute labor time. Their relatively low social status and sense
of powerlessness engendered attitudes of subservience toward authority in
general, and traditional authority in particular.[5] These attitudes persisted during the autocratic phases of colonialism, especially in the rural areas, thanks to
their subjection to canton chiefs and French colonial officials.

When electoral politics were extended to the interior after World War II,
candidates from noble backgrounds when appealing to rural voters often
cited their family pedigrees as descendants of royalty to support their can-
didacy. Nobles engaged in politics were expected to act like a *Samba
Linguère* noble—the man of honor who generously rewarded and took care
of his following.

Slaves, Artisans, and Griots

As late as 1904, the slave population in Senegal was estimated to be over
30 percent of the total population by the colonial authorities.[6] Along the
Senegal River, slaves comprised more than 50 percent of the population.

Despite the formal abolition of slavery, former slaves in many rural areas continued to remain highly dependent upon their former masters who provided them with access to land and assistance in times of need. Servile relationships remained strongest in the Senegal River basin where the nobility still retained control over much of the cultivable land and in parts of the peanut basin where former slaves depended on nobles for access to land. On the other hand, the destruction of the military power of the old nobility meant that slave-owners could no longer force their slaves to remain. Following their emancipation, former slaves from other parts of Senegal and French Soudan gravitated toward the new peanut lands to work as *navétanes*. Thousands of former slaves returned to their villages of origin, settled in new areas, or migrated to the towns where one could more easily shake off the stigma of being slaves.

The French urban settlements of Saint-Louis and Gorée, where slaves comprised more than half the population had a larger percentage of slaves than many African territories in the interior before emancipation.[7] The emancipation of slaves in the Communes, the flight of runaway slaves to Saint-Louis and other areas under French direct rule, and the heavy migration of former slaves to the towns after the demise of slavery in the interior meant that Senegal's urban areas had a high percentage of former slaves.

Before the abolition of slavery in French Senegal in 1848, male slaves worked in various nonagricultural occupations as sailors, masons, weavers, tailors, laborers, servants, carpenters, and cooks while female slaves worked as seamstresses, laundresses, cooks, and domestics.[8] When emancipated, many slaves continued to work for their former masters while some went out on their own and prospered. Slavery was abolished in Dakar in 1877 and in Rufisque in 1879, before they obtained the status of full communes.

The abolition of slavery posed fewer problems for Senegalese societies than for Tocqueville's America.[9] In the first place, slavery in precolonial Senegal was not based on racial ideologies that pitted white masters against black slaves.[10] To be a slave was largely a matter of bad luck and had little to do with being a member of an inferior race. Second, the destruction of the slave economy did not bring about great economic hardship. On the contrary, the emergence and rapid expansion of Senegal's peanut export economy brought relative prosperity to large numbers of the Senegalese population, including former slaves who found new economic opportunities. Third, emancipated slaves in Senegal had greater social and economic mobility than their counterparts in America where former slaves encountered racial discrimination and were treated poorly by the white population in the North before the Civil War.

In precolonial aristocratic societies, the stigma of caste relegated artisans and griots to inferior social status. Artisans and griots had to live in separate villages and residential quarters from the rest of the population.[11] Griots were not allowed to be buried in cemeteries for fear that they would pollute the land and were often interred in the hollow trunks of baobab trees. Like slaves, artisans were attributed to have negative character traits and to be of inferior blood. Nobles and commoners regarded slaves and people of caste as men without honor.

During colonial rule, access to Western education enabled members of the artisan castes to enter new occupations and hold important positions in colonial society despite their lowly-traditional-social status. Through Western education, low caste individuals and former slaves could rise in colonial society. However, those from lowly social origins who entered the colonial service and held posts in the territorial administration as canton chiefs frequently experienced difficulties in administering their districts because they were not respected by the local populations.

Under colonial rule, taboos preventing freemen from exercising occupations previously monopolized by members of specialized castes declined. Thus, while many artisans became textile and tannery workers, furniture makers, and mechanics, these areas also became open to freemen and former slaves. In time, non-griots could also aspire to become prominent singers, dancers, and musicians, areas that had traditionally been restricted to griots in aristocratic societies.

Colonial rule and the destruction of the old nobility, however, did little to change traditional attitudes toward caste and taboos against intermarriage. Nobles and commoners rarely married members of the artisan caste. Popular prejudices also often excluded former slaves and individuals from the artisan castes from becoming Imams of local mosques.

Although persons of caste were no longer excluded from participating in political life and could run for public office on their own in the Four Communes, one's slave and caste origins made it more difficult to be nominated and elected.

Elders and Youth

Social hierarchies based largely on age characterized social structures in Senegal's precolonial acephalous societies. Elders dominated family and village structures, allocated land, and participated in public affairs. Elder brothers exercised considerable authority over younger brothers. The eldest male descendant of the founder of the village usually held the post of village chief while the eldest male headed the extended family and represented them in village councils. At the village level, Senegal's precolonial aristocratic societies also had similar gerontocratic political and social structures.

Control over family land permitted family patriarchs to exercise strict control over their children who received from their fathers parcels of land to cultivate, which married men inherited after the death of their father. Under colonialism, Western education, migration, and fragmentation of landholdings contributed to the decline of male parental authority over their sons. The development of commercial agriculture coupled with the monetarization of the bride-price provided incentives for young unmarried males to earn money on their own to get married. Young men increasingly preferred to cultivate cash crops on the parcels of land allocated to them by their fathers rather than contribute labor time to cultivate food crops on family land controlled by the head of the extended household.

Modern politics was one area in which age was relatively less important. In the Four Communes, politicians with Western education could aspire to public office at a relatively early age. Blaise Diagne was only forty-two when he became Senegal's first Black African deputy. Lamine Guèye became mayor of Saint-Louis at the age of thirty-four.

During the late 1940s and early 1950s, secondary school and university students became highly politicized and active in Senegalese politics. In the mid and late 1950s, Senegalese political parties began to establish youth wings as auxiliary party organizations. Membership in the party's youth wings was extended to Senegalese males up to the age of thirty-five and above. Apprenticeship in party youth wings served as stepping-stones for ambitious young people to rise in the party hierarchy. Before independence, members of the youth wing rarely challenged their elders.

Women

In Senegal's precolonial aristocratic societies, women from royal dynasties shared the privileges of royalty. Women from noble families campaigned for the election of rulers and distributed gifts to enlarge their family's clientele.[12] In the Wolof kingdoms, the *linguère*, usually the mother or sister of the ruler, served as the head of the community of women, received gifts when they married, levied fines on promiscuous women, and controlled large tracts of land.[13] With the demise of the Old Order, women from the nobility lost their special privileges and status in society. Women of caste, former slaves, and descendants of commoners generally shared the social status of their male counterparts, but could move up socially if they married above their group.

The Sufi brand of Islam that emerged in Senegal was less oppressive than its fundamentalist counterparts in the Arab world.[14] Women moved freely, did not wear the veil, and engaged in market activities. Ibrahima Niasse, head of the Niassene Tijanis, strongly believed in educating women and trained his own daughters who became outstanding religious teachers.

The French colonizers did little to improve the status of women. The demands for equality expressed during the French Revolution did not apply to women.[15] In France, the status of French women actually declined after the French Revolution. The Napoleonic Code established the legal framework for subordinating women to their husbands. France exported its negative attitudes toward women to the colonies.[16] Colonial officials rarely dealt with women or women's issues and perpetuated Western gender stereotypes.[17]

Unlike their male counterparts in the Four Communes, Senegalese women did not receive the right to vote until 1946, two years after France finally gave this right to French women. When French women got the right to vote in 1944, Senegalese male politicians responded with a campaign to extend suffrage to Senegalese women based on racial equality rather than gender equality.[18] Despite their newfound suffrage, Senegalese women did not run for public office or hold important posts in Senegal's postwar political parties.

In the Four Communes, Senegalese women were highly active in Senegal's two main political parties contesting power during the postwar era. In Dakar, the percentage of women joining political parties was almost as high as that for men.[19] Women organized and actively participated in political rallies in the communes garbed in their party's colors and strongly supported the 1947 Dakar–Niger rail workers strike against their French colonial bosses.[20]

Senegalese women had fewer opportunities to rise in colonial society because of their lack of formal education. As late as 1958, girls accounted for less than 28 percent of the total number attending Senegalese public schools.[21] In the rural areas, few girls went to school. Very few women held positions in the French colonial bureaucracy, even as secretaries, until the last years of colonialism. And no women served in the territorial administration.

Political and Social Equality after Independence

All Senegalese constitutions, since independence, have proclaimed the equality of all citizens before the law without distinction of origin, race, sex, or religion and the legal equality of men and women. The revised 2001 constitution went even further than earlier constitutions in declaring that all human beings, not just citizens, were equal before the law.[22] The new constitution also explicitly proclaimed the access of all citizens without discrimination to the exercise of power at all levels and affirmed its rejection of inequality and discrimination. Senegalese constitutions thus provided a legal framework for promoting political and social equality and insuring liberty—all crucial elements in meeting Tocqueville's requirements for a vibrant democracy.

The steady movement toward political and social equality in Senegal continued after independence. It evolved rather slowly during the Senghor era, picked up speed in the 1980s and has accelerated rapidly since the 1990s. The spread of literacy and democratic ideals coupled with economic stagnation in the rural areas and large-scale migration to the towns, other parts of Africa, and Europe undermined Senegal's precolonial aristocratic social structures and permitted former slaves, persons of caste, women, and youth to rise in society and hold public office on a scale not possible in the past. However, the pace of the march toward greater political and social equality varied considerably in different parts of the country. In some rural areas, traditional social structures survived with relatively little change. In other rural areas, previously excluded social groups now played a more important role in public affairs. However, in all rural areas, social distinctions based on age, gender, and caste diminished.

Nioro

In the rural *arrondissement* of Médina Sabakh located in the Saloum near the Gambian border, movement toward political and economic equality has been slow. The local power structure has not changed much since the seventeenth century.[23] When the French established their sovereignty over Saloum in 1887, they left the traditional social structures intact. Approximately half the population were slaves while 10 percent of the population belonged to the caste of artisans and griots. With the development of peanut cultivation, many former slaves came into the Saloum area, some joining *daras* that eventually became transformed into villages, while others worked as farm laborers.

During the 1930s, the slaves left their former masters to become independent farmers. Most ex-slaves preferred to live in their former villages or in nearby hamlets. Rural notables and freemen continued to monopolize the office of village chief and imam. Parents were reluctant to send their children to a secular school and preferred to send them to Koranic schools. The first public school in Médina Sabakh did not open until 1954.

After independence, social structures evolved slowly. The number of artisans practicing their profession declined as most became full-time farmers. Unlike the case in rural areas in the Senegal River Valley or in the Casamance, few young males left to migrate to the towns. As a result, Médina Sabakh *arrondissement* had no hometown associations. Most of the area's new associations were initiated by the state or by foreign NGOs.

In 1974, the government established three rural councils in the *arrondissement*. Although the top leadership positions on the Rural Councils continued to be dominated by village chiefs, rural notables, and elders, former slaves and casted people also served as elected officials. The composition of Kaymor's Rural Council, where slaves actually outnumbered freemen, accurately reflected social divisions in the population. However, in practice, the former slaves in the rural council tended to follow the lead of the rural notables and rarely took any initiatives on their own. Traditional notables comprised most of the members of Médina Sabakh's Rural Council, which included three former slaves and one artisan. Only one woman and one youth served on each of the *arrondissement's* three Rural Councils. Male dominance was reflected in the fact that women's groups were often started by men and that men served as secretaries and treasurers of these associations. The wives of rural notables also tended to control women's associations.

The party bosses of the PS representing factions contending for power at the Nioro department level exerted considerable influence over rural council officials who sided with one or the other faction. The clientelist relations so characteristic of Senegalese politics prevailed at the local level. The population remained largely dependent upon the state, which initiated most of the new development activities and brought foreign aid projects and

NGOs to the area. Thanks to the patronage provided by Nioro-based party leaders like Moustapha Niasse who held high government and party posts, Médina Sabakh received more than its fair share of development projects.

In the 1990s, younger men with some secondary school education began to exert more influence in public affairs. Former slaves who became successful merchants and transporters rose in the economic hierarchy. Social distinctions became blurred as friendships and cooperation developed across class and caste lines. It became increasingly less appropriate to refer to someone's social origins. In the 1996 local government elections, members of opposition parties won seats on the Rural Councils and the number of women and young males on the Councils increased sharply. By the end of the century, new forces were coming into play while the power and social prestige of the old power structure was slowly eroding.

Fouta Toro

Fouta Toro had the most rigid caste structures in precolonial Senegal. During the colonial era, descendants of the families of the *Grands Electeurs* served as canton chiefs. Before independence, members of caste and former slaves played little or no role in Senegalese politics. During the early years of independence, Halpulaar ministers from Fouta Toro like Cheikh Hamidou Kane and Ibra Wane came exclusively from *torodo* noble families.

Mass migration of former slaves and members of the artisan castes from Fouta Toro to the towns and other parts of Senegal and later to other African countries and Europe deprived the region of a pool of manpower. Few incentives existed for former slaves to stay since they had access only to marginal land. The best lands near the Senegal River flood plain remained in the hands of the nobility. Members of the old nobility who had traditions of Islamic learning soon saw the advantages of Western education and sent their children to French schools. After independence, many entered the liberal professions, staffed the higher echelons of the civil service, and became active in national and local politics using their home area as a political base.

The introduction of irrigated agriculture in the 1970s on government-controlled lands further reduced the nobility's control over the local economy. The majority of people cultivating rice in the irrigated perimeters were former slaves and fishermen who became more involved in the management of these perimeters even though nobles continued to hold many of the leadership positions.

Despite their lowly social origins, some merchants, transporters, and diamond dealers working in other African countries acquired immense wealth and became influential figures in Fouta Toro by giving large sums of money to build mosques, health centers, and other social infrastructure and by funding the political campaigns of their favorite candidates.

Sparked by drought and expanding European economies seeking labor for factory and other menial jobs, migration to France and Europe from Fouta Toro increased in the 1970s. Slaves and members of the artisan castes were able to hold leadership roles in the Senegalese workers organizations that sprung up in France and, to a lesser extent, in other *émigré* associations. Members of the local nobility grudgingly recognized the importance of working with low caste and former slave leaders of *émigré* organizations to improve living conditions and infrastructure at home.

By the mid-1990s, members of lowly social origins had begun to rise in the political hierarchy in Fouta Toro. The mayor of Matam came from the group of freed slaves; the secretary-general of the Socialist Party in Podor and a deputy in the National Assembly was a member of the weaver's caste; and a prominent Socialist politician in Kanel belonged to the caste of griots.[24] Despite the ascent of some members of lowly social origins and their greater representation in local and national political institutions, members of the old nobility still tended to hold most of the top leadership positions in rural councils in Fouta Toro. In the future, their grip on these institutions is likely to decline further.

Lower Casamance

The majority of the indigenous populations in the political and administrative region of Ziguinchor encompassing the Lower Casamance belonged to acephalous societies with strong egalitarian and individualistic traditions. Age and wealth were linked to the individual. Diola villages were largely juxtapositions of families living in proximity to each other but not dependent on each other. Diola societies had no hereditary inferior social categories. Slaves captured in raids and wars against neighboring societies thus became prisoners of wars and a source of wealth to be exchanged for cattle and other goods rather than to be kept as labor to cultivate land or to serve as domestic servants in the home. Descendants of slaves were integrated into the village. Although generally poorer than their fellow villager because they had smaller rice fields, they were not considered to be social inferiors. Diola society also had no attachments to caste and specialized hereditary occupations like warriors, blacksmiths, griots, and leatherworkers. Any Diola peasant could become an artisan without having a social sigma attached to this.

The high school attendance rates among the Diola, the spread of commercial agriculture, and migration to the towns undermined the traditional Diola rice-based economy. Migration of large numbers of young Diola men and women to the cities to work as domestics, laborers, clerks, and civil servants deprived the local economy of sufficient labor needed to properly tend to the rice fields and to sustain food production. The migration of young women to the towns reflected a higher degree of independence for Diola women than among the Islamized societies in the north of the country or among the neighboring Mandinka. Ironically, the majority of independent young Diola women going to Dakar wound up working as domestics for Europeans and wealthier Senegalese.

The pattern of Diola participation in modern electoral politics also reflected their fierce desire for equality and autonomy. Emile Badiane, a Diola primary schoolteacher, was one of the founders of the MFDC in 1947, which protested the dominance of Senegalese politics by the citizens of the Four Communes. After independence, Badiane served in the government and held high posts in the party. His death in 1972 deprived the Diola of one of its few authentic political leaders who had the confidence of the people. The highly centralized administrative and patronage system set up by the PS party-state based on clientelism and state largesse was ill-suited to represent effectively a highly fragmented, egalitarian population, fiercely proud of its autonomy. The absence of autonomous, local government institutions, the domination of the territorial administration operating in the Lower Casamance by culturally insensitive northerners, and the over-representation of non-Diola and civil servants in local party structures were also important factors leading to the outbreak of hostilities against the government in 1982.

The Cap Vert Peninsula

Metropolitan Dakar with a population of well over two million people encompasses the Cap Vert peninsula and has a rich blend of political and social egalitarian traditions not found in the countryside. The movement toward political and social equality began with the settlement of the sparsely populated Cap Vert peninsula by the Wolof-speaking Lebu community in the eighteenth century and their success in achieving political independence from the Damel of Cayor. It gained momentum with the granting of political and civil rights to the inhabitants of the Four Communes and the rise of the Layenne Brotherhood toward the end of the nineteenth century. The influx of Senegalese migrants from all parts of the interior, many of whom were former slaves and of low caste status, and the spread of Western education during the first two decades of the twentieth century transformed Dakar from a small Lebu village into a heterogeneous and cosmopolitan city that by 1910 had surpassed the old colonial capital of Saint-Louis in population. The higher degree of social and economic mobility permitted many former slaves and those of low caste status to rise in society, weakened old social structures based on hierarchy, and provided a more suitable climate for the propagation and spread of political and social equality.

Although governed according to Islamic law adapted to pre-Islamic Lebu customs, the Wolof-speaking Lebu who settled in the Cap Vert peninsula during the eighteenth century had relatively egalitarian social structures when compared with the aristocratic order prevailing in Cayor when they obtained their independence. The Lebu had no high nobility or warrior class. The class of freeman—patriarchs, clan leaders, fishermen, and farmers—constituted the core of society.

Shortly after establishing a foothold in Cap Vert in 1857, the French began seizing Lebu villages and expropriating land. The loss of their independence and disruptions caused by colonial rule set the stage for the rise of a millenarian movement during the 1880s and 1890s among the

Lebu led by Limamou Laye who preached egalitarian ideals:

> All disciples of Limamou must consider themselves as equals and make
> a *table rasa* of their racial origins, social rank or caste. Superiority does
> not lie with these differences. The better person is the person who
> fears God the most.[25]

Laye's efforts to promote women and youth and the lack of formality and
submissive relationships between Layenne marabouts and their disciples
reflected the egalitarian thrust of the Brotherhood.

Egalitarian norms infused Dakar's municipal politics after Blaise Diagne's
victory in 1914. Frenchmen, Afro-Europeans, and Africans worked together
in the same political parties as equals. During the colonial period, elite status
was based largely on French education and restricted to a relatively small
group. After independence, the number and percentage of children attending
schools increased rapidly in Dakar. Primary school education was open to
members of all groups, regardless of social origins. Former slaves coming to
Dakar from the interior found it easier to shed their former identities than
those from the griot and artisan castes because they often had the same
names as their former masters whereas members of the griots and the
artisan castes generally kept their family names.

One indicator of the higher degree of political and social mobility and
equality prevailing in Dakar can be seen in the disproportionate number of
persons of caste and women in government from this region. Slightly less
than 10 percent of the 187 ministers in the government from 1957 to 2000
came from the griot and artisan castes.[26] Six ministers from caste origins,
comprising one-third of the total number of ministers of caste, were born,
raised, and went to school in Dakar. Out of the fourteen women serving in
the government as ministers during this period, five were born and raised in
Dakar. The relatively large percentage of Dakar women in government
reflected their greater access to education and the higher degree of female
participation in politics and public life in comparison with the rest of the
country.

After independence, the rise of Mouride influence in the so-called informal
sector in Dakar also contributed to improving the social and economic
status of people of caste in Dakar. Mouride traders, transporters, and
artisans, many of whom came from the artisan castes and other humble
origins, came to play an increasingly important role in Dakar's economic
life. Their frugality, work ethic, and piety combined with an aggressive
entrepreneurial spirit transformed some into millionaires and provided
sustenance for thousands more who would have remained unemployed and
unproductive.

The social stigma attached to caste is clearly in decline. A newspaper poll
taken in Dakar in January 1995 identified Youssou Ndour, a popular
Senegalese world music singer of humble origin, as the most admired person
in 1994. In this poll, Ndour scored higher than President Abdou Diouf and

Abdoulaye Wade put together. Ndour's father was a Serer mechanic while his mother was a Halpulaar praise singer. His music emphasized remembering one's roots, respecting one's parents, and praising all mothers and women. Like many of Senegal's most popular singers and musicians, Ndour was a Mouride and has written songs in praise of Ahmadou Bamba. Starting his career as a young singer with a local band in the late 1970s, by the end of the century, he had become a rich and famous international super-star. Ndour's success pointed to the importance of talent and hard work in rising in society and served as a model for Senegalese youth.

Ascribed social status has become less important for Dakar's youth. Throughout the city, young people have organized neighborhood cultural and sports associations that bring together young people of all origins who choose their leaders on merit rather than social origins.

Gender and Equality in Independent Senegal

Tocqueville who regarded women as the moral and intellectual equals of men[27] saw the movement toward democracy as raising the status of women and reducing inequality between men and women:

> [T]he same social impetus which brings nearer to the same level father and son, master and servant, and generally every inferior to every superior does raise the status of women and should make them more and more nearly equal to men.[28]

One of the most striking developments in Senegal since independence has been the general movement toward greater gender equality and the increased participation of women in politics, civil society, and economic activities.

Women in Public Office

The ascent of women in Senegalese politics did not gain momentum until the declining years of the Senghor regime. During the 1960s, Senegal had only one woman as a deputy out of 100 deputies in Senegal's National Assembly. This number increased to eight in 1978. Senghor appointed the first two women ministers in March 1978. Caroline Diop, Senegal's first female deputy and the president of the women's wing of the ruling party, became the Minister for Social Action. Senghor also chose Maimouna Kane, a former judge, as a junior minister charged with Women's Affairs. Kane represented a new breed of educated women (*femmes phares*) who provided a symbolic representation of women in the government and the ruling party.[29]

When he became president, Abdou Diouf made a conscious effort to recruit more women into the party and in 1982 introduced a quota system in the PS party that reserved 25 percent of all party posts below the political bureau for the women.[30] The number of PS female deputies in the National Assembly after the 1983 legislative elections climbed to twelve. Among the new deputies was Arame Diène, the first illiterate woman elected to the National Assembly. Unlike many of the women nominated for public office, Diène had strong grassroots support and headed the women's national party section as well as the Cap Vert regional women's party organization.

During his presidency, Abdou Diouf increased the number of women in ministerial level posts in the government and put some of them to head ministries previously reserved for men. Most women ministers owed their post to the support they received from the president rather than to their having a strong political base of their own. One of the few exceptions to that rule was Mata Sy Diallo, a Halpulaar of humble social origins and a native of Kaffrine, who rose to become the political boss of Kaffrine, the largest department in the peanut basin, second vice president of the National Assembly, and president of Kaolack's Regional Council. As a local party leader in her own right, she was one of the few women "serving as a man" in Senegalese politics and thus not dependent upon the largesse of the party's male leadership for access to party resources and offices.[31]

At the local level, particularly in the rural areas, the number of women holding public office remained low. Men did not see women holding public office while most women were reluctant to challenge traditional social norms. During the 1996 local government elections, the percentage of women elected to municipal and rural councils increased sharply. However, this reflected more the decision of the major political parties to put a higher percentage of women on the party lists than a surge in support for women's participation. Nevertheless, the elections revealed some movement toward acceptance of women as local government leaders. For the first time, a woman served as the president of a Rural Council. More significant was the fact that she was chosen largely on the basis of the trust and support of the people in her constituency rather than being handpicked by a prominent male party leader. In the greater Dakar metropolitan area, four women emerged as mayors of the newly created *communes d'arrondissement*.

During the 1990s, Wade's PDS made a strong bid for the support of women voters. After his victory in the March 2000 presidential elections, the number of women in government increased dramatically. When Ibrahima Niasse left the government in March 2001, Wade replaced him with Mame Madior Boye, who became Senegal's first woman prime minister. During the April 29, 2001 legislative campaign, Wade promised the women of Senegal that he would name a woman as prime minister in the new government.[32] After the elections in which women won 19 of the 120 seats in the National Assembly, he kept his promise by retaining Mame Madior Boye as prime minister.

As Prime Minister, Boye had little influence within her government. A year later, Wade replaced Boye with Idrissa Seck, the number two man in the PDS and the person widely considered as Wade's dauphin. Seck's government had seven women ministers, most of whom were *femmes phares*, recruited from civil society who had little influence in PDS party circles. Despite the greater visibility of women in the government, men continued to dominate the inner circles of power.

In 1977, Senegal had no women ministers. A quarter of a century later, Senegalese women constituted nearly a quarter of the cabinet. Despite these gains for women, politics and key government posts remained largely dominated by men now more aware of the importance of the female electorate. Although women were far from reaching equality with men in the holding of public office and control over public resources, they had made great strides in being recognized as equals.

Women and Civil Society

At independence, few Senegalese men had attained the level of education needed to enter the liberal professions and the upper echelons of the state administration. What was true for men was even more so for women because of the much lower rates of young women attending postsecondary education institutions. During the early 1960s less than 5 percent of the Senegalese attending the University of Dakar were women.[33] Moreover, certain professions and activities seemed to be reserved for men. The *École Nationale d'Administration*, an institution created shortly after independence to train Senegalese civil servants, was almost exclusively male. As in France, males dominated the teaching profession. At independence, male nurses were more numerous than female nurses. Becoming a midwife constituted the principal channel open to women in the health professions. Women were trained to teach home economics and to serve as typists and secretaries in the lower levels of the state bureaucracy.

During the first decade of independence, Senegal's predominantly male Western-educated elite placed more emphasis on placing Senegalese males in posts and positions that had been previously held by Frenchmen. This meant having Senegalese lawyers, judges, secondary school and university teachers, journalists, engineers, agronomists, economists, bankers, and businessmen replacing Frenchmen. The drive for Africanization of all sectors of society on the part of Senegalese nationalist reflected the belief that Africans were the equals of Europeans and could perform just as well when given the same level of education.

Males dominated Senegal's liberal professions, trade unions, economic associations, student organizations, the media, and the higher echelons of the administration. Senegalese women were predominantly housewives, farmers, and petty traders. Nearly all women in the monetized sectors of the economy served in subordinate positions as midwives, nurses, primary schoolteachers, salesclerks, secretaries, typists, maids, seamstresses, laundresses, and cooks. Few worked as lawyers, doctors, engineers, civil servants, and secondary schoolteachers. Although a national survey of women taken during the mid-1960s revealed that most Senegalese women wanted work outside the home, their aspirations remained very limited.[34] The survey also revealed that most Senegalese women agreed that males should head the household and take the lead in making family decisions and accepted the notion that males, for various reasons—more education, their higher social status in society, and natural intelligence—were generally superior to women. Women in Dakar and other urban areas expressed a greater desire for more equality between men and women than women in rural areas.

Greater access of women to higher education during the first two decades of independence created the preconditions for women to enter the higher echelons of civil society on an equal basis with men. By the end of the century, women had entered and thrived in occupations previously reserved for men. The teaching corps became increasingly feminized, particularly in Dakar and especially at the elementary school level. But even in rural areas in the interior, the number of women teachers increased. Significant numbers of women became doctors, lawyers, pharmacists, economists, university professors, and writers.

Women in Dakar and the Interior

Gaps in perception persisted between the better educated and more politically sophisticated women in Dakar and the larger towns and the less educated women in the Dakar and the interior. Dakar's educated women were more likely to push for political and functional equality with men while the largely unschooled rural women were more concerned with improvements in their economic well-being and quality of life.

The steady decline of the agricultural sector, massive rural exodus, and the loss of thousands of jobs resulting from structural adjustment programs led to a major shift in family structures as Senegalese families became more dependent upon resources generated by women. At the same time, more and more women became the head of the household and responsible for making family economic decisions. The percentage of women in Dakar heading a household rose from 19 percent in 1988 to 27 percent in 1994.[35] However, even when women assumed responsibility for the family, Senegalese family law continued to extend recognition only to male members as the legal head of the household.

In metropolitan Dakar, variations in occupation, level of education, and economic status were more differentiated than in the rural areas. Illiterate women and those with little education worked primarily in the informal sector, served as maids, or remained unemployed. Women accounted for the majority of Senegalese participating in the rapidly expanding informal sector. Market women sold fish, fruits, vegetables, and condiments and ran fast food stalls and mini-restaurants. Some women toiled in the canneries that transformed Dakar's fish catch into canned tuna and other fish products. A large number of young women with no schooling worked as maids in Dakar where 30 percent of households had maids.

The percentage of Dakar women with at least secondary school education jumped from 17 percent in 1988 to 31 percent in 2001. Due to the economic crisis and cut back in government recruitment, university-educated women in Dakar found it difficult to find a job commensurate with their level of education as employers gave preference to men over women in their hiring practices. While the growing number of well-educated women increased the pool of women aggressively seeking political and social equality with men, less educated women living in metropolitan Dakar remained more attached to familiar family roles that maintained the man as the undisputed head of the household. Nearly all the women's rights advocacy groups were based in Dakar and run by university-educated women.

The status of women has also increased in the eyes of Senegalese men. However, while accepting the need to improve conditions for women and to provide women with greater access to religious and secular education, most men and the leading religious authorities balk at giving women equal legal status within the family and changing family, property, and inheritance practices based in Islamic law. These views have created tensions between the urbane secular Senegalese elite, male and female, advocating political and social equality and the more traditionalist elements in Senegalese society who still saw men as the natural leaders of the family, society, and the nation.

CHAPTER ELEVEN

Democracy in Senegal: A Balance Sheet

> Among democratic peoples it is only through association that the
> citizens can raise any resistance to the central power.[1]

This book has traced the evolution of Senegal from a predominantly
aristocratic order toward a more democratic order. Rather than placing
the emphasis primarily on national elites, political parties, elections, and
the state, we have also looked at the movement toward social equality, local
liberties, associational life, and ethnic and religious tolerance as crucial
components of the democratization process.

This chapter summarizes the state of democracy in Senegal after more
than four decades of independence, examining strengths and weaknesses
and the impact of globalization.

Cracks in Senegalese Democracy

Persistence of Patrimonial Mores: Personalization of Power

Despite the movement toward greater social equality and political democracy,
patrimonial norms and mores have not disappeared. Rulers and bureaucrats
still treat state resources as their own while many ordinary citizens expect
those in power to be generous in distributing state resources and offices to
their families, friends, place of origin, and supporters. Given the persistence
of patrimonial mores, it should not be surprising that many Senegalese
political leaders see criticism as personal attacks, have difficulty sharing
power and delegating authority to others, and seek to win support and popularity by generously rewarding their followers and constituents with money,
jobs, and other material benefits.[2]

Paradoxically, the 2000 presidential elections that established Senegal's
credentials as a full-fledged electoral democracy also led to a surge in mores
typical of neopatrimonial regimes. Once in power, Wade increasingly
personalized the office of president and centralized power in his hands at
the expense of other national and local government institutions.

Wade blurred the distinction between public and private resources by distributing monthly supplements to the salaries of governors and other officials in the territorial administration and giving leaders of political parties in his coalition monthly stipends. It wasn't always clear whether the money came from Wade's own personal fortune or the state's resources.[3] Wade also held meetings of his party in the presidential palace thus blurring boundaries between his role as president and party leader while the state controlled media and friendly newspapers often gave the impression that government projects and assistance reflected the personal generosity of the president.

His personal and idiosyncratic style of governing, bypassing of legal and constitutional norms despite his training as a lawyer, and disdain for traditional protocol drew the fire of critics who accused Wade of weakening the office of the presidency, deinstitutionalizing the structures of the state, and needlessly antagonizing other African leaders.[4]

The concentration and personalization of power in the hands of the president also aroused some concern that Senegal was already in, or in danger of, becoming an authoritarian regime.[5] By mid-2002, the president and his supporters controlled the executive, legislative, and judicial branches of government as well as most local government councils, which had only three years earlier been dominated by the PS.

Despite his position as undisputed leader of his party and immense presidential powers, Wade was not able to impose his will and act without checks on his power. An increasingly better informed public opinion frequently forced Wade to reconsider his actions when his behavior and policies went against popular norms and interests.

Despite his authoritarian tendencies, Wade's liberal ideals and personal history of struggle to expand the Senegalese opposition's political and civil rights[6] coupled with his desire to maintain his international reputation as an apostle for democracy make it less likely that he will use force and repression to impose his views on the country or that Senegal will reverse its trends toward greater democratization.

Political Parties and Clientelism: Sharing the Spoils

Senegalese political parties traditionally have regarded control of the presidency as the main stake in politics, access to state resources as the main spoils of victory, and positions as ministers and heads of state agencies as important sources of revenue for party leaders and their party. This attitude, which reflects Senegalese political realities, helps explain the ease with which so many political leaders rally to the president's party after the national presidential elections.

The heavy concentration of power in the hands of the presidency and the president's personal control over state resources and jobs provided incentives for politicians to join the winning camp. Ministerial posts and formal leadership positions in the National Assembly were highly coveted and afforded the fortunate few with lucrative salaries and perks. During the Diouf era, many members of Wade's PDS succumbed to temptation and joined the PS. Once in power, it was Wade's turn to encourage what Senegalese call *transhumance*—the movement back and forth between different political parties. After Wade's victory in the 2000 presidential elections, a significant number of political leaders affiliated with the PS and other political parties left to join the ranks of the PDS.

The smaller political parties reflected old patterns of clientelist politics. Political leaders organized highly localized political parties based largely on their own personal following and used their party as an instrument for negotiating advantages for themselves and their followers with the leader of the ruling party heading the government.

The leaders of former opposition parties that had formed an alliance with Wade to bring down Diouf shared in the fruits of power, becoming ministers and holding prominent positions in the National Assembly. Despite their misgivings about Wade's policies, the leaders of parties like LD-MPT and *And Jef* (AJ) have been reluctant to leave the coalition and lose their access to jobs and resources. Their parties are now faced with the dilemma as to what they should do in the future. Should they remain junior partners in the governing coalition or should they again seek to conquer power on their own as principled opposition parties offering an alternative to Wade's liberal economic policies and idiosyncratic style of governing?

Given Senegal's long traditions of patrimonial and neopatrimonial politics, clientelism is likely to remain a central feature of Senegalese political life for many years to come—as long as access to state resources remains the main objective of Senegal's political class, the presidency continues to control state resources, and the state remains the country's primary employer.[7]

Parliament and the Judiciary: Weak and Dependent National Institutions

Traditions of executive dominance under colonialism and the transformation of Senegal into a de facto one-party state shortly after independence sharply restricted the potential for the National Assembly to become a strong independent institution. Ironically, the last major act of the National Assembly to assert its authority as an autonomous institution took place when the deputies deposed a formal motion of censure against Mamadou Dia, in December 1962, for abusing his powers and ignoring the prerogatives of the National Assembly. The censure motion eventually led to the demise of Dia and the emergence of Senghor as Senegal's undisputed national leader. Under Senghor, the National Assembly did little more than rubber stamp the legislation introduced by the government.

Although the restoration of unrestricted multiparty competition during the 1980s brought new blood into the National Assembly and allowed for greater public debate of the issues, the National Assembly remained a weak legislative body used by the government to ratify laws and treaties initiated by the government.

During the 2000 electoral campaign, Wade promised to strengthen the powers of the National Assembly and to abolish the Senate as a second legislative body on the grounds that it was too costly and a haven for PS politicians. Once in power, Wade made little effort to strengthen the National Assembly. Although the Wade regime abolished the Senate as promised, it created a new hybrid institution, the *Conseil de la République*, as a second legislative body that served primarily to provide offices for Wade's political clientele. Rather than working to strengthen their institution's powers vis-à-vis the executive and to introduce legislation on their own initiative, most Senegalese deputies have little attachment to the National Assembly as an institution and have devoted more time and energy to increasing their perks—salaries, vehicles, and other benefits. As in the past, the National Assembly remains a weak institution with poor attendance and little will and capacity to check the powers of the president or to initiate legislation on its own.

Looking at the past record, it is clear why the judicial branch of government remains one of the Achilles heels of Senegalese democracy. Under colonial rule, the judiciary was exclusively run by Frenchmen working for the colonial administration, and metropolitan laws applied to only a small fraction of the population. Unlike the case in France, where the legal system had evolved slowly and had its roots in Roman and French jurisprudence and customary law, the legal system left by the French had no roots in Senegal society and was largely devoid of Senegalese jurists. At independence, Senegal had only a handful of Senegalese magistrates and not many more lawyers to operate the court system, a fact that underscored the weakness and alien nature of the legal system.

Following the French Constitution, the 1960 Senegalese Constitution proclaimed that the judiciary constituted a third independent power alongside the executive and legislative powers. In fact, the judiciary was neither independent nor on a separate but equal footing with the executive and legislative branches.[8]

Although competent to rule on disputes concerning the conduct of elections, the judiciary showed little independence from the executive branch. In nearly every instance in which the opposition went to court before 2000 (often at the initiative of Abdoulaye Wade) to contest alleged election irregularities, the courts invariably rejected these claims and rarely overturned or ruled against the government.

In campaigning for the presidency in 2000, Wade promised to strengthen the independence of the judiciary vis-à-vis the executive branch. However, while reaffirming the judiciary power's independence, the 2001 Senegalese Constitution provided fewer protections for judges than the 1963 Constitution that nominated Supreme Court judges for life. In practice, the judiciary remained subordinated to the president who nominated all judges and to the minister of justice who headed the legal system and who was responsible for taking the lead in prosecuting criminal cases. Although the Wade regime has made efforts to improve the material and working conditions of Senegalese jurists, judges are still reluctant to make controversial decisions that contradict the will of the president and tempted to take bribes because of low salaries and lack of transparency in judicial processes.

While the number of lawyers and magistrates has multiplied and urban elites are using the courts more often, the courts remain an alien institution for the great majority of the Senegalese population, and the judiciary an appendage of the executive branch. As a result, the formal legal system constitutes one of the weakest aspects of Senegalese democracy.

The Casamance Insurrection, Ethnic Violence, and Insecurity

The insurrection of separatists in the Casamance demanding independence, which began in 1982, has been a major sore spot for the central government. Overcentralization, northern domination of the territorial administration, the influx of merchants, transporters, and fishermen from the North and their domination of the local economy, flawed development projects, and disputes over land tenure and land use have all contributed to the uprising.

Since the beginning, the insurrection has been predominantly Diola-based and concentrated in the Lower Casamance. Although Diola separatists claimed to be part of a broader multiethnic Casamance independence movement, they often played on Diola ethnic solidarity and hostility to northerners to win support in predominantly Diola areas. Diola separatists have attacked members of ethnic groups from Northern Senegal who migrated to the Casamance.

For its part, the government has often reacted to the insurgency with considerable force. In the process of attempting to put down the rebellion, the Senegalese government has engaged in acts that violated human rights such as arbitrary imprisonment, torture, and summary execution of rebels that represent one of the few blemishes on Senegal's otherwise excellent human rights record. On the other hand, the rebels have also been guilty of pillaging villages, planting land mines that have killed and maimed civilians, and intimidating local officials.

The fighting remained localized in the Casamance and did not spread to Dakar, which has a sizeable Diola community. Intercommunal ethnic rioting did not break out in the Senegalese capital between the Diola and other ethnic groups in retaliation for what was happening in the Casamance. The Casamance insurrection has had little of the intensity characteristic of intercommunal ethnic conflicts in other parts of Africa.[9] The majority of the population does not seem to support the rebel demands for independence and are putting more pressure on the rebels and the government to make peace. Decentralization has provided both sides with a way out of the conflict. Decentralization satisfies some of the Diola demands for more local liberties while also preserving national unity.

The outbreak of violence directed against the Moors in 1989 was a major exception to the general rule of ethnic tolerance and harmony in Senegal. The most serious outbreak of ethnic violence in postcolonial Senegal took place in April and May 1989, following incidents along the Senegalese–Mauritanian border, which pitted Mauritanian herders against Senegalese farmers. The killing of two Senegalese villagers by Mauritanian soldiers escalated into full-scale pogroms in both countries when Moors attacked, mutilated, and killed hundreds of Senegalese and black-skinned Wolof, Halpulaar, and Soninke Mauritanians in Nouakchott and other areas.[10] Mobs of unemployed youth in Dakar retaliated by looting Mauritanian shops and attacking their owners, leaving many dead Moors in the streets. By the end of May, the Moors who had constituted approximately 1.5 percent of the population at the time of independence[11] and who controlled much of the petty retail trade in Senegal's towns had been repatriated to Mauritania while thousands of Halpulaar of Mauritanian nationality had fled to Senegal and lived in refugee villages along the Senegalese side of the border.

Animosity toward Moors was stronger in Dakar and the larger towns where the Moors controlled much of the neighborhood petty retail trade. Unlike the Lebanese, the Moors rarely married Senegalese women, kept to themselves, showed little respect toward their customers, and were perceived by many Senegalese as exploiters, unfriendly, and racially biased. The Moors also had a long precolonial history of fighting with Senegalese for control over land in the Senegal River Valley.

Insecurity and crime have increased in metropolitan Dakar and in the interior, touched off by rapid urban growth, high levels of unemployment in general and among youth in particular, and a declining rural economy. Armed crime that was largely absent from Senegal until the 1990s has become more frequent. The inability of government institutions to provide security has led to the emergence of various anticrime groups and vigilante justice that pose threats to the rule of law.

The Bright Side of Senegalese Democracy

Traditions of Ethnic Tolerance

Many parts of Africa have been wracked by ethnic conflicts and divisions leading to war and bloodshed, for example, genocide in Rwanda, civil war in Nigeria, oppression of ethnic minorities in Sudan, etc. For the most part, Senegal has been spared from these horrors, thanks to the survival of norms and mores dating back to many centuries.

Precolonial Senegambia was a multiethnic society with a good deal of ethnic intermarriage and intermingling of cultures. Ethnic minorities enjoyed a high degree of autonomy, the right to choose their own chiefs and leaders, and representation in political institutions. Hospitality (*teranga*) toward strangers constituted a cardinal virtue in most Senegambian societies before colonial rule. Host societies had few qualms about granting land-use rights to stranger communities.

During the colonial area, Senegal was one of the few European colonies in Africa where race and ethnicity were not major sources of conflict.

The urban neighborhoods that emerged in Dakar were multiethnic in nature. Although the Lebou, the original inhabitants of the Cap Vert peninsula quickly became an ethnic minority, they displayed relatively little resentment toward the new immigrants to Dakar. As a result, Dakar did not experience the kinds of antistranger riots and interethnic conflicts that have taken place in the Ivory Coast.

Ethnicity was a relatively minor factor in postcolonial politics or society where caste biases remained stronger than ethnic biases. Senghor's emphasis on dialogue as the main instrument for preventing and resolving conflicts, his philosophy concerning the complementarity of human civilizations, and the convergence of different civilizations toward a universal civilization contributed to preserve and strengthen Senegalese traditions of ethnic tolerance.[12] During the 1960s, Senegal welcomed large numbers of immigrants from Mali, Guinea, and Guinea-Bissau who came to settle in Senegal.[13] Although recognizing ethnic and regional identities in his distribution of ministerial posts and party offices, Senghor downplayed ethnic politics and identities and focused on building a national Senegalese identity.

Senegalese nationalist sentiments during the Senghor era were directed primarily against the French and Lebanese. Anti-French sentiments declined with the Africanization of the Senegalese Civil Service and Dakar University, the nationalization of key sectors of the economy previously controlled by the French, and the departure of thousands of French *petits blancs*.[14] Senegalese resentment of Lebanese domination of certain sectors of the economy was not expressed in outbreaks of ethnic violence against the Lebanese community who kept a low profile and adapted to changes in their economic status resulting from the Africanization of the economy.[15]

Abdou Diouf encouraged greater public expression of ethnic identity and actively promoted ethnic pluralism and cultural diversity as a manifestation of Senegalese democracy. In opening a colloquium on cultural convergence in Senegal, Diouf affirmed that Senegalese national culture was a product of a "long tradition of intermingling, cultural cross-fertilization and respect of pluralism in all its dimensions—ethnic, linguistic, and religious."[16]

Abdoulaye Wade continued past policies of promoting ethnic tolerance and harmony and accelerated the government's efforts to end the fighting in the Casamance. Wade was also one of the few African leaders to publicly condemn the Ivorian government's ethnic policies that had brought that country to the brink of civil war by discriminating against ethnic groups originally from Burkina Faso.

Senegal's national leaders from Senghor to Wade have downplayed ethnic affiliation as a source of political conflict while recognizing and valuing the importance of ethnic affiliation and traditions in contributing to cultural diversity. At the grassroots level, the resurgence in expressions of ethnic identity in Senegal among different ethnic groups has not been accompanied by a rise in ethnic conflicts.

The Spirit of Religion: Religious Tolerance, Peaceful Coexistence, and State–Church Relationships

In Senegal, Muslim religious leaders attempting to impose Islam through the sword during the nineteenth century failed. The leaders of the Sufi Brotherhoods that emerged during the latter part of the nineteenth century renounced *jihad* as an appropriate means for spreading Islam in Senegal.

During the colonial era, Christians and Muslims lived side by side in peace. Violence among Muslims was rare. Although occasionally raised during the heat of election campaigns, religion was not a major issue in Senegalese politics. Senghor's Catholicism did not prevent him from winning the support of most of the major Sufi Brotherhoods and keeping it after independence.

Abdou Diouf, Senegal's first Muslim president, presided over a Muslim renaissance and attempted to maintain good ties with the Sufi Brotherhoods while also recognizing reformist and orthodox tendencies supported by Saudi Arabia and other Arab nations. Efforts by radical Islamists to stir up trouble failed. Under Diouf, Senegal preserved its reputation for religious tolerance and peaceful coexistence. Despite the presence of only a small Christian minority, Christian holidays were maintained and celebrated.

Although attracting some intellectuals, radical Muslim fundamentalist movements made few inroads among the mass of Senegalese Muslims who remained faithful to the Sufi Brotherhoods. Senegal's religious tolerance and coexistence had much to do with the successful integration of traditional precolonial religious beliefs and practices with those of Islam and Christianity. A popular Senegalese witticism affirmed that Senegal was 95 percent Muslim, 5 percent Christian and 100 percent Animist.

Religious toleration continued into the first decade of the new millennium. In his frequent travels abroad, Wade has presented Senegal as a land of religious moderation and tolerance. Senegal's Muslim leaders have consistently insisted that Islam is a religion of peace and strongly support efforts to settle the conflict in the Casamance.

After the September 11, 2001, attack on America launched by Al Qaeda, Senegal's Muslim religious authorities expressed their condemnation of terrorist acts in the name of Islam as contrary to the spirit of Islam. For their part, Senegalese religious leaders have, on many occasions, organized national seminars and participated in international conferences stressing the role of religion in fostering peace and reconciliation, thus enhancing the country's reputation for religious tolerance.[17] When interviewed by the press after returning from the World Conference for Religion and Peace held in Abuja in 2003, the Catholic Abbey of Dakar and the president of the *Féderation des Associations Islamiques du Sénégal* affirmed that religions were essentially artisans of peace and must resist efforts to be taken over by people advocating violence.

Despite the advance of Islam since independence, Senegal has maintained its status as a secular state. In the Senegalese context, the secularism of the state (*laïcité*) did not imply hostility or even indifference to religion. It simply meant that Senegal would treat all religions equally and not impose a state religion on its people.

During the late 1970s and 1980s, radical Senegalese Islamists influenced by the example of Iran demanded that Senegal become an Islamic state governed by the Sharia in all matters. Although the heads of the Sufi Brotherhoods wanted autonomous Muslim courts to rule on family matters according to Muslim law, they had no intentions of calling for the establishment of a theocratic Islamic republic.

When he came to power, it appeared that Wade might eliminate the term secular in referring to the state in the 2001 Constitution. In the end, the 2001 Constitution retained the wording of previous constitutions that defined Senegal as a secular and democratic state. But the issue flared up again in 2003 when a broad coalition of Islamic leaders called for the revision of the 1972 Family Code to restore Muslim courts and to formally recognize the Sharia as the main source of family law for Muslims.[18]

Unlike Muslim Islamists in Nigeria, Senegalese advocates of a Muslim personal status insisted that Islam respect the rights of religious minorities to live under their own religious system and would not force Christians to submit to Muslim law. In Nigeria, the Sharia was imposed on Christian minorities and sparked religious conflicts in several regions where the Muslim majority had imposed Islamic law on the entire population.

After remaining silent on the issue, Wade declared in a press conference held in Japan that he would never accept any revision of the 1972 Family Code as long as he was president.[19] Wade maintained that revision of the code to conform to Muslim law could cast doubts about Senegalese democracy that was predicated on religious tolerance while tarnishing Senegal's image as a country of peace, tolerance, and an advocate of freedom and women's rights.[20] He argued that many practices described in the Koran, for example, flagellation, cutting off the hands of thieves, etc.—had been abandoned. Wade also implied that the Christian minority felt uneasy about revising the code and that the proposed legislation that clearly submitted Senegalese women to the authority of their fathers and spouses contradicted their aspirations for greater equality with men.[21]

The debate over revisions in the Family Code pitted the Senegalese political class against the marabouts who, while comfortable with a secular state that guaranteed religious tolerance and pluralism and displayed no favoritism to one sect over another, demanded that the state recognize the right of Muslims to follow the precepts of religion in personal matters. However, the version of the Personal Status Code presented by the marabouts encompassed a strict orthodox interpretation of Islamic law that restricted women's rights and conflicted with Senegalese laws and policies affecting the status of women.

Despite the Islamic renaissance in Senegal and the support of the marabouts for more Islamic religious education and revisions of the Civil

Code, it is highly unlikely that Senegal will become a theocratic Islamic republic bent on imposing the Sharia as the law of the land. The growing commitment of Senegal's religious leaders to good citizenship norms, the decline of the *ndiguel* as an instrument for influencing elections, and frequent interventions of religious leaders to mediate conflicts and preserve social peace all bode well for the future of democracy in Senegal.

Freedom of the Press and Media

Freedom of the press has steadily advanced in Senegal since the mid-1970s. This trend has been accompanied by the proliferation of daily and weekly newspapers in the capital, the appearance of newspapers published outside the capital devoted to the discussion of local political issues, and the emergence of a wide range of newspapers and newsletters reporting on political, economic, cultural, religious, and sports events, activities, and themes. The media in general has also assumed an increasingly important role in promoting a democratic culture in Senegal by emphasizing citizenship, public debate, and transparency in government operations and giving various sectors of Senegalese society an outlet to freely express their views.

The emergence of private FM radio stations in 1994 ushered in a new era of media freedom that offered alternative and independent news coverage, information about public affairs, and political debates that reached the great majority of the Senegalese population. By the year 2000, independent radio stations like *Sud-FM* and *Walfadri FM* had set up stations in most of Senegal's regional capitals and were reaching more than 90 percent of the population.

A national survey taken after the 2000 presidential campaign indicated that 62.2 percent of those questioned in the survey looked to radio as their main source of information as opposed to the 2 percent of those polled who looked to the written press as their primary source of information.[22] Media coverage of the 2000 presidential and 2001 legislative elections disseminated information about the political candidates and also exerted pressure on the government to insure that the elections were conducted in an honest and transparent manner. During these campaigns, the media informed the Senegalese public about voting procedures while exhorting voters to go to the polls to fulfill their civic duties as good citizens. By its physical presence and coverage, the independent media discouraged fraud and the use of political violence during the campaigns.[23]

The state-controlled audio-visual media under Wade still tends to give more coverage to the party in power and to be less critical of the government than the independent media.[24] Under Wade, the state radio and TV news coverage gives a disproportionate attention to the activities of the president and his entourage. Although television remains the last bastion of state monopoly over the media, pressures are mounting to liberalize television broadcasting in order to present more diversified programming.

Though often beset with financial difficulties, the media in Senegal have become increasingly more independent and fearless. During the last years of the Diouf regime, PS politicians complained that the independent press was working for the opposition. Through its criticism of the Diouf regime and comprehensive reporting of election results, the media clearly contributed to his loss in the 2000 presidential elections. After Wade's election, the independent media continued its watchdog role and maintained a highly critical stance toward Wade and government policies rather than succumb to the temptation of flattering the new president and his regime and over-looking its mistakes. Rather than intimidating journalists the arrest of Madiambal Diagne, the editor of a popular daily independent newspaper in 2004 for publishing a story critical of the Wade government's handling of the judicial system and not revealing his sources led to the launching of a massive media campaign to demand the release of their colleague.[25] The campaign rallied public opinion around the jailed editor and led to his release after two weeks in prison. Pressure from the media and public opinion not only insured Diagne's release, but it also prodded Wade to promise to repeal provisions in the penal code that enabled government to jail journalists.

Freedom of Association

The trend toward greater autonomy of civil associations that began under Diouf has continued under Wade. With the proliferation of civil associations, it has become increasingly more difficult for the government or political parties to capture or dominate peasant organizations, economic and professional associations, and youth groups.

The growing number, density, scope, and democratic nature of most Senegalese associations provide counterweights to state power and alternative mechanisms to the state and markets for meeting people's needs. Several trends concerning associational life bode well for the future of Senegalese democracy:

1. *National urban-based urban advocacy, interest, and civic-minded groups have grown in size, scale, and professionalism.* Many of these national-level associations have become forceful advocates for democracy, good governance, human rights, and social equality. Originally concentrated almost exclusively in the capital, some of these organizations are now establishing branches at the regional level, increasing their communications with community-based grassroots associations at the local level, and becoming more familiar with local conditions and priorities.

2. *A wide range of national level associations are also forging coalitions to pro-mote citizenship, monitor public policies in different sectors, and to fight corruption.* In 2000, RADDHO, the Forum Civil, *Environment et Développement du Tiers-Monde* (ENDA), *Siggi Jiginn*, a women's group, and *Oxy-jeunes*, joined together to launch what proved to be a very successful voter registration campaign. In December 2003, eight major national level civil society organizations signed a protocol to define a framework for collaborating to

promote the active participation of civil society in the elaboration, implementation, monitoring, and evaluation of public policies. A month later, the *Forum Civil* took the initiative to create a broad-based Coalition against corruption out of sixteen national level civil associations consisting of private sector associations, trade unions, NGOs, religious associations, and national organizations working on democracy and good governance issues.[26]

3. *National level organizations are no longer exclusively urban-based and organized around the interests and concerns of urban elites.* In 1968 Senghor trucked in hundreds of peasants from the countryside to Dakar to demonstrate their support for him and his government, which had been under attack by students and workers in 1968. Thirty-five years later, the CNCR mobilized over 30,000 peasants from all over the country to come to Dakar to peacefully express their demands for changes in the government's policies toward the rural world and to ask the government to open frank and sincere negotiations on their concerns.[27]

4. *Autonomous self-governing community-based associations are increasingly federating with similar groups in their sector and forming coalitions and working groups with other grassroots organizations to participate in development planning, local government, and civic education activities.* Nineteen community radio stations recently formed the *Alliance des Radios Communautaires de Sénégal* (ARC/Sénégal) to pool resources and promote community radio.[28] Neighborhood credit and savings associations are federating and pooling their resources. Representatives of grassroots associations are becoming increasingly active in participation in local government affairs and demanding more and better information.

5. *The gap between national-level urban-based elitist associations and local grassroots community-based associations also seems to be diminishing.* For example, national level women's groups advocating an end to violence against women and female genital mutilation are discussing these issues in the larger interior towns and with village-based women's groups throughout the country.

Local Liberties and Self-Governance

One of the most interesting manifestations of the exercise of local liberties has been the expansion and consolidation of informal local governance institutions based on community solidarities. These have been organized as voluntary associations rather than formal local government entities. Village development and hometown associations brought together the residents of villages and groups of villages and those who had left the village to go to the towns and abroad but who had maintained their ties with the home locality.

Though taking new forms, the hometown and village development associations were built on traditional Senegalese values stressing group solidarity, sharing of resources, public discussion of community issues, respect for the wisdom of elders, and consensus rules for decision-making to reduce conflict. Members of these self-governing communities have sought to prevent politicization and capture of their associations by local politicians and political parties. They hope to avoid much of the factionalism that plague Senegalese political parties and undermine the functioning of many formal local government bodies.

The trend toward greater local liberties continued after Wade took office despite his efforts to recentralize the country and abolish some of the local government institutions established by his predecessor. Senegalese public opinion forced Wade to drop his plans to eliminate regional councils and the *communes d'arrondissement* in metropolitan Dakar.

Another recent development boding well for the consolidation of Senegalese democracy has been the growing participation of women, young people, people of caste and former slave status, and members of local grassroots association in local government and the growing responsiveness of the local politicians to the concerns of their constituencies.

Movement Toward Social Equality

Social inequality based on birth and other ascriptive criteria are on the decline. In the larger cities, the stigma attached to being a slave descendant is rapidly disappearing. Former slaves in the rural areas are no longer dependent on their former masters. Caste prejudices are also declining. Although Senegalese youth still show respect to their elders, they are less inclined to obey them blindly. Senegalese women are boldly asserting their prerogatives and entering professions previously reserved for men.

As Tocqueville predicted, social equality has been one of the historic forces serving to promote democracy in Senegal. The end of slavery and the decline of caste prejudices, the spread of Western and Islamic education to the masses, the rising social status of youth and women, and universal suffrage have reinforced political and social equality, which in turn have oriented the habits and hearts of more and more Senegalese toward democratic principles and practices. During the past decade, Senegalese have moved from demanding the government to grant more freedom and fair elections to calling for Senegalese citizens to exercise the obligations of citizenship in a democratic society. Senegalese from all walks of life and groups representing different interests are now demanding a greater voice in national and local decision-making and insisting that the government not take decisions affecting their lives without consulting them.

The movement toward great social equality, however, has not been accompanied by significant declines in economic inequality and income gaps between rich and poor. As late as the mid-1970s, non-Africans received more than 28 percent of wages and salaries even though constituting only 5 percent of the modern labor force.[29] However, during the 1970s, and 1980s, Africanization and the shrinking of the European population permitted Senegalese to sharply increase their share of the income in the salaried sectors of the economy. Much of the salaried sector that constitutes less than 10 percent of the economy is concentrated in Metropolitan Dakar. The huge gap in wealth and services between metropolitan Dakar and the rural areas has contributed to a massive rural exodus that has deprived the countryside of some of its most productive elements. Structural adjustment policies also depressed incomes in metropolitan Dakar and led to loss of jobs in the state and industrial sectors. Although Senegal has had economic growth rates averaging 4 to 5 percent since 1995, this has not done much to alleviate poverty or to reduce income gaps among the Senegalese.

Globalization and Senegalese Democracy: Updating Tocqueville

Processes of globalization were beginning to accelerate before Tocqueville died. He predicted the spread of democracy in the Western world even though he did not live to see it in its fullest fruition. Since Tocqueville, the world has become more interdependent as revolutions in transportation and communication have brought peoples closer together for better or worse in many areas—politics, economics, culture, and religion—and facilitated the transmission and exchange of ideas and ideologies.

Until now, we have limited our discussion of the forces shaping Senegalese democracy to those taking place largely within the country. The following is a list of some of the external influences affecting Senegalese society as a result of globalization:

1. *Greater access to and integration with a global network of human and civil rights organizations promoting democracy and good governance.* Senegalese are now closely tied to international organizations like Amnesty International, Transparency International, and scores of other Pan-African and International professional organizations.

2. *More connections with the Muslim world outside of Africa.* The Sufi Brotherhoods are increasingly being influenced by currents from the Muslim world and are doing more to establish their credentials as legitimate Muslim movements by showing their solidarity with the Arab world in international political matters.[30] These developments may be blurring the distinctions among Sufis, Islamists, and other Muslims. It remains to be seen whether this aspect of globalization will have a negative affect on the traditional tolerance of the Sufi Brotherhoods. On the other hand globalization has also brought Sufi marabouts in touch with global interfaith dialogue groups.

3. *The growing importance and influence of the Senegalese diaspora émigré communities.* Senegalese in the diaspora have been playing an increasingly important role in community development associations through their financial support and connections with their host country institutions and international donors. Money repatriated by *émigrés* is now almost the equivalent of all the foreign international aid going to Senegal. *Émigrés* are

also seeking to play a more active and progressive role in Senegalese politics in promoting democratic political reforms. With greater access to financial resources, they are less dependent upon political parties and those in power and therefore less likely to be integrated into clientelist political machines and more likely to become political brokers themselves with the ability to mobilize the constituents in their home communities.[31]

4. *The movement toward greater cultural and artistic interchanges.* Senegalese scholars are teaching in European and North American Universities. American popular cultural influences are influencing Senegalese society, especially its youth culture that has adapted rap and hip hop to Senegalese conditions with great enthusiasm. Senegalese musicians like Youssou Ndour and Baaba Maal have integrated and synthesized Western and indigenous African forms of music and become international super stars of World Music. Rather than alienating Senegalese these external cultural influences have contributed to a growing identity of Senegalese as citizens of the world and part of the worldwide movement toward democratization and greater solidarity.

Tocquevillian Analytics and Democracy in Senegal: A Balance Sheet

In applying Tocquevillian analytics to the study of democracy in Senegal, it is clear that Senegal, despite its many flaws, has made considerable gains along the road to democracy.

In looking at Senegal from a predominantly top-down state-centered perspective, we find that the country still suffers from a host of problems—the concentration of power in the hands of the president, the personal nature of presidential authority, a still highly centralized government, a plethora of political parties not elevated and sustained by lofty purposes, factionalism, corruption, the persistence of clientelism and dependency relationships, and a rise in crime rates and personal insecurity.

However, if we look beyond the state and the arena of electoral politics, the foundations for the future of democracy in Senegal look more promising. Today, democracy in Senegal is no longer the exclusive preserve of a tiny minority of Western-educated urbanized French-speaking elite. Democratic values have spread throughout Senegalese society. Thanks to the expansion of the independent media and literacy, Senegalese at the grassroots level are better informed and involved in public matters. They are increasingly demanding more accountability from Senegal's political class and the state, a greater voice in making national policies, and fair play and civility in political competition. They also have managed to synthesize and integrate traditional religious and cultural values stressing tolerance, coexistence, and hospitality with Western-style concepts of *démocratie* and indigenous concepts of *demokarassi*.

The Sufi Brotherhoods, the major counterweight to state power, have embraced democratic norms like the sovereignty of the people, religious tolerance and pluralism, freedom of speech, and a high degree of separation of church and state. Although the potential for religious intolerance is present, religion in general has generally played a positive role in preaching reconciliation and peace and in stressing social solidarity and the obligation to take care of the poor and needy in Senegalese society. In Tocqueville's terms, the spirit of religion in Senegal is favorable to the promotion of democracy.

Many of the numerous village development, neighborhood, and savings and loans associations now flourishing throughout the country meet Tocqueville's criteria for the self-governing local community bodies and associations constituting the foundation and building blocks for democracy. However, Senegal's self-governing voluntary associations organized at the grassroots levels according to traditional African values and modes of organization (*demokarassi*) also have different decision-making rules and priorities than those found in the Western democracies. These differences stress consensus over majority decision-making rules, the importance of sharing benefits and burdens over maximizing profits, and solidifying social relations and networks over attaining specific economic objectives.

Western forms of democracy are also flourishing as reflected in the holding of fair and competitive elections, the growth of an independent free press and media, the proliferation and autonomy of human and civil rights groups, professional, economic, and civic associations, and NGOs engaged in development activities. Senegal has also succeeded in institutionalizing and maintaining Western democratic traditions subordinating the military to civilian authority. It has been the only country in West Africa not to have experienced a military coup since obtaining independence.

Senegal's relatively poor economic performance since independence, the impoverishment of large segments of the population due to the decline of the rural economy and the adverse effects of structural adjustments, and the country's heavy economic dependence on foreign donors for development capital have, surprisingly enough, not slowed down the march toward greater political and social equality and democratization.

Senegalese democracy is not and cannot be a carbon copy or blend of American and European democratic systems, which have different histories, traditions, and physical environments. Nor is it a model of democracy that can be easily exported to other parts of Africa. Shaped by its point of departure and historic development, democracy in Senegal has evolved as a hybrid mix of institutions and mores that combines Western forms and norms of democracy/*démocratie* with African forms and norms of demokarassi.

CHAPTER TWELVE

The Future of Democracy in Africa

A great democratic revolution is taking place in our midst; everybody sees it, but by no means everybody judges it in the same way.[1]

In studying the evolution of democracy in Senegal, we attempted to systematically apply the main components of Tocquevillian analytics. Having done so, we concluded that the foundations for democracy have been strengthened in Senegal and that the prospects for democracy there look reasonably good. Rather than presenting Senegalese democracy as an ideal model to be exported to other African countries, following Tocqueville, we shall emphasize some of the main principles contributing to Senegal's success. Building on Tocquevillian analytics, what can one say about the state of democracy in Africa today and its prospects for the future?

The Failure of the Nation-State in Postcolonial Africa

The legacy of the nation-state has been one of the major obstacles to building viable democratic societies in postcolonial Africa.

As a political system, colonialism imposed a highly centralized and autocratic state on the African peoples under its jurisdiction. The boundaries drawn up by the colonizer became the framework for the new African nation-states at independence.

Colonialism often brought peoples together under the same jurisdiction that had no previous contact with each other or had been engaged in conflict as members of different political entities. Rather than seeking to integrate the different peoples under their jurisdiction, the colonial system practiced a divide and rule policy, pitting different communities against each other and favoring some groups over others.

Western commentators referred to the growing demand for independence after World War II as nationalism. However, the term nationalism did not accurately reflect African sentiments. Few African colonies had only one group of people sharing a common language, history, and territory who sought independence like Greece did from the Ottoman Empire in the nineteenth century. Nearly all colonial societies in Africa were plural in nature encompassing several ethnic and linguistic groups. For most Africans, independence meant freedom from foreign rule.

During the drive to independence, African leaders like Kwame Nkrumah, and Léopold Sédar Senghor called for some form of Pan-African or federal government. In the end, the European nation-state model prevailed as early efforts to achieve viable Pan-African and federal political institutions transcending national boundaries failed. Federations set up during the colonial period like the French West African, French Equatorial African and East African Federations disintegrated shortly after independence while efforts to create new Federations like the Mali Federation and the *Conseil de l'Entente* also collapsed.

Africa's difficulties in maintaining the formal institutions of democracy left by the French, British, and Belgian colonizers have been attributed to different factors. Some have blamed this failure on neocolonialism, imperialism, and other forms of economic dependency and exploitation. Others have blamed this failure on the survival of neopatrimonial political systems; the attachments of Africa's peoples to primordial sentiments, for example, kinship, ethnicity, and religion; or the absence of a democratic culture and civil society sharing and advocating democratic values.

None of the above explanations have looked to the design of the African nation-state itself as a potential cause of the dysfunction of democracy in Africa today.[2] Since independence, Africans have been admonished to change their behavior to fit the requirements of the nation-state and Western models of democracy handed down to them. Rather than letting African peoples work out their own frameworks for living together, Western commentators insisted that African peoples had to fit into a nation-state framework that had no historical precedents.

Gambia became a nation-state distinct from Senegal even though the two territories had similar peoples and precolonial traditions simply because they had different colonial rulers. The Belgian Congo became a nation-state even though many of the peoples historically had little, if any, contact with each other before Belgian rule. The Tuaregs who lived independently in the Sahara were forced to become citizens as marginalized minority groups in Algeria, Mali, and Niger because of the focus on the nation-state.

Much of the early political science literature on independent Africa focused on themes like *national* integration[3] and *national* development rather than on democracy. Under the nation-state model, the state was the primary instrument for achieving both national integration and national development. Therefore, it was essential to strengthen and modernize state bureaucracies, elaborate national development plans, provide universal education in the official national language (which was that of the colonizer), and create a new national identity at the expense of traditional group identities.

By the 1980s, it seemed evident that the nation-state framework was not working well or at least that the postcolonial state was doing a poor job.

By then much of Africa was governed by military regimes, one-party systems, or personal dictatorships, and experiencing civil wars and predatory violence with the breakdown of inappropriate political orders. In many African countries, the people responded by disengaging from the state and developing their own institutions and parallel economies.[4]

During the 1980s and 1990s, one began to see a shift in attitude toward the state as the principal agent of change. The development literature now spoke of the need for economic disengagement of the state, free market economies, nongovernmental organizations and popular participation. Political scientists placed more emphasis on democracy, civil society, and governance issues. Despite this movement away from identifying and supporting the state as the main vehicle for promoting democracy and development, the nation-state remained the main frame of reference.

While free, competitive elections and political competition among political parties became the defining characteristics of democracy, most of the emphasis was placed on *national* elections—presidential or legislative—and capturing control of the *national* government, that is, the state. Even when civil society was defined as encompassing all institutions between the family and the state, the term was most often used in analyses of democratization processes to refer to Western-educated and urbanized advocacy or interest groups seeking to influence and change *state* policies to promote human and civil rights, gender equality, the rule of law, open elections, etc. Again the focus was on the state.

Limitations of State-Centered Frameworks
for Studying Democracy in Africa

Since the late 1980s and early 1990s, much has been written about democracy in Africa.[5] Following Huntington, scholars have referred to the burst of political change that led to the demise of personal and military dictatorships in Africa as part of the Third Wave of democratization. During the Third Wave of democratization, bilateral and multilateral aid agencies identified democratization as a major objective of their assistance programs and pressured African governments to democratize as conditions for receiving aid.

Elections and Multiparty Systems as the Litmus Test for Democracy

In measuring the state of democracy in Africa, analysts have identified free elections, and multiparty competition as the hallmark of democratic regimes. By these criteria, there has been a tremendous surge in multiparty competition and the holding of free elections during the Third Wave. By the end of 1997 only four countries in Sub-Saharan Africa had not held competitive elections during the 1990s.[6]

Multiparty competition and free elections do not shore up democracy if the victors once in power are not committed to preserving public liberties and political competition. Electoral regimes based on the principle of majority rule can also be used to legitimize the "Tyranny of the Majority" and subject minorities to the whims of the majority. In extreme cases, the principle of majority rule can also be used to legitimize and facilitate the subjugation and destruction of minorities by providing the majority control over the state and the "legitimate" use of violence.

On the eve of independence in 1959, the victory of the Hutu parties in Rwandan national elections was followed by massacres of the Tutsi. During the early 1990s, the Hutu-dominated regime "liberalized" the political system by permitting other political parties to organize and holding national elections, thus enabling Rwanda to improve its standing with the international donor community and its ratings with Freedom House.[7] At the same time, extremist elements were systematically planning genocide and using the media to demonize the Tutsi minority that led to the 1994 genocide in which 500,000 to 800,000 Tutsi and moderate Hutu perished.[8]

Alternation or changing the party in power has also been cited as an important criterion for evaluating democracy because losing an election provides concrete evidence that the party in power has indeed held reasonably free elections. Holding two consecutive elections in which power changes hands through the ballot box has been considered a vital indicator for the consolidation of democracy.[9]

After being forced to hold presidential elections in 1992–1993 and losing them in the first truly free elections since independence, Didier Ratsiraka, the former Afro-Marxist dictator of Madagascar made a political comeback and narrowly won the 1996 presidential elections. Rather than indicating the consolidation of democracy, Ratsiraka's victory reflected disillusionment with the incumbent president. Back in power, Ratsiraka systematically used the powers of the state to strengthen his own party, take over all the other branches of government, intimidate potential opponents, and enrich his own family. Ratsiraka was eventually ousted from power in 2002, but not before bringing the country close to the brink of civil war because of his refusal to accept the results of the December 2001 presidential elections.

Changing governments through the ballot box only indicates that the people have the power to oust incumbents. It does not reflect their power to make laws, to hold government officials accountable for their actions, or to participate in the management of their own affairs.

Civil Society and Civil Liberties in Illiberal Democracies

Since the mid-1990s, the notion of elections and multiparty competition as the central feature of democracy has increasingly come under challenge because many of the regimes in power have restricted rather than expanded public liberties after winning the elections. This had led to the growing popularity of the term "illiberal democracies" to describe regimes that restrict public liberties.[10] Liberal democracies protect the rights of its individual citizens. Illiberal democracies merely reflect procedures for electing rulers that involve the participation of the people; they do not offer protection of individual and minority rights or insure that rulers are not above the law.

Recognition of these differences has led students of democracy in Africa to place a greater emphasis on civil liberties and a strong civil society as the hallmarks of democracy. From this perspective democratization requires the strengthening of civil society vis-à-vis state structures. Rather than the state imposing its will on civil society, civil society should hold the state accountable for its acts and influence state policies. However, the state still remains the main reference point.

The state-centered definition of civil society stressing Western-style advocacy and interest groups implies that democracy is primarily or exclusively the affair of urban Western-educated middle-class elites. The emphasis on Western-style civil society organizations has led to underestimating the existing and potential contribution of rural grassroots-based voluntary associations to democratization.[11] Although Western-style civil society organizations clearly serve a positive role as advocates for democratization, from a Tocquevillian perspective, the number and quality of local level and community-based voluntary associations and their capabilities for self-governance may be more useful indicators for evaluating the progress and depth of democracy in Africa than the number of Western-style advocacy groups.

Neopatrimonialism and the State

The term neopatrimonialism to describe contemporary political regimes in Africa provides many useful insights concerning African political behavior rooted in precolonial history and modes of political organization.[12] Most analyses of neopatrimonialism focus on the state and how those gaining control of the state use its resources to offer rewards to their clients in exchange for their political support.

Since the imposition of structural adjustment programs, analyses of neopatrimonial regimes have speculated on the impact of the corresponding decline in state resources on clientelist relationships. While it is true that declining state resources will likely reduce the capacity of personal rulers and governing political parties to offer patronage to a steadily growing number of potential clients, it is more problematic whether a relative reduction in state resources in itself will erode clientelist relationships in general.

Clientelism in neopatrimonial regimes is based on more than just the state as patron; it is based on the kinds of personalized hierarchical relationships found in aristocratic orders. Its decline will depend more on the general advance of economic and social equality than the decline of state resources. Analyses of neopatrimonial regimes generally don't look at the emergence of more egalitarian modes of social organization outside the state and their impact on clientelism.

Tocquevillian Analytics: A Valuable
Tool for the Study of Democracy in Africa

One of our main premises has been that Tocqueville provides us with tools, concepts, and principles for understanding the evolution of democracy in Africa—the importance of history, physical environment, equality of social conditions, local liberties, and self-governing capabilities—usually absent in the approaches described in the previous section. The incorporation of these categories into analyses of democracy in Africa will deepen our understanding of how African societies actually work as well as the processes of democratization.

Bringing Back History

Studies of democracy in Africa often deal with Africa's past in a superficial manner, if at all. Many of the divisions and conflicts taking place in Africa had their roots in precolonial times. Others were created or reinforced under colonialism. History can tell us a great deal about why democracy and stable political orders have greater difficulty in taking hold in some African countries than in others and why the nation-state framework inherited by many African countries has been the cause of many of their problems.

Bringing back history into contemporary analyses of democracy in Africa is essential to putting Africa back into the mainstream of world history as an actor in its own right and not a simple appendage of European history. It would also do much to correct the stereotypes that Africa had no history before the coming of the European, that Africa's problems lie in its peoples' attachment to "primordial sentiments," and that its success in the future depends upon its adopting carbon copies of Western political and economic systems.

Africa's precolonial history provides many examples of self-governing societies and associations, larger-scale political institutions offering local communities and populations under their jurisdiction local autonomy, and peaceful coexistence among different ethnic and religious communities.[13] Under the Mali Empire, diverse groups of people from the Atlantic coast to the Niger River Bend enjoyed long periods of peace and prosperity. After defeating his enemies Sundiata Keita, the founder of the ruling dynasty of Mali, elaborated the Mande Charter that provided the basis for diverse peoples to enjoy a high degree of local autonomy and religious freedom. The relative absence of violent ethnic and religious conflicts among the peoples constituting the Mali Empire compared to those occurring in other parts of Africa may be one of the positive legacies of a political system initiated more than seven centuries ago.

The peoples of precolonial Africa demonstrated immense self-governance capabilities, especially at the grassroots level. Despite the rise of centralized monarchies, the ravages of the slave trade, and the destruction of their independence under colonialism, many local African communities have been remarkably resilient in adapting to adverse political, economic, and ecological conditions. The emphasis on national level institutions in most studies of democracy has detracted us from looking at the extent to which self-governing capabilities based on indigenous modes of organization have survived and adapted to changing conditions.

To present some of the positive features of precolonial African societies handed down through the generations is not to deny the darker side of precolonial African history. The Atlantic and East Coast African slave trade ravaged the African continent. In West Africa, the slave trade contributed to the rise and consolidation of centralized monarchies and chiefdoms and an aristocratic order built on violence and engaged in constant wars. During the precolonial era, Africans defined freedom as the antithesis of slavery.[14]

The colonial era constituted a second major "point of departure." The imposition of colonial rule overthrew the old order in Africa and established Europeans as the new masters. The duration of colonial rule varied considerably and its impact on African societies depended on many factors, for example, the policies and political systems of the colonizer; the extent to which Africans were treated as subjects and denied basic political, civil, and economic rights; the length of the period in which Africans could exercise political and civil rights; the degree of direct penetration of the colonial state and its economic institutions; and the conditions in which African colonial territories obtained their independence.

Though formally abolishing slavery, colonialism introduced new forms of predatory behavior and servitude such as forced labor, pass laws, and involuntary conscription in colonial armies. For many years, the Belgian Congo was the personal property of King Léopold of Belgium whose agents looted the territory and terrorized its people before world public opinion forced the King to transfer control over the Belgian Congo to the Belgian government in 1908. For many years, the French used forced labor to build and maintain roads and railroads, uprooting tens of thousands of Africans from their homes to work under horrible conditions in other territories. Forced labor was even more severe in Portuguese Africa where Africans remained in virtual servitude. Many Africans regarded colonial rule itself as a form of slavery.[15]

European colonial administrators, businessmen, missionaries, and farmers comprised an "aristocratic" elite based on race and nationality. Like aristocrats in aristocratic societies, they exercised privileges denied to their social inferiors. In providing Western education in the language of the métropole to a relatively small number of Africans, the colonizer created an auxiliary elite to serve the colonial state and its interests. Because of their relatively small numbers, these men constituted a new indigenous "aristocracy," based on mastery of the colonial language and their status within the colonial system. From their ranks came the first generation of "inheritance elites" who came to power with independence.[16] The peaceful transfer of sovereignty to the indigenous inheritance elite was accompanied by the adoption of constitutions patterned on those in the metropole.

Africans living in the Portuguese colonies, on the other hand, had to launch wars of national liberation in order to gain their independence as did the populations of Algeria, Zimbabwe, South Africa, and Namibia, all countries with large European minorities that did not readily want to give up their privileges. Portugal's nondemocratic regime used force to suppress the independence movements until a military coup in April 1974 established a democratic regime in Portugal that granted independence to all its overseas colonies—Cape Verde, Guinea-Bissau, Angola and Mozambique in 1974 and 1975 respectively.

Tocqueville asserted that where traditions of freedom had not been firmly established, democracies could become easily transformed into tyrannies. In fact, democracy had a great deal of difficulty in taking hold and being maintained in African countries that had experienced relatively short periods in which Africans enjoyed full public liberties and participated in representative institutions. For example, none of the former Belgian colonies—Rwanda, Burundi, and Belgian Congo have had stable democratic regimes since independence. Belgium had the most repressive and paternalistic colonial policies of the three European democratic colonial powers in Africa and did not grant its subjects public liberties and limited voting rights until the mid- to late-1950s. Countries that won their independence through armed struggle have experienced difficulty in nurturing and sustaining democratic institutions and have been prone to civil wars (Angola and Mozambique), coups (Guinea Bissau), and dictatorships (Algeria and Zimbabwe).

The Physical Environment

Most comparative analyses of democracy and political change in Africa don't consider environmental factors and electoral geography.[17] Many of the most acute conflicts afflicting Africa today pit peoples against each other from different ecological zones cast together within the framework of nation-states and boundaries artificially created by European colonialism and preserved by postcolonial states. The physical environment also had a major impact in shaping colonial society. European settlers were more numerous in countries like Algeria, South Africa, Zimbabwe, and Kenya where the climate was more temperate.

The great diversity of the peoples of Africa mirrors the enormous diversity found in Africa's physical environment—tropical forests, deserts, highlands, savannah lands, and coastal plains. These differences have spawned communities of farmers, pastoralists, fishermen, and hunters and gatherers who have organized their societies to adapt to their physical environment and worked out mechanisms to exchange resources and to resolve conflicts concerning access to natural resources and land use.

In the tier of countries running from Mauritania to Sudan's north–south cleavages, for example, reflect tensions and differences between desert peoples and sedentary agrarian populations resisting domination by the other group. The ex-Belgian Congo's vast expanses and the effort to integrate groups having no past history of living and working together before the advent of Belgian autocratic colonial rule into a nation-state provided the background to political instability and frequent revolts against central authority.

The harsh Sahelian climate combined with poor soils have made it extremely difficult for countries in that ecological zone to move out of poverty and has stimulated massive migrations of people seeking employment in other parts of Africa, Europe, and more recently in America. The movement of several million people from Burkina Faso to work in the more prosperous Ivory Coast during the colonial era and after independence created a north–south split in that country that brought the Ivory Coast to the brink of civil war.

Citizen Sovereignty and Self-Governance: Freedom of Association, Local Liberties, and an Informed Citizenry

The exercise of citizen sovereignty as opposed to state sovereignty requires freedom of association and an end to state tutelage over associational life. The reduction of state tutelage facilitated the creation or revitalization of local community-based indigenous institutions. Using social capital accumulated from the past and integrating a mixture of indigenous modes of social organization adapted to modern conditions, these associations have often been extremely effective in accomplishing their modest goals.[18]

In many parts of Africa, the decline or collapse of the state has facilitated the creation of relatively autonomous self-governing voluntary associations whose members developed their own internal governance rules, criteria for membership, and mechanisms for sanctioning members who violated the rules. Many of these associations constitute the kinds of civic communities essential to the development of democratic norms and society. In some African countries—Somalia, Liberia, Sierra Leone, and the Congo—the collapse of the state has led to chaos, civil war, and the rise of warlords.

With the loosening of state tutelage and the overthrow of repressive regimes, peasants in many rural areas of Africa have organized self-governing grassroots associations to deal with their daily problems. Paradoxically, these groups are often more democratically governed than many of the Western-styled civil society organizations like the trade unions, human rights organizations, employers' associations, etc. Moreover, despite the generally low levels of wealth and formal education of the membership, grassroots-based voluntary associations often experience less embezzlement of funds because of the high level of trust developed among its members.

The exercise of citizen sovereignty also requires an informed citizenry and modes of communication that enable citizens to follow the conduct of government business and to make their opinions known to government officials. Tocqueville noted that in democracies, governments were highly responsive to public opinion, which was often expressed through the press, public meetings, and petitions. The development of an independent press and radio throughout much of Africa has greatly improved the flow of information concerning political matters and created forums to discuss and debate public issues. The spread of literacy and the introduction of civic education stressing democratic norms in school curricula are creating the foundations for a democratic culture and greater citizen participation in public affairs.

Tocquevillian analytics also makes a distinction between "local liberties," which refers to the desire and ability of local communities to manage their own affairs and decentralization, which transfers powers previously exercised by the state to formal local government units, which may themselves have been created by the state. The granting of local liberties to different ethnic groups and regions has contributed to ending conflicts and rebellions in Mali where the regime offered greater regional autonomy to the Tuareg populations in the north through broad decentralization reforms. Conversely, the failure to offer more autonomy to regionally based ethnic and religious groups has been one of the major causes of civil war in countries like the Sudan. In Chad, where civil war weakened central government structures and led to the collapse of state services outside the capital, villages throughout the southern part of the country have mobilized their own scarce resources to recruit and pay teachers, construct schools, and provide materials for the students.[19] By the end of the century, community schools accounted for more than one-third of Chad's schools.

Although an improvement over continuing state tutelage over local communities, decentralization policies still reflect a top-down approach in which the central government for the most part still determines governance rules and the boundaries delimiting local government units.[20] One of the major problems arising from this approach is that it artificially brings together many local communities who, if they had a choice, would not join the specific local government jurisdiction set up by the state. Local liberties, on the other hand, lets the naturally constituted communities themselves determine how they will be governed and which groups will be part of their community.

The failure of the state to deliver adequate basic goods and services has created an environment in which local communities are reconstituting themselves and developing their self-governing capabilities. The most striking examples of this phenomenon can be seen in the emergence of village-level development associations and the redefinition of community to include native sons and daughters who have moved elsewhere but who retain strong ties to their home community. Because they are not formal local government units, these associations have not received much attention by those writing about decentralization and democratization processes in Africa. Yet, many of the associations exhibit the attributes of a democratic local government. They establish governance rules, they elect officers and hold public meetings to deliberate on the needs of their community whether in the home village itself or among its members working in the towns and abroad, they levy taxes, and they enforce sanctions.

Although some of these associations are still dominated by "big men" and members of the old aristocracy in the community, even these have become more receptive to the participation of formerly excluded groups in decision-making.

Equality of Social Conditions

Most discussions about equality in Africa are ahistorical and refer primarily to disparities in income between the ruling elites and the rest of the country or the growing income gap between Africa and the industrialized countries. They rarely examine the extent to which aristocratic structures and values still survive and their impact on democratization processes.

Slavery was perhaps the most pernicious institution in perpetuating hierarchical and dependency relationships and undemocratic practices. While it is widely assumed that European colonization ended slavery, this was not true in many parts of Africa. The French did not start to make a serious effort to uproot slavery until the first decade of the twentieth century in Senegal, French Soudan, and Guinea. They made no effort to eliminate slavery in Mauritania. Slavery persisted in Northern Nigeria into the 1930s. Emancipated slaves who remained in their areas often stayed in quasi-servitude to their former masters upon whom they were dependent for access to land. Democracy has had great difficulty in establishing a foothold in countries like Mauritania where master–slave relationships have persisted well after independence.

One of the major social revolutions going on in Africa has been the rising social status of young people and women throughout the continent. These two groups, which had muted voices in precolonial and colonial societies, are emerging as increasingly important actors in politics and associational life. Young people and women have organized thousands of associations engaged in a variety of activities—sports, religion, recreation, popular culture, and economic activities. Their associations are also usually organized along relatively egalitarian lines. The extension of education to women has opened up many areas previously reserved to men—politics, the civil service, teaching, and the liberal professions.

The growing power of young people in African societies also has a dark side, especially in areas where political order has broken down. In places like Liberia, Sierra Leone, and the Congo, young men and even children have served as the storm troops of predatory warlords, terrorizing and pillaging surrounding communities.

Religion as a Positive Force in Promoting Democracy

The overwhelming majority of the people of Africa professes and practices some form of religion. In most African societies, it is very difficult to find an atheist. Although in decline, traditional African religions continue to influence the practice of Islam and Christianity in Africa.

Studies of political change in Africa rarely look at the application of religious principles of equality, peace, solidarity, and justice held in common by the Abrahamic-based religions as a potentially powerful force for promoting democracy. Instead, they tend to analyze religious institutions as political actors and focus primarily on their relationships with the state or on conflicts caused by religious differences between Christians, Muslims, and Animists.[21] The ongoing conflict in Sudan, for example, is often explained in terms of religious differences between the Muslim North and the Christian and Animist South. However, the tragedy in Darfur indicates that conflict in that region where Arab Muslim militias have been slaughtering and expelling thousands of darker-skinned Muslims is largely a struggle over land.

With few exceptions like Algeria, Sudan, and Northern Nigeria, Islam in Africa has been moderate, tolerant of other religions, and receptive to democracy and human rights. There is little evidence in Africa to indicate that Islam is incompatible with democracy. Public opinion polls indicate that Muslims are no less inclined to support democracy than Christians.[22] History shows that Muslims in Sub-Saharan Africa have not generally engaged in *jihads* to convert others or to impose Muslim law on non-Muslims. The eighteenth and nineteenth century *jihads* conducted by radical religious leaders were exceptions to this rule.

Most of West Africa has longstanding traditions of peaceful coexistence between Muslims and Christians[23] Mali has an even longer tradition of religious tolerance than Senegal.[24] In Rwanda, the head of the Muslim religious community in Kigali has opened the doors of its school facilities to Christian children in a gesture of good will and worked for reconciliation between Hutus and Tutsis.

During the colonial era, most Christian churches aligned themselves with the colonial authorities and were dominated by Europeans.[25] Many Africans, recruited primarily from the ranks of those adhering to traditional African religions joined Christian churches to have access to schools provided by the missionaries and to upgrade their social status vis-à-vis the colonial administration. Other African Christians reacted to the complicity of the church with colonialism by joining separatist Christian churches and messianic movements that sharply opposed colonial rule. Given the association of Christianity with colonial rule, it is not surprising that Islam has grown faster than Christianity since independence.

After independence, the Africanization of the Catholic Church and the post-Vatican II Third World orientation of the Catholic Church contributed to making the Church a more progressive force with the creation of peace and justice centers in many African countries that lobbied for human rights and democracy and an end to violence. The Protestant-based Council of Churches also adopted policies fostering human rights and democracy in many African countries in the 1980s and 1990s.

Christian churches and religious leaders have taken the lead in championing human rights and democracy in many African countries—Kenya, Madagascar, and South Africa. Although the European-dominated Catholic hierarchy in Rwanda did little to stop the genocide in 1994, since then Protestants and Catholics are cooperating to promote reconciliation between Hutus and Tutsis at the national and grassroots level.

Because of the universality of principles of human equality and peace embedded in Islam and Christianity, these principles can be applied to check and overcome the high degree of interethnic conflict that plagues so many parts of Africa. Islam has definitely contributed to the relative absence of ethnic conflicts in Sahelian countries. Christian values have been invoked to oppose apartheid in South Africa. Where Islam has been fundamentalist and aligned with repressive regimes as for example in Northern Nigeria and the Sudan, Islam has used its majority status to take power and to oppress minorities.

Those still adhering to traditional Animist religions are not necessarily hostile to other religions. In Liberia, for example, the leaders of Poro secret societies and Muslim clerics have traditionally respected each other's religious institutions.[26] During the Liberian civil war, they worked together to protect the people against plunder and pillage by marauding bands in northwestern Liberia and to rebuild their villages when peace returned.

The Future of Democracy in Africa: Afro-Pessimism or Afro-Optimism?

Tocqueville asserted that democracy would take different paths that reflected a specific society's historical traditions, mores, and physical environment, relative equality of social conditions and status, degree of administrative centralization, and commitment to local liberties and individual freedom.

Despite the positive conclusions concerning Senegalese democracy found in chapter 11, we are not advocating Senegal's unique form of democracy as the ideal model to be exported to other countries. As we have seen, Senegal has its flaws and weaknesses similar to those found throughout Africa—the tremendous concentration of power in the hands of the president, clientelism, corruption, the weakness of the rule of law, and the failure to maintain peace throughout the country.

Instead, we will briefly highlight some of the principles that we have discovered to be operating in Senegal that give cause for hope for the rest of the continent and provide an antidote to Afro-pessimism that focuses primarily on what is not working in Africa and foresees only a bleak future for Africa. The application of Tocquevillian analytics to Senegalese society has helped us to discover positive traits of Senegalese society that are often not highlighted in other studies of democracy in Senegal and that can be found elsewhere in Africa.

If Tocqueville is correct in asserting that movement toward equality of conditions is a critical element in democratic societies, then one can identify powerful trends in this direction throughout the continent since the middle of the nineteenth century. The stigma attached to slave and caste status is waning. Youth and women have reached new heights of participation in public life. Education is becoming increasingly accessible to all categories of society. The information and language gap between elites and society has been decreasing. Perhaps just as important, more and more Africans are affirming social equality as an important value. People demand equitable treatment of all groups and are increasingly rejecting *ceddo* ethics and lifestyles.

Although vestiges of slavery and aristocratic orders still exist in some African countries, these residues of the past are clearly in decline. The establishment of a multi-racial democracy in South Africa in the early 1990s after more than half century of apartheid rule represented a major advance toward political and social equality on the African continent.

Tocqueville warned that concentration of power in the hands of those controlling the state and the state's tutelage over society would lead to democratic despotism. Throughout much of Africa, there has been a steady trend away from this phenomenon since the 1980s and 1990s. While enormous power remains concentrated in the hands of the president, African rulers remain more beholden to listen to public opinion and have less leeway to act brutally. Although long-standing dictators like Biya, and Mugabe are still around, Africa has no more Emperor Bokassas or Idi Amins or Camp Boiros where rulers like Sékou Touré can torture and starve to death their political opponents.

While power remains concentrated in the hands of the president in most African countries, the number of one-man and military dictatorships has decreased considerably. Abacha's death in 1999 and the return to civilian rule in Nigeria marked the end of one of Africa's most brutal military dictatorships and raised hopes for a more democratic future despite the continuation of intense religious conflicts between Christians and Muslims.

Throughout Africa, more and more people are openly expressing their views and exercising freedom of association. People are less afraid to criticize their government or their leaders in many African countries. Radio talk shows proliferate. The press and media expose government scandals and incompetence. Communication between the government and the people is no longer exclusively top-down and one-way. Resistance to government policies has forced governments to revise and liberalize their policies. Farmers' groups organize peaceful marches and meetings to express their dissatisfaction with government policies. Women stand up and take part in village and neighborhood meetings.

Although it is still dangerous to be a journalist or to openly criticize the government in some African countries like Burkina Faso, Zimbabwe, and the Ivory Coast, freedom of expression is generally on the rise throughout the continent. Africans themselves increasingly perceive democracy primarily in terms of freedom of expression.[27] Much of the democratization that took place in the 1990s resulted from popular protests against authoritarian regimes and demands for greater freedom. By facilitating the dissemination of information and the development of ties among journalists and those fighting for human and civil rights in Africa, the Internet revolution has made it more difficult for rulers to get away with murder in secret.

Perhaps the most promising development has been the rapid rise and flourishing of associational life and the resurgence of grassroots based self-governing communities that Tocqueville identified as so vital to a democratic society. Africa's peoples are taking advantage of the political and economic space opened up by political and economic liberalization. Africa's Western-educated civil society has grown in size, made considerable advances in becoming more professional, pragmatic, and less dependent upon the state. Africans from all walks of life throughout the continent have created a myriad of functional voluntary associations and community-based associations built on indigenous modes of organization and patterns of trust to find collective solutions to a wide range of every day problems. Informal local government communities such as village and neighborhood development associations are often doing a better job of providing public goods and services than their formal local government counterparts.

Hometown associations with links to their members' community of origins can be found throughout west Africa and to a lesser extent elsewhere on the continent. The African diaspora working in Europe and North America is sending large amounts of money and other resources back to their families and communities and lobbying for freedom and democracy. The resurgence of associational life in Africa clearly demonstrates the self-governing capabilities of Africans, and their ability to adopt organizational modes incorporating old and new mores and ways of doing things. In the end, this bottom-up manifestation of democracy is bound to strengthen the foundations for a democratic culture in Africa.

Freedom entails the right of minorities to pursue their own religious beliefs, to speak their own languages, and to organize their own communities in peace. It is becoming increasingly clear that ethnic conflicts in Africa are not rooted in "tribalism" but in efforts of elites seeking power to mobilize their ethnic groups on their behalf. Reconciliation committees in South Africa and Rwanda are seeking to heal the wounds of past racial animosities and genocide. In Monrovia, Liberians from every ethnic group took to the streets in 2003 to demand peace, the end of violence, and the departure of Charles Taylor. In Somaliland, once warring clans work together to rebuild their country from scratch.

Looking at the future of democracy in Africa from a Tocquevillian perspective, there is room to be optimistic despite the fragility of so many African regimes. Aristocratic orders are disappearing. More dictatorships are falling by the wayside. Africans are demanding more freedom and using their freedom to develop their self-governance capabilities. They are demonstrating their skills in the art of association, reaffirming their taste for local liberties, and returning to the sources to build new forms of democracy from the bottom-up.

Tocqueville wisely noted that democracy, like Rome, was not built in a day but was the result of long historical processes. It took France 700 years to reach the stage of equality that set off the French Revolution. Those who deplore the fragility of democracy on the African continent often forget that it took many decades after the French Revolution for liberal democracy to take hold in France and Western and Central Europe. Most African countries have had less than a half century of national independence—less than the sixty years between the French Revolution of 1789 and the 1848 revolution, a period which Tocqueville described as one in which all the nations of Europe were "ravaged by war or torn by civil strife."[28]

Modern democracy in Europe during the twentieth century has also had its examples of backsliding, repression of basic freedoms, oppression of ethnic and religious minorities, and return to authoritarian rule. We should not forget that little more than seventy years ago, following the collapse of the Weimar Republic in Germany, Germans embraced a fascist regime that declared its hatred of democracy while affirming its right to enslave and exterminate other peoples.

Rather than imposing Western models and forms of democracy on Africa, we might do better, in the spirit of Tocqueville, to let Africans work out their own version of the democratic revolution and learn from their experiences.

NOTES

Chapter One   Tocquevillian Analytics in Africa

1 Alexis de Tocqueville, *Democracy in America*. Edited by J.P. Mayer (New York: Harper & Row Publishers, 1988), p. 9.
2 For some of the rare examples of scholars systematically using Tocqueville to understand democracy in the non-Western world see Vincent Ostrom, *The Meaning of Democracy and the Vulnerability of Democracies: A Response to Tocqueville's Challenge* (Ann Arbor: The University of Michigan Press, 1997); Carlos A. Forment, *Democracy in Latin America, 1760–1900* (Chicago: University of Chicago Press, 2003); and Sombat Chantornvong, "Tocqueville's *Democracy in America* and the Third World," in Vincent Ostrom, David Feeny, and Hartmut Picht (eds.), *Rethinking Institutional Analysis and Development: Issues, Alternatives and Choices* (San Francisco: Institute for Contemporary Studies, 1988), pp. 69–99.
3 The metaphor of waves to describe movement toward and away from democracy in modern societies was first popularized by Robert Michels, the German sociologist in 1911, in his *Political Parties: A Sociological Study of the Oligarchical Tendencies of Modern Democracies* (New York: Free Press, 1966).
4 According to Huntington, the Third Wave began with the overthrow of the Salazar regime in Portugal in 1975 and was followed by the demise of authoritarian regimes and their replacement by democratic regimes in Europe, Asia, and Latin America. *The Third Wave: Democratization in the Late Twentieth Century* (Norman, Oklahoma: University of Oklahoma Press, 1990), p. 17. Huntington had little to say about Africa because the Third Wave did not begin there before 1990. For an overview of the Third Wave in Africa, see Larry Diamond, "Introduction," in Larry Diamond and Marc F. Plattner (eds.), *Democratization in Africa* (Baltimore: The Johns Hopkins University Press, 1999), pp. ix–xxvii.
5 Tocqueville, *Democracy in America*, pp. 58–60.
6 For a discussion of Tocqueville's overturning of the prevalent European idea of the state and sovereignty, see Larry Siedentop, *Tocqueville* (New York: Oxford University Press, 1994), pp. 41–43.
7 Samuel P. Huntington, *Political Order in Changing Societies* (New Haven: Yale University Press, 1968), p. 26.
8 Huntington, *The Third Wave*, p. 16.
9 For a vigorous defense of Tocqueville's approach affirming the importance of decentralized politics and local self-government in fostering freedom, see Michael Hereth, *Alexis de Tocqueville: Threats to Freedom in Democracy* (Durham: Duke University Press, 1986), pp. 39–44.
10 Huntington, *The Third Wave*, p. 9.
11 James T. Schleifer, *The Making of Tocqueville's Democracy in America* (Chapel Hill: The University of North Carolina Press), pp. 263–274. Equality was such a major component of his definition of democracy that Tocqueville once thought of naming the second volume of his study of American democracy, which appeared in 1840, *Equality in America*.
12 For example, there are no entries for equality in the index of *The Third Wave*.
13 Tocqueville, *The Old Régime and the French Revolution* (Garden City, NY: Doubleday & Company, Inc., 1955), pp. xiv–xv.
14 Huntington, *Political Order in Changing Societies*, pp. 7–8.

15 Ostrom, *The Meaning of Democracy and the Vulnerability of Democracies*, p. 17.
16 Democratic despotism came to France during the course of the French Revolution. The liberal phase of the French Revolution gave way to the Reign of Terror, Napoleon, and the Bourbon Restoration. The 1830 Revolution failed to transform France into a democracy because it restricted participation to a tiny minority of educated men of wealth and property. As a deputy in the French Parliament (1839–1851), Tocqueville witnessed the overthrow of the July Monarchy in the 1848 Revolution and the 1851 *coup d'état* engineered by Louis Napoléon that shelved the Second Republic's embryonic democratic institutions. France did not become a liberal democracy until the establishment of the Third Republic (1879–1940) until twenty years after Tocqueville's death in 1859.
17 For the coining of the concept and its implication, see Mahmoud Mamdani, *Citizen and Subject: Contemporary Africa and the Legacy of Colonialism* (Princeton: Princeton University Press, 1996), pp. 62–108.
18 Tocqueville, *The Old Regime and the French Revolution*, pp. 146–147.
19 This section owes a great debt to the work of Frederick C. Schaeffer's *Democracy in Translation: Understanding Politics in an Unfamiliar Culture* (Ithaca: Cornell University Press, 1998). His book, a linguistic inquiry that uses Senegal as a case study, looks at the interaction of culture and institutions and the formation and use of social science concepts like democracy in different cultural settings.
20 *Merriam-Webster's Collegiate Dictionary*, Tenth Edition (Springfield, MA: Merriam-Webster Incorporated, 1993), pp. 446, 670.
21 Schaeffer, *Democracy in Translation*, pp. 1–20.
22 Scholars have described countries that hold free and fair elections but restrict civil rights and other basic freedoms as illiberal democracies. Fareed Zakaria, "The Rise of Illiberal Democracy," *Foreign Affairs*, Vol. 76, No. 6 (1997), pp. 181–195.
23 For an analysis of the trend to differentiate among different strands of democracy by adding an adjective in front of the term, see David Collier and Steven Levitsky, "Democracy 'with Adjectives': Conceptual Innovation in Comparative Research," *World Politics*, Vol. 49 (April 1997), pp. 430–451. For a review of the literature on these themes and a spirited defense of the use of clientelist democracy, see Linda Beck, *Clientelist Democracy*, Unpublished paper for a conference on "Mapping the 'Gray Zone': Clientelist Democracy and the Boundary between Democratic and Democratizing," Columbia University, April 4–5, 2003.
24 For critiques of the Western developmental model based on the nation-state, see Basil Davidson, *The Black Man's Burden: Africa and the Curse of the Nation-State*, 1992; Sheldon Gellar, "State-Building and Nation-Building in West Africa," *Building States and Nations: Models, Analyses, and Data Across Three Worlds*, Vol. 2 (Beverly Hills: Sage Publications, 1973), pp. 384–426.
25 Gerti Hesseling, *Histoire Politique du Sénégal* (Paris: Karthala, 1985), p. 349.
26 For a detailed discussion and analysis of the different usages of the term *démocratie* by politicians from the ruling party and the opposition, see Schaffer, *Democracy in Translation*, pp. 21–36.
27 In recent years, there has been a new literature arising that looks at local understandings of democracy in Africa. For example, see Maxwell Owusu, "Democracy and Africa—A View From the Village," *The Journal of Modern African Studies*, Vol. 30, No. 3 (1992), pp. 369–396; Mikael Karlstrom, "Imagining Democracy: Political Culture and Democratization in Buganda," *Africa*, Vol. 66, No. 4 (1996), pp. 485–505; and Davidson, *The Black Man's Burden*.
28 Schaeffer, *Democracy in Translation*, p. 84.

Chapter Two   Point of Departure

1 Tocqueville, *Democracy in America*, p. 26.
2 For discussions of Senegal's geographical features and the physical environment shaping Senegalese history and culture, see George E. Brooks, *Landlords and Strangers: Ecology, Society, and Trade in Western Africa, 1000–1630* (Boulder: Westview Press, 1993); Philip D. Curtin, *Economic Change in Precolonial Africa: Senegambia in the Era of the Slave Trade* (Madison: University of Wisconsin Press, 1975), pp. 13–29 and Paul Pélissier, *Les Paysans du Sénégal: Les Civilisations Agraires du Cayor à la Casamance* (Saint Yrieux: Imprimérie Fabregue, 1966).

3   Nehemia Levtzion, *Ancient Ghana and Mali* (London: Methuen, 1973) and Djibril Tamsir Niane, *Le Soudan Occidental au temps des grands empires (XIe-XVIe Siècles)* (Paris: Présence Africaine, 1975).

4   The tiny band of fertile land touched by the overflowing of the Senegal River was called *walo*, while the land outside the flood plain was designated diéri.

5   Even today, these regions remain relatively marginalized, especially in the political arena. Inhabitants of the Casamance region still speak of going to Senegal when leaving for visits to Dakar and other locations to the north.

6   For a detailed description of the Diola rice civilization, see Pélissier, *Les Paysans du Sénégal*, pp. 646–689.

7   On this point, see Pathé Diagne, "Pluralism and Plurality in Africa," in Dov Ronen (ed.), *Democracy and Pluralism in Africa* (Boulder: Lynne Rienner Publishers, Inc., 1986), pp. 68–69.

8   For more on this theme, see Sheldon Gellar, "State-Building and Nation-Building in West Africa," pp. 384–426.

9   See Cheikh Anta Diop, *L'Afrique Noire précoloniale* (Paris: Présence Africaine, 1960).

10 The term Halpulaar refers to people who speak the Pulaar language. For many years, distinctions were made between the sedentarized Halpulaar, called Tukulor and the nomadic Halpulaar called Fulbe or Peul in French. Today, the census statistics list both groups as Halpulaar.

11 For the history of Tekrur, see Abdourhamane Ba, *La Takrur, des origines à la conquête par le Mali (VIe-XIII siècles)* (Nouakchott: Imprimerie Nouvelle, 2002).

12 Gajaaga was reputed to be what was left of the ancient Ghana Empire. Boubacar Barry, *La Sénégambie du XVe au XIXe siècle: Traite négrière, Islam, conquête coloniale* (Paris: L'Harmattan, 1988), p. 40.

13 Jean Boulégue, *Le Grand Jolof (XIII–XVIe)* (Blois: Editions Facades, 1987).

14 For the evolution of the two Serer kingdoms, see Pathé Diagne, *Pouvoir traditionnel en Afrique occidentale* (Paris: Présence Africaine, 1967), pp. 56–94.

15 Charlotte Quinn, *Mandingo Kingdoms of the Senegambia: Traditionalism, Islam, and European Expansion* (London: Longman, 1972).

16 For details on the revolt of the Lebus, see Mamadou Diouf, *Le Kajoor au XIXe siècle: pouvoir ceddo et conquête coloniale* (Paris: Karthala, 1990), pp. 96–103.

17 Malick Ndiaye has labeled this school the Dakar school and has been critical of historians like Boubacar Barry, Abdoulaye Bathily, and Mamadou Diouf for exaggerating the impact of external forces on Senegalese society. See Malick Ndiaye, *L'Ethique Ceddo et la Société d'Accaparement ou les conduites culturelles des Sénégalais d'audjourd'hui* (Dakar: Presses Universitaires de Dakar, 1996), pp. 79–86.

18 For examples of the other school, which puts the emphasis on indigenous forces shaping Senegalese society, see Diagne, *Pouvoir traditionnel en Afrique occidentale* and Cheikh Anta Diop, *L'Afrique Noire pré-coloniale*.

19 On this point, see Mamadou Diouf, *Histoire du Sénégal: Le Modéle islamo-wolof et ses péripheries* (Paris: Maisonneuve & Larose, 2001).

20 For an analysis of the emergence of caste in West Africa, see Tal Tamari, *Les castes de l'Afrique occidentale: Artisans et musiciens endogames* (Nanterre: Société d'ethnologie, 1997).

21 The description of Wolof social structures is taken from Abdoulaye-Bara Diop, *La Société Wolof, Tradition et Changement: Les Systèmes d'inégalité et de Domination* (Paris: Editions Karthala, 1981).

22 Tocqueville, *Democracy in America*, pp. 535–536.

23 For more on African and Afro-European traders and middlemen, see Curtin, *Economic Change in Precolonial Africa*, pp. 59–152.

24 For discussion of the system of Wolof values, see Assane Sylla, *La philosophie morale des Wolof* (Dakar: Sankoré, 1978).

25 For the relationships of the marabouts among the Wolof with power, see Abdoulaye-Bara Diop, *La Société Wolof*, pp. 214–245.

26 For a portrait of the marabouts as social reformers during the precolonial era, see Christian Coulon, *Le marabout et le Prince: Islam et Pouvoir au Sénégal* (Paris: Editions A. Pedone, 1981), pp. 115–163.

27 For more on this theme, see Martin Klein, *Islam and Imperialism in Senegal, Sine Saloum 1847–1914*. (Stanford: Stanford University Press, 1968).

28 For a classic work of Fouta Toro's response to Umar Tall, see David Robinson, *Chiefs and Clerics: The History of Abdul Bokar Kane and the Fouta Toro* (Oxford: Clarendon Press, 1975).

29 However, the British left more of an impact in what is now Gambia where they established their trading posts and took control when Africa was carved up. For a history of the Gambia and British influence, see John Milner Gray, *A History of the Gambia* (London: Frank Cass, 1966).

Chapter Three The Old Order and Colonialism

1 Tocqueville, *The Old Régime and the French Revolution*, p. vii.

2 Ibid., pp. 1–5. Tocqueville began his great work on the French Revolution with a section entitled "Conflicting Opinions of the Revolution at Its Outbreak."

3 For a discussion of French ideologies and interests justifying colonialism, see Henri Brunsweig, *Mythes et Réalités de l'Imperialism Colonial Français, 1871–1914.* (Paris: Armand Colin, 1960); and Alice L. Conklin, *A Mission to Civilize: The Republican Idea of Empire in France and West Africa, 1895–1930* (Stanford: Stanford University Press, 1998).

4 For examples, see George A. Almond and James S. Coleman (eds.), *The Politics of Developing Areas* (Princeton: Princeton University Press, 1960) and Lucian W. Pye, *Aspects of Political Development* (Boston: Little, Brown, & Company, 1966).

5 Rupert Emerson, *From Empire to Nation* (Cambridge, MA.: Harvard University press, 1960), pp. 272–292.

6 For an analysis of Marx's views toward colonialism and excerpts from his writings, see Shlomo Avineri (ed.), *Karl Marx on Colonialism and Modernization* (New York: Doubleday, 1969). For more recent Marxist interpretations of the impact of colonialism on Africa, see Jean Suret-Canale, *L'Afrique Noire: L'Ére Colonial: 1900–1945* (Paris: Editions Sociales, 1964) and Walter Rodney, *How Europe Underdeveloped Africa* (Washington, DC: Howard University Press, 1974).

7 See Samir Amin, *Accumulation on a World Scale* (New York: Monthly Review Press, 1974); André Gunder Frank, *Capitalism and Underdevelopment in Latin America* (New York: Monthly Review Press, 1967), and Colin Leys, *Underdevelopment in Kenya: The Political Economy of Underdevelopment* (London: Heineman, 1975).

8 William B. Cohen, *Rulers of Empire: The French Colonial Service in Africa* (Stanford: Stanford University Press, 1971), p. 9.

9 For the best account of this period, see Barry, *La Sénégambie du XVè au XIXè Siècle*.

10 David Robinson, *Chiefs and Clerics.*

11 For a detailed account of how the rulers of Sine and Saloum came to terms with superior French military might, see Martin A. Klein, *Islam and Imperialism in Senegal.*

12 Boubacar Barry, *La Sénégambie du XVe au XIXe Siècle*, pp. 298–214; Mamadou Diouf, *Le Kajoor au XIXe Siècle*, pp. 247–286.

13 For a monumental study of the impact of French rule on slavery, see Martin A. Klein, *Slavery and French Colonial Rule in French West Africa* (New York: Cambridge University Press, 1998.

14 Klein, *Islam and Imperialism in Senegal*, p.170.

15 For the economic changes taking place in Senegal, see Sheldon Gellar, *Structural Changes and Colonial Dependency: Senegal, 1885–1945* (Beverly Hills: Sage Publications, 1976).

16 David Robinson, "French Islamic Policy and Practice in Late Nineteenth Century Senegal," *Journal of African History*, Vol. 29, No. 3 (1988), pp. 185–211.

17 For the Muslim Brotherhoods' relations with the French colonial state, see David Robinson, *Paths of Accommodation: Muslim Societies and French Colonial Societies in Senegal and Mauritania, 1880–1920* (Athens, Ohio: Ohio University Press, 2000); Paul Marty, *Etudes sur l'Islam*, 2 vols. (Paris: Leroux, 1917); Christian Coulon, *Le marabout et le Prince: Islam et Pouvoir au Sénégal* (Paris: A. Pedone, 1981); Lucy C. Behrman, *Muslim Brotherhoods and Politics in Senegal* (Cambridge, MA.: Harvard University Press, 1970); and James E. Searing, "*God Alone is King*": *Islam and Emancipation in Senegal, The Wolof Kingdoms of Kajoor and Bawol, 1859–1914* (Portsmouth, New Hampshire: Heinemann, 2002).

18 For a general study of the Tijani movement, see Jamil Abun-Nasr, *The Tijaniyya: A Sufi Order in the Modern World* (New York: Oxford University Press, 1965) and Jean-Louis Triaud and David Robinson (eds.), *La Tijaniyya, Une confrérie musulmane à la conquête de l'Afrique* (Paris: Karthala, 2000).

19 The Mourides have been the most studied of all the Senegalese Brotherhoods. For three important studies, see Donal Cruise O'Brien, *The Mourides of Senegal: The Political and Economic Organization of an Islamic Brotherhood* (London: Oxford University press, 1971); Cheikh Tidjiane Sy, *La confrérie sénégalaise des Mourides* (Paris: Présence Africaine, 1969); Jean Copans, *Les Marabouts de l'Arachide: la Confrérie Mouride et les paysans du Sénégal* (Paris: Le Sycamore,1980).

20 Tocqueville, *The Old Régime and the French Revolution*, pp. 57–58.

21 For a description of the system set up by Faidherbe, see Cohen, *Rulers of Empire: The French Colonial Service in Africa*, pp. 9–17.

22 M.D. Lewis, "One Hundred Million Frenchmen: The Assimilationist Theory in French Colonial Policy," *Comparative Studies in Society and History*, Vol. 4, No. 2 (1962), pp. 48–61.

23 Raymond Buell, *The Native Problem in Africa*, Vol. 1 (New York: McMillan, 1928), p. 984.

24 For an idealized version of the role of the village chiefs, see Robert DeLavignette, *Service Africain* (Paris: Gallimard, 1946).

25 For a discussion of the patterns of territorial control in precolonial Africa and the primacy of the exit option, see Jeffrey Herbst, *States and Power in Africa: Comparative Lessons in Authority and Control* (Princeton: Princeton University Press, 2000), pp. 35–57.

26 A treaty signed in Paris in August 1889 between France and Great Britain gave Great Britain sovereignty over the Gambia River and a small band of land on both sides of the riverbank, which became the British colony of Gambia. A few years earlier, in 1886, the Portuguese signed agreements that gave France control over Ziguinchor and established the current boundaries between Senegal and Portuguese Guinea. For a discussion of the demarcation of boundaries and administrative districts and accompanying maps, see *Atlas national du Sénégal*, 1977, pp. 58–63.

27 For a comprehensive study of the movement of labor to Senegal, see Philippe David, *Les Navétanes: Histoire des migrants saisonniers de l'arachide en Sénégambie des origins à nos jours* (Dakar: Les Nouvelles Editions Africaines, 1980).

28 L. Gray Cowan, *Local Government in West Africa* (New York: Columbia University Press, 1958), p. 40.

29 G. Wesley Johnson, Jr., *The Emergence of Black Politics in Senegal: The Struggle for Power in the Four Communes, 1900–1920* (Stanford: Stanford University Press, 1971), p. 228.

30 Michael Crowder, *Senegal: A Study of French Assimilationist Policy* (New York: Oxford University Press, 1967).

31 Nicole Bernard-Duquenet, *Le Sénégal et le Front Populaire* (Paris: L'Harmattan, 1985).

32 For a description of Vichy practices in Senegal, see Francois Zuccarelli, *La Vie Politique Sénégalaise (1940–1988)*, Vol. 2 (Paris: CHEAM, 1989), pp. 13–25 and Jean Suret-Canale, *Afrique Noire occidentale et centrale: L'Ere Colonial, 1900–1945*, pp. 567–600 for an account of the war years (1939–1945) in France's Black African colonies.

33 For a detailed analysis of French postwar colonial reforms, see Ruth Schachter-Morgenthau, *Political Parties in French-Speaking West Africa*, (New York: Oxford University Press, 1964), pp. 37–74.

34 William J. Foltz, *From French West Africa to the Mali Federation* (New Haven: Yale University Press, 1965), pp. 21–26.

35 For an extensive analysis of postwar Senegalese politics, see Schachter-Morgenthau, *Political Parties in French-Speaking West Africa*, pp. 135–165 and Kenneth Robinson, "Senegal" in W.J.K. Mackenzie and Kenneth Robinson (eds.), *Five Elections in Africa* (London: Oxford University Press, 1960), pp. 281–390.

Chapter Four   Centralization and Democratic Despotism

1 Tocqueville, *Democracy in America*, p. 693.

2 For one of the best studies of the emergence of one-party states during the early years of independence, see Aristide R. Zolberg, *Creating Political Order: The Party-States of West Africa* (Chicago: Rand McNally & Company, 1966). For an analysis of African political parties during the last phases of decolonization and early days of independence, see Thomas Hodgkin, *African Political Parties* (London: Penguin Books, 1961).

3 Hodgkin, *African Political Parties*, p. 159.

4 Thus, one saw party-state regimes emerge in such diverse countries as Mali, Ghana and Guinea (Marxist); Senegal and Tanzania (African Socialist); and the Ivory Coast, Cameroon, Malawi, and Zaire (State Capitalist).

5 The elections pitted Senghor and the UPS against a unified list of opposition elements—partisans of Mamadou Dia, PRA-Senegal, elements of the outlawed PAI, and the *Bloc des Masses Sénégalaises* (BMS). The official election results gave the UPS 94.2 percent of the vote, a figure that surely exaggerated its degree of popular support.

6 During the decolonization era, regional party leaders had a strong popular base and were not dependent upon the party executive for their power. They also lobbied intensely to promote regional interests when serving as ministers or deputies.

7 With no opposition to run in or to monitor elections and state officials loyal to the regime responsible for organizing the elections, the UPS was able to claim fantastic results. For example, the results

showed that 99 percent of registered voters turned out to vote in the 1973 national elections and that virtually everyone voted for Senghor and the UPS. Zuccarelli, *La vie politique sénégalaise (1940–1988)*,Vol. 2, p. 124.

8   The PDS had to accept the label of liberal democratic even though its leaders at the time felt that they were closer to the English labor party in doctrine. Majhemout Diop's resurrected PAI became the officially sanctioned Marxist-Leninist party.

9   For a detailed portrait of Senghor's technocratic approach to governance, see Irving L. Markowitz, *Léopold Senghor and the Politics of Negritude* (New York: Atheneum, 1969) and Mamadou Diouf, Le clientelisme, la "technocratie" et après," in Momar Coumba Diop (ed.) *Sénégal: Trajectoires d'un Etat* (Paris: Karthala, 1992), pp. 233–278.

10 Gil Blanchet, "L'Evolution des Dirigeants du Sénégal: De l'Indépendance à 1975," *Cahiers d'Etudes Africaines*,Vol. 18, No. 1–2 (1978), pp. 49–78.

11 For the genesis of Tocqueville's two kinds of centralization, see Schleifer, *The Making of Tocqueville's Democracy in America*, pp. 135–139.

12 See Elliot J. Berg, "The Economic Basis of Political Choice in French West Africa," *The American Political Science Review*,Vol.54, No. 2 (June 1960), pp. 397–398 for data on the composition of the colonial service in French West Africa. Many had been trained at Ecole William Ponty in Senegal, which also trained schoolteachers.

13 For an idealistic version of the role of the *administrateur civil*, in the territorial administration, see Abdourahmane Konaté, *Le cri du mange-mil: Mémoires d'un Préfêt Sénégalais* (Paris: L'Harmattan, 1990).

14 In increasing the state's control over municipal affairs, Senghor evoked the same pretext—the maladministration of their finances—used by Louis XIV in his efforts to destroy the municipal liberty of towns. Tocqueville, *The Old Régime and the French Revolution*, p. 249.

15 For Dia's rural development program in the early 1960s, see Sheldon Gellar, "Circulaire 32 Revisited: Prospects for Revitalizing the Senegalese Cooperative Movement in the 1980s," Mark Gersowitz and John Waterbury (eds.), *The Political Economy of Risk and Choice in Senegal* (London: Frank Cass, 1987), pp. 123–130.

16 For the functioning of Senegal's Rural Councils, see Richard Vengroff and Alan Johnston, *Senegal's Rural Councils: Decentralization and the Implementation of Rural Development* (Dakar: CAIDS, 1985).

17 A survey of African students studying in France showed that more than 80 percent embraced some form of socialist ideology and an even larger percentage looked to the state as the main actor in promoting economic development. See Jean-Pierre Ndiaye, *Enquête sur les étudiants noirs en France* (Paris: Editions Réalités Africaines, 1962). Another survey showed that 72.1 percent of African students studying in France intended to enter government service. Cohen, *Rulers of Empire*, p. 202.

18 For analysis of the rural development institutions that emerged during the 1960s and early 1970s, see Edward J. Schumacher, *Politics, Bureaucracy, and Rural Development in Senegal* (Berkeley: University of California Press, 1975).

19 Tocqueville, *The Old Régime and the French Revolution*, pp. 40–41.

20 For the development of the concept of democratic administration as an alternative to bureaucratic administration, see Vincent Ostrom, *The Intellectual Crisis in American Public Administration*, Second Edition (Birmingham: University of Alabama Press, 1989), pp. 74–99.

21 Ibid., pp. 80–81.

22 For the principles underlying this innovative state agency and its evolution, see Sheldon Gellar, Robert A. Charlick and Yvonne Jones, *Animation Rurale and Rural Development: The Experience of Senegal* (Ithaca: Cornell University, 1980).

23 For a discussion of the position of Senegalese law vis-à-vis corruption, see Malick Ndiaye, *L'Ethique Ceddo et la Société d'Accaparement*, pp. 61–63.

24 For the rise and fall of ONCAD and its impact on the rural economy, see Nim Casswell, "Autopsie de l'ONCAD: La politique arachidière du Sénégal, 1966–1980," *Politique Africaine*, No. 14 (1984), pp. 38–73.

25 Ousemane Sembène's film, *The Money Order*, documents this form of corruption in following the travails of an illiterate Senegalese in Dakar seeking to cash a money order sent by a relative working in France.

26 Malick Ndiaye, *L'Ethique Ceddo et la Société d'Accaparement*,Vol. 1, passim.

27 Ibid. This style of negotiations (*waxtane* in the Wolof language), has roots in precolonial cultural practices. Ndiaye also describes the different forms of *ceddo* behavior in contemporary Senegalese society and their antecedents in precolonial Senegalese society.

28 Also see Peter Ekeh's classic article on popular attitudes toward raiding public resource, "Colonialism and the Two Publics in Africa: A Theoretical Statement," *Comparative Studies in Society and History*, Vol. 17, No. 1 (1975), pp. 91–112.

29 Tocqueville, *The Old Régime and the French Revolution*, pp. 157–169.

30 Ibid., p. 162.

31 For a discussion of the three ideological models and their failure to be disseminated outside the intelligentsia, see Mamadou Diouf, "Les intellectuals et l'Etat au Sénégal: La Quête d'un paradigme," in Mamadou Diouf and Mahmoud Mamdani (eds.), *Liberté Académique en Afrique* (Paris: Karthala, 1994), pp. 241–271.

32 For a sample of Senghor's writings on this topic, see *On African Socialism* (New York: Frederick A. Praeger, 1964). For the evolution of Senghor's philosophy, see Jacques Hymans, *Léopold Sédar Senghor* (Edinburgh: Edinburgh University Press, 1971).

33 For a sample of a Marxist ideological analysis, see Majhemout Diop's *Histoire des classes sociales dans l'Afrique de l'Ouest: Le Sénégal* (Paris: François Maspero, 1972). Diop was the founder and leader of the PAI.

34 For a sampling of Cheikh Anta Diop's works see *Nations Négres et Culture* (Paris: Présence Africaine, 1954); *L'Unité Culturelle de l'Afrique Noire* (Paris: Présence Africaine, 1959); *L'Afrique Noire Pré-coloniale* (Paris: Présence Africaine, 1960); and *Civilisation et Barbarie* (Paris: Présence Africaine, 1981). Translations of his work into English also sparked the development of a vigorous Afrocentric movement in the United States among African American intellectuals and cultural nationalists.

35 The first administrative reform referred to the 1972 reform establishing the groundwork for Senegal's Rural Councils.

36 The 1996 decentralization code transferred power from the central government to local government bodies in several areas including education and literacy programs, health, urbanism and housing, economic development planning, management and protection of the environment, land use management and planning, and sports, culture, and youth activities. République du Sénégal *Textes de Lois de la Décentralisation* (Dakar, 1996).

37 The exception to this rule took place during the late 1970s when the PDS contested local elections and managed to win control over two rural councils.

38 For example, the National Council for the Development of Local Government had thirty-five members of which twenty-five were ministers, directors of government services, and other state officials while only six members represented the three levels of local government.

Chapter Five   Local Liberties

1 Tocqueville, *Democracy in America*, pp. 62–63.

2 Ibid., p. 62.

3 Ibid., p. 47.

4 Robert T. Gannett, Jr., "Bowling Ninepins in Tocqueville's Township," *American Political Science Review*, Vol. 97, No. 1 (February 2003), p. 2. Gannett identifies four different kinds of associations evoked by Tocqueville: permanent associations, political associations, civic associations, and private associations.

5 Autonomous self-governing urban communities like Timbuktou and Djenné, nevertheless, emerged in other areas of West Africa during the heyday of the Trans-Saharan trade between North and West Africa and in Nigeria during the nineteenth century.

6 Pathé Diagne, "Le Pouvoir en Afrique," in UNESCO, *Le Concept de Pouvoir en Afrique* (Paris: Les Presses de l'UNESCO, 1981), p. 45. Diagne describes west Africa's village democracies in much the same terms used by Tocqueville to describe self-governing village communities in feudal France.

7 Pélissier, *Les Paysans du Senegal*, pp. 197–203.

8 Emmanuel Ndione et al., *Avenir Des Terroirs: La Ressource Humaine* (Dakar: Enda-Editions, 1992), pp. 23–28.

9 David Boilat, *Esquisses Sénégalaises* (Paris: Editions Karthala, 1984), pp. 59–60. The None are considered to be a sub-group of the Serer.

10 Ibid., pp. 42–43.

11 Feudal nobles also championed local liberties in the more limited sense of defending the autonomy of their realm against the encroachments of centralizing rulers. Although opposing centralization,

aristocratic notions of local liberties were not equalitarian. Liberty and the right to govern were the prerogatives of the nobility and not a natural right.

12 The Senegal River Valley was divided into *leydis* that constituted largely autonomous political, social, and economic management units over lands governed by the dominant families in the area. For more details, see Catherine Boone, *Political Topographies of the African State: Territorial Authority and Institutional Choice* (Cambridge: Cambridge University Press, 2003), pp. 286–291 and Jean Schmitz, "Cités Noires: les Républiques villageoises du Fuuta Tooro (Vallée du Fleuve Sénégal)," *Cahiers d'études africaines*, Vol. 34, No. 1–3 (1994), pp. 419–461.

13 Johnson, *The Emergence of Black Politics in Senegal*, pp. 40–41.

14 Ibid., p. 42.

15 Ibid., pp. 197–205.

16 In 1885, Saint-Louis had a population of 18,620, Dakar 4,929, Rufisque 3,127, and Gorée 1,744.

17 In Senegal, as elsewhere in French West Africa, the French also created local government institutions known as mixed communes in urban areas. These communes, however, differed from the full communes because French colonial officials directly administered them and restricted African representation in municipal councils.

18 For the historical evolution of the communes in French Africa during the post war period, see Cowan, *Local Government in West Africa*, pp. 112–118.

19 Momar-Coumba Diop and Mamadou Diouf, "Pouvoir Central et pouvoir local: la crise de l'institution municipale," in Sylvy Jaglin and André Dubresson (eds.), *Pouvoirs et cités d'Afrique noire. Décentralisation en question* (Paris: Karthala, 1993), pp. 101–125.

20 *Info-Sénégal*, October 1961.

21 Robert DeLavignette, *Freedom and Authority in French West Africa* (London: Oxford University Press, 1950), p. 75.

22 The December 14, 1789 law transformed the 44,000 parishes of the Old Regime into an equivalent number of municipalities, all built on the same model regardless of size. The Convention officially abolished the categories of towns (*bourgs*), cities, and villages, which all became communes. Dominique Turpin, *Droit de la Décentralisation: Principes-Institutions-Compétences* (Paris: Gualino Éditeur, 1998), p. 19.

23 Sheldon Gellar, "Circulaire 32 Revisited: Prospects for Revitalizing the Senegalese Cooperative Movement in the 1980s," pp. 123–136.

24 Rural Communities could have anywhere between fifteen and sixty-five villages and a population ranging from 5,000 to 30,000 people. Village populations in Senegal varied tremendously reflecting different patterns of ecological conditions and economic organization with villages smaller in the Sylvo-Pastoral Zone and larger in the more densely populated agricultural parts of the country.

25 For more on this phenomenon, see Franck Petiteville, *La Coopération Décentralisée: Les Collectivités locales dans la Coopération Nord-Sud* (Paris: L'Harmattan, 1995).

26 See Claude Dupuy, "Les Associations Villageoises au Sénégal: Functions Economiques et Modalités de Financement," *Revue Tiers Monde*, Vol. 31, No. 122 (Avril–Juin 1990), pp. 351–375.

27 Projects financed by urban migrants were often not well thought out or languished because of poor implementation and lack of maintenance of equipment. Michael C. Lambert, *Longing for Exile: Migration and the Making of a Translocal Community in Senegal, West Africa* (Portsmouth NH: Heinneman, 2002), pp. 108–116.

28 Jean Schmitz, "Cités Noires: les Républiques villageoises du Fuuta Tooro (Vallée du fleuve Sénégal)," pp. 419–461.

29 For an analysis of Halpulaar village associations in the towns and their contributions to their home villages, see Claude Reboul, "Les Associations de Village de la Vallée du Fleuve Sénégal," *Revue Tiers Monde*, Vol. 28, No. 10 (April–June 1987), pp. 435–440.

30 This phenomenon seems to be prevalent throughout much of West Africa and not peculiar to Senegal.

31 For the genesis of Touba, its development, and its role as spiritual capital of the Mouride Brotherhood, see Eric Ross, "Touba: A Spiritual Metropolis in the Modern World," *Canadian Journal of African Studies*, Vol. 29, No. 2 (1995), pp. 222–259.

32 For the growth of Touba, see Cheikh Guèye, "Touba: les marabouts urbanisans," in Monique Bertrand and Alain Durbresson (eds.), *Petites et Moyennes Villes d'Afrique Noire* (Paris: Karthala, 1997), pp. 179–203.

33 For a discussion of Touba's city government, see Ross, "Touba: A Spiritual Metropolis in the Modern World," pp. 245–248.

34 Serigne Sailihou Mbacké, *Touba (Sénégal): Du "Ndiguel" de Cheikh Ahmadou Bamba Mbacké aux Réalisations de ses Khalifes ou une Voie Communautaire vers la Maitrise de la Croissance Urbaine Rapide* (Istanbul, Turkey, June 1996).

35 See, for example, Leonardo A. Villalòn, *Islamic Society and State Power in Senegal: Disciples and Citizens in Fatick* (New York: University of Cambridge Press, 1995).

36 For a discussion of the responsiveness of the Grand Khalife to criticism of his choice as president of the Conseil Rural in Touba in the late 1990s, see Linda Beck, "Reining in the Marabouts?: Democratization and Local Governance in Senegal," *African Affairs*, No. 100 (2000), pp. 601–621.

37 For the rise of this religious community see, Moriba Magassouba, *L'Islam au Sénégal: Demain les mollahs?* (Paris: Karthala, 1985), pp. 48–53.

38 This section owes much to the lucid summing up of the contribution of Tocqueville's analysis of the contribution of the township in forging democracy by Gannett in "Bowling Ninepins in Tocqueville's Township," pp. 14–15.

39 For example, Mont Rolland has a very dynamic Local Development Committee that includes representatives from all the villages within the Rural Community. Most of these villages had long traditions of working with each other dating back to the pre-colonial era when they were part of the None Republic described by Boilat. In the Fouta Toro, Halpulaar villages within the Agnams have also organized *Association pour la liason et le Développement des Agnams* (ALMA), a Rural Community wide development association.

40 For the potential for building democracy from the ground up in Africa, see James S. Wunsch, "Refounding the African State and Local Self-Governance: The Neglected Foundation," *The Journal of Modern African Studies*, Vol. 38, No. 3 (2000), pp. 487–509 and James S. Wunsch and Dele Olowu, *Local Governance in Africa: The Challenges of Democratic Decentralization* (Boulder: Lynne Rienner, 2003).

Chapter Six   Political Associations, Parties, and the Press

1 Tocqueville, *Democracy in America*, p. 698.

2 Ibid., p. 522.

3 For the evolution of *L'Aurore* and the *Jeunes Sénégalais*, see Zuccarelli, *La Vie Politique Sénégalaise (1789–1940)*, Vol. 1, pp. 90–93 and Johnson, *The Emergence of Black Politics in Senegal*, pp. 149–155.

4 Diagne also received heavy support from the Afro-European community of Gorée, disciples of Ahmadou Bamba, and the Lebu community in Dakar for championing their land rights.

5 Zuccarelli, *La Vie Politique Sénégalaise (1940–1988)*, Vol. 2, pp. 117–118.

6 Guèye was allied with Leon Blum, the leader of the French S.F.I.O (*Section Française de l'Internationale Ouvrière*) and head of the Popular Front government that initiated colonial reforms in Africa.

7 Going back to Lamine Guèye, the losers in Senegalese elections have usually blamed their defeat on the intervention of the administration on the side of their opponents or to electoral fraud.

8 Zucarrelli, *La Vie Politique Sénégalaise (1940–1988)*, Vol. 1, pp. 62–65.

9 For Senegalese clan politics and patron–client relationships, see Robert Fatton, Jr., "Clientelism and Patronage in Senegal," *African Studies Review*, Vol. 29, No. 4 (December 1986), pp. 61–78 and William J. Foltz, "Social Structure and Political Behavior of Senegalese Elites," in Steffen W. Schmidt, James C. Scott, Carl Landé, and Laura Guasti (eds.), *Friends, Followers and Factions* (Berkeley: University of California Press, 1977), pp. 242–250.

10 For the political struggles revolving around the September 28 referendum, see Foltz, *From French West Africa to the Mali Federation*.

11 For the Senghor's regime's restrictions on freedom of the press, association and assembly during the 1960s and 1970, see Gerti Hesseling, *Histoire politique du Sénégal, Institutions, Droit et Société*, pp. 307–325.

12 For the history and content of the debates, see *Club Nation et Développement* (Paris: Présence Africaine, 1972).

13 For a review of the history of the political press in Senegal after independence, see Moussa Paye, "La Presse et le Pouvoir," in Momar Coumba Diop (ed.), *Sénégal: Trajectoires d'un État* (Paris: Karthala, 1992), pp. 331–337.

14 Ibid., pp. 355–356.

15 Hesseling, *Histoire politique du Sénégal*, p. 308.

16 For the organization and platforms of Senegal's fifteen political parties in 1983, see Jacques Mariel Nzouankeu, *Les Partis Politiques Sénégalais* (Dakar: Editions Clairafrique, 1984).

17 Opposition demands for electoral reform increased sharply after the 1988 elections. See Crawford Young and Babacar Kanté, "Governance, Democracy, and the 1988 Senegalese Elections," in Goren Hyden and Michael Bratton (eds.), *Government and Politics in Africa* (Boulder: Lynne Rienner Publishers, 1992) p. 65. For the provisions of the 1991 electoral code, see *L'Unité*, No. 195 (September 1991), p. 4.

18 For the political dynamics underlying the entry of opposition parties into the government coalition, see Linda Beck, "Patrimonial Democrats: Incremental Reforms and the Obstacles to Consolidating Democracy in Senegal," *Canadian Journal of African Studies*, Vol. 31, No. 1 (1997), pp. 1–31.

19 The disintegration of the Soviet Union in the late 1980s and the collapse of communist regimes in Eastern Europe in the early 1990s had much to do with the decline of the influence of Marxist ideology throughout the third world.

20 Mamadou Niang, the military officer who headed ONEL eventually became minister of the interior under Wade.

21 Sheldon Gellar, "Pluralisme ou jacobinisme: quelle démocratie pour le Sénégal," in Momar-Coumba Diop (ed.), *Le Sénégal Contemporain* (Paris: Editions Karthala, 2002), pp. 523–525.

22 For a comparison of the French and American press in Tocqueville's day, see *Democracy in America*, pp. 182–188.

23 These included newspapers like *Thiès Tribune, Louga Infos, Saint-Louis J*, and *Le Courrier du Sud*, which appeared irregularly and reported on local politics and events.

24 Oxy-Jeunes, *Présentation de la Radio Oxy-Jeunes* (Dakar, 2003).

25 Political class refers to those members of Senegalese society seeking to take and retain power through the vehicle of political parties and the ballot box. It includes the leaders of opposition political parties as well as leaders of the party (ies) in power.

26 After independence, Afro-European Senegalese quickly faded from the political scene. By the end of the millennium, only one Afro-European sat in the National Assembly and none held cabinet posts.

27 At independence, Senegal had fewer than 1,000 university students. By 1980, this number had climbed to over 10,000. Today, Senegal has more than 25,000 students enrolled in Senegalese universities and thousands more abroad.

28 On this point, see Pathé Diagne, "La Liberté des candidatures: un imperative de la démocratization de l'État-Parti," *Prospective Alternative Africaine*, Bulletin No.3, (1998), pp. 4–10.

29 In referring to civic associations, I specifically exclude charitable or fraternal organizations such as Rotary, Optimists, and Kiwanis clubs.

30 For a detailed analysis of these associations, see Momar-Coumba Diop and Mamadou Diouf, *Le Sénégal sous Abdou Diouf: État et Société* (Paris: Karthala, 1990), pp. 115–148.

31 A recent survey indicated that 77 percent of the Senegalese population opposed a one-party system. The survey also indicated that Senegalese believe that there are too many political parties in the country today and support limiting the number of political parties. Zeric Kay Smith, Babaly Sall and Mady Dansonko, *Liberalisme, Patrimonialisme, ou Authoritarianisme Attenué: Variations autour de la Démocratie Sénégalaise*, Draft Report produced by Afrobarometer, December 2002.

32 Tocqueville, *Recollections* (Garden City: Doubleday & Company, 1970), pp. 32–33.

33 Ibid., p.33.

34 Abdou Latif Coulibaly, *Wade, un opposant au pouvoir: L'alternance piégée?* (Dakar: Les Éditions Sentinneles, 2003).

35 Tocqueville, *Democracy in America*, pp. 180–188.

36 Ibid, p. 186.

37 For more on this theme, see Sidy Lamine Niasse, *Un arabisant entre presse et pouvoir* (Dakar: Editions Groupe Wal Fadjri, 2003), pp. 78–82.

38 Programme des Nations Unies pour le Developpement (PNUD), *Rapport National sur le Développement Humain au Sénégal*, 2001, pp. 45–46.

Chapter Seven   The Art of Association

1 Tocqueville, *Democracy in America*, p. 517.

2 Ibid., p. 517.

3 Robert D. Putnam, *Making Democracy Work: Civil Traditions in Modern Italy* (Princeton: Princeton University Press, 1993), pp. 89–91. Putnam built on Tocqueville's analysis to develop his thesis that civil associations provided the foundation for democratic culture.

4 Tocqueville, *Democracy in America*, p. 522.

5 Article 291 of the 1810 Napoleonic penal code stated that no association of over twenty people could be formed without the authorization of the government and remained in effect until 1901. For more on laws restricting associational life in France, see Carol E. Harrison, *The Bourgeois Citizen in Nineteenth Century France: Gender, Sociability, and the Uses of Emulation* (Clarendon: Oxford University Press, 1999), pp. 24–33.

6 On the origins of Senegalese trade unions and workers associations, see Nicole Bernard-Duquent, *Le Sénégal et le Front Populaire*, pp. 37–52.

7 For the impact of William Ponty graduates on postwar French West African politics, see Schachter-Morgenthau, *Political Parties in French-Speaking West Africa*, pp. 18–19.

8 Robert L. Tignor, "Senegal's Cooperative Experience, 1907–1960," in John Waterbury and Mark Gersovitz (eds.), *The Political Economy of Risk and Choice in Senegal* (London: Frank Cass, 1987), pp. 90–122.

9 Senegal had the largest trade union movement in Francophone West Africa in 1955 with 55,700 members. Schachter-Morgenthau, *Political Parties in French-Speaking West Africa*, p. 157.

10 Charles, Diané, *La FEANF et les grandes heures du mouvement syndical étudiant noir* (Paris: Editions Chaka, 1990).

11 For the diverse types of associations in Dakar, see Michèle O'Deyé-Finzi, *Les Associations en Villes Africaines, Dakar-Brazzaville* (Paris: Editions L'Harmattan, 1985).

12 For an excellent survey of the literature on voluntary associations in Africa during the colonial period, see Immanuel Wallerstein, "Voluntary Associations," in James S. Coleman and Carl Rosberg, Jr. (eds.), *Political Parties and National Integration in Tropical Africa* (Berkeley: University of California Press, 1964), pp. 318–339.

13 Thomas Hodgkin, *Nationalism in Colonial Africa* (New York: New York University Press, 1957), pp. 84–92.

14 Robert Tignor, "Senegal's Cooperative Experience, 1907–1990," pp. 114–122.

15 For the role of Senegal's trade union movement during the Senghor era, see Magatte Lo, *Syndicalisme et Participation Responsable* (Paris: L'Harmattan, 1987). For a more critical interpretation of the significance of the "unification" of the trade union movement imposed by the state, see Abdoulaye Ly, *Les regroupements politiques au Sénégal (1956–1970)* (Paris: Karthala, 1992), pp. 308–333.

16 For the party-state in Mali's attempts to organize the population into a comprehensive network of official associations, see Claude Meillasoux, *The Urbanization of an African Community: Voluntary Associations in Bamako* (Seattle: University of Washington Press, 1968), pp. 69–72.

17 For a description of this transformation of Diola age-grade work parties to village-level youth associations, see Francis F. Snyder, *Capitalism and Legal Change: An African Transformation* (New York: Academic Press, 1981), pp. 173–197.

18 These included peasant movements like the *Association des Jeunes Agriculteurs de Casamance* (AJAC), which was founded in 1974 by young farmers. For more on AJAC, see Daniel Descendre, *L'Autodétermination Paysanne en Afrique: Solidarité ou Tutelle des O.N.G. Parténaires?* (Paris: Editions L'Harmattan, 1991), pp. 79–105.

19 For the founder's story of his association, see Abdoulaye Diop, 'Une Expérience Associative du Foyer de Ronkh à l'Amicale Economique du Walo, *Archives de Sciences Sociales de la Coopération et du Développement*, No. 62 (Octobre–Décembre 1982), pp. 108–127. Also see Dominique Gentil, *Les Mouvements Coopératifs en Afrique de l'Ouest* (Paris: L'Harmattan, 1986), pp. 206–236.

20 For details on the spread of weekly markets in Senegal, see Regina Van Chi-Bonnardel, *Vie de Relations au Senegal: La circulation des biens* (Dakar: IFAN, 1978), pp. 643–680 and Donna Perry, "Rural Weekly Markets and the Dynamics of Time, Space and Community in Senegal," *Journal of Modern African Studies*, Vol. 38, No. 3 (2000), pp. 461–486.

21 See Robert Putnam's chapter on the Progressive Era in *Bowling Alone* (New York: Simon & Schuster, 2000), pp. 367–401.

22 For a detailed analysis of these forces, see Ibrahima Thioub, Momar-Coumba Diop, and Catherine Boone, "Economic Liberalization in Senegal: Shifting Politics of Indigenous Business Interests," *African Studies Review*, Vol. 41, No. 2 (September 1998), pp. 63–89.

23 If fact, opposition intellectuals had founded several NGOs and played important roles in the NGO movement.

24 Sheldon Gellar, "Circulaire 32 Revisited: Prospects for Revitalizing the Cooperative Movement in the 1980s," pp. 136–159.

25 The decline of the state-initiated producer groups was especially strong in the Senegal River Delta and Valley when peasant associations and producers groups were able to gain access to land and credit without having to go through SAED, the state water and irrigation agency.

26 For the impact of FONGS in the creation of a broad-based peasant movement see Gudrun Lachenmann, "Civil Society and Social Movements in Africa," in Jean-Pierre Jacob and Philippe Lavigne Delville (eds.), *Les Associations paysannes en Afrique: Organisation et dynamiques* (Paris: Karthala, 1994), pp. 74–77.

27 CNCR, *Declaration of Thiès March 17*, 1993, p. 4.

28 The CNCR opposed several elements of the *Projet de loi d'Orientation Agricole et Rurale* drafted by the Wade government in 2003 and succeeded in having the government drop clauses giving the president sweeping powers to allocate land to agribusinesses. See CNCR, *Séminaire National des Ruraux sur la Reforme Foncière* (Dakar: January 2004).

29 Momar-Coumba Diop, *La lutte contre la pauvrété à Dakar: Ver sune définition d'une politique municipale* (Dakar: Nouvelles Imprimeries du Sénégal, 1996), pp. 175–177.

30 For a glowing description of the *Set Setal movement, see ENDA, Set Setal; des murs qui parlent nouvelle culture urbaine à Dakar* (Dakar: ENDA, 1991).

31 Tocqueville, *Democracy in America*, p. 527.

32 Robert Putnam, a neo-Tocquevillian, has effectively used the concept of social capital to examine the vitality of associational life and its impact on democracy in Italy and in America in *Making Democracy Work Alone.*

33 Quoted in Frederick C. Schaeffer, *Democracy in Translation*, p. 55.

34 Scholars and development practitioners like Emmanuel Ndione have demonstrated that it is better to work with existing associations based on traditional modes of organization, which reflect indigenous values and interests, than to create new ones based on imported values and organizational structures. Emmanuel S. Ndione, *Dynamique Urbaine d'une Société en Grappe: Un Cas, Dakar* (Dakar: ENDA, 1987) and *Le Don et le Recours: Ressorts d'une Économie Urbaine* (Dakar: ENDA, 1992).

35 Ndione, *Dynamique urbaine d'Une Société en Grappe*, p. 154.

36 Ndione provides a very interesting metaphor to describe this process of circulation of resources. Individuals seek to create numerous "drawers" (*tiroirs*) based on social relationships. The more people in your network, the more drawers are available that one can open to resolve a problem—for example, paying for a wedding, providing a gift at some life-cycle problem, repaying a debt, purchasing a stock of goods to sell in the market, etc. On the other hand, reciprocity norms oblige individuals to dig into their own drawers to come up with money and other resources requested by others in the network.

Chapter Eight   Spirit of Religion

1 Tocqueville, *Democracy in America*, p. 290.

2 Ibid., p. 287.

3 Tocqueville believed that Islam would decline in ages of democracy and enlightenment because people would not be willing to follow all its prescriptions outside the purely religious realm. Ibid., p. 445.

4 For Ahmadou Bamba's ideas during the early development of the Mouride Brotherhood, see Cheikh Anta Mbacké Babou, "Autour de la Génèse du Mouridisme," in *Islam et Sociétés au sud du Sahara*, Vol. 13, No. 1 (1999), pp. 5–38.

5 Jean Copans, *Les marabouts de l'Arachide*, pp. 109–115.

6 Ibid., p. 123.

7 Leonardo Villalòn, *Islamic Society and State Power in Senegal*, pp. 151–199.

8 Seymour Lipset makes this point for the United States in *The First New Nation: The United States in Historical and Comparative Perspective* (London: Heinneman, 1963) pp. 160–161.

9 Villalòn, *Islamic Society and State Power in Senegal*, pp. 129–135.

10 However, relationships were not always good. Tijanis regarded the Mourides as ignorant while Mourides sometimes proclaimed the spiritual superiority of Ahmadou Bamba. For tensions

between the Brotherhoods, see Khadim Mbacké, *Soufisme et Confréries Religieuses au Sénégal* (Dakar: Publifan, 1993), pp. 84–90.

11 For the importance of tolerance for Tijanis, see Amadou Makhtar Samb, *Introduction à la Tariqah Tidjniyya ou voie spirituelle de Cheikh Ahmad Tidjani* (Dakar: Imprimerie Saint-Paul, 1994), pp. 94–97.

12 Ibid., p. 96.

13 The majority of the more than 50,000 students attending Catholic private schools were Muslims.

14 Leonardo Villalòn, *Islamic Society and State Power in Senegal*, p. 127.

15 However, relationships have not always been smooth. Marabouts opposed an earlier visit of the Pope to Senegal and Abdoul Aziz Sy, the Grand Khalife of the Tivouane Tijanis refused to give permission to the Catholic Church to rebuild an historic chapel in Tivouane in 1984.

16 This description of the Senegalese Catholic community's commitment to religious freedom and separation of church and state echoes Tocqueville's comments about the democratic credentials of the Catholic minority in America. *Democracy in America*, pp. 288–290.

17 For the place of Christians in a predominantly Islamic society, see Augustin Simmel Ndiaye, "Une Minorité confessionnelle dans l'État laic: Point de vue d'un chrétien," in Momar-Coumba Diop (ed.), *Le Sénégal Contemporain* (Paris: Karthala, 2002), pp. 601–616.

18 Tocqueville was highly critical of what today is called Islamic fundamentalism, which obliterates distinctions between church and state and imposes specific political maxims, criminal and civil laws, and scientific theories to all of society under its jurisdiction. See Tocqueville, *Democracy in America*, p. 445.

19 For a detailed analysis of the conflicts among orthodox Muslims and the Qadiri and Tijani Brotherhoods in Nigeria, see Roman Loimeier, *Islamic Reform and Political Change in Northern Nigeria* (Evanston: Northwestern University Press, 1997).

20 By 1981, it was estimated that Dakar had a population of 50,000 blind people, 60,000 handicapped, and 45,000 lepers. Robert Vuarin, "L'Enjeu de la Misère pour l'Islam Sénégalais," *Revue de Tiers Monde*, Vol. 31, No. 123 (July–September 1990), p. 606.

21 Ibid., pp. 610–615.

22 Ibid., p. 609.

23 For the roots of these Islamic Associations, see Muriel Gomez-Perez, "Associations Islamiques à Dakar," *Islam et Sociétés au Sud du Sahara*, No. 5 (November 1991), pp. 5–19.

24 For Dièye's activities in France, see Donal Cruise O'Brien, "Charisma Comes to Town: Mouride Organization 1945–1986," in Donal Cruise O'Brien and Christian Coulon (eds.), *Charisma and Brotherhoods in African Islam* (Oxford: Clarendon Press, 1988), pp. 146–147.

25 For the origin and spread of Wahabi influences in West Africa, see Lansiné Kaba, *The Wahabiyya: Islamic Reform and Politics in French West Africa* (Evanston: Northwestern University Press, 1974).

26 For the rise of the Moustarchadine Movement, see Leonardo Villalòn, "Senegal: The Crisis of Democracy and the Emergence of an Islamic Opposition," in Leonardo Villalòn and Phillip Huxtable (eds.), *Critical Juncture: the African State between Disintegration and Reconfiguration* (Boulder: Lynne Rienner, Publishers, 1998), pp. 143–166.

27 Cheikh Anta Mbacké Babou, "Autour de la Génèse du Mouridisme," p. 31.

28 For more on this phenomenon, see Malick Ndiaye, *Les Móodu-Móodu ou l'éthos du développement au Sénégal* (Dakar: Presses Universitaires de Dakar, 1998).

29 One shouldn't exaggerate differences between the *móodu-móodu* businessman and Senegalese civil servants. Many civil servants were also pious Muslims who lived simple, exemplary lives, worked hard, and did not steal from the public coffers. And not everyone working in the informal sector led exemplary lives. Some made their fortunes by dealing in contraband and other illegal activities.

30 Wade himself was the author of an article comparing the Mouride work ethic with the Protestant ethic. See his "La doctrine économique Mouride," *Annales Africaines* (1967), pp. 175–208.

31 Magassouba, *L'Islam au Sénégal*, p. 98.

32 For a copy of the letter and critique of the Family Code's violation of Islamic law, see *Deggel*, No.1, and November 23, 1998.

33 Roman Loimeier, "The Secular State and Islam in Senegal," p. 187.

34 As a student at the *École Nationale de la France D'Outre-Mer*, Diouf wrote a paper that adopted a highly critical stance toward the marabouts in Senegal. Many young cadres of his generation shared his negative views toward Senegal's Muslim establishment.

35 In time, the "Ayatollah" moderated his views and wound up supporting Abdou Diouf in the 2000 presidential elections.

36 Dièye won slightly less than 1 percent of the vote in the 2000 presidential elections and lost his seat in the National Assembly in 2002. His political career tragically ended after his death in a car accident in 2003.

37 Changes have already occurred within the Niasse branch of the Tijanis where Hassane Cissé, the son of a close associate of Ibrahima Niasse, rather than a direct descendant of the founder, seems to have taken charge.

38 The former Soviet Union was an extreme example of the first model. Overtly hostile to organized religion, which it regarded as the opium of the masses, the Soviet regime closed down religious schools and preached antireligious doctrines in the public schools. Of the Western democracies, France is closest to the first model. The forbidding of Muslim girls to wear head coverings in public schools and nonrecognition of religious schools are just two examples of how France insists upon keeping the state education system secular.

39 For positions taken by diverse Senegalese parties on the secular state during the late 1970s and early 1980s, see Magassouba, *L'Islam au Sénégal*, pp. 145–151.

40 For a detailed critique of the secular state in Senegal and Western-style democracy and discussion of the principles underlying the Islamic state, see Cheikh Oumar Tall, *Islam: Engagement politique et Démocratie* (Dakar: Les Presses de la Sénégalaise de l'Imprimerie, 1997).

41 Moustapha Sy, leader of the Moustarchadines, used language close to that of the Islamists in attacking the Diouf regime in 1993. For a translation and discussion of Sy's 1993 speech attacking Diouf, see Leonardo Villalòn and Ousemane Kane, "Entre confrérisme, réformisme, et Islamisme, les mustarshidin du Sénégal," in Ousemane Kane and Jean-Louis Triaud (eds.), *Islam et Islamismes au Sud du Sahara* (Paris: Karthala, 1998), pp. 263–310.

Chapter Nine   Language

1 Tocqueville, *Democracy in America*, p. 33.

2 Ibid., p. 477.

3 Ibid., p. 33.

4 For the importance of language in constituting self-governing communities, see Ostrom, *The Meaning of Democracy and the Vulnerability of Democracies: A Response to Tocqueville's Challenge*, pp. 157–164.

5 Tocqueville, *Democracy in America*, p. 478.

6 Ibid., p. 478.

7 For the relationship between ethnicity and language in Senegal, see Makhtar Diouf, *Sénégal: Les Ethnies et la Nation* (Dakar: les Nouvelles Editions Africaines du Sénégal, 1998), pp. 73–78.

8 Senegal has 36 different living languages, some spoken by as few as 1,500 people. *Sud Quotidien* No. 2829, Monday, September 9, 2002.

9 The Wolof in eastern Senegal often speak Mandinka and Bambara while many Diola in the Casamance also understand Mandinka, thanks to their proximity to and long contacts with the Mandinka.

10 Wolof has often been described as a cross between Serer and Pulaar while the Serer language appears to have been the original prototype for Wolof and Pulaar.

11 A shared language, of course, is not sufficient to prevent ethnic conflict. The fact that Hutu and Tutsi in Rwanda shared a common language (Kinyarwanda) did not prevent the horrendous genocide of the Tutsi minority by the Hutu.

12 See, for example, Diop, *Afrique Noire Pré-coloniale* and *Les fondements économiques et culturels d'un Etat féderal d'Afrique noire*.

13 Much of the Western Soudan also experienced a high degree of ethnic intermingling under the Ghana and Mali empires.

14 For a list of nearly 1,300 Pulaar proverbs and comments on their meaning, see Henry Gade, *Proverbes et Maximes, Peuls et Toucouleurs traduits, expliqués et annotés* (Paris: Institut d'Ethnologie, 1931).

15 Kocce Barma, the seventeenth century Wolof philosopher coined some of the best known proverbs concerning rulers. For a sample of Wolof proverbs, see Sylla, *La philosophie morale des Wolof*, pp. 213–219.

16 For French government policies to impose French as the sole language in France, see Brian Weinstein, *The Civic Tongue: Political Consequences of Language Choices* (New York: Longman, 1983), pp. 85–86 and 141–142.

17 For more on French language policy in France, see James E. Jacob "Language Policy and Political Development in France," in Brian Weinstein (ed.), *Language Policy and Political Development*, (Norwood: Ablex Publishing, 1990), pp. 43–65.

18 Weinstein, *The Civic Tongue*, pp. 141–142.

19 From 1887 until 1939 only twelve percent of colonial administrators spoke an African language. In 1933, less than one out of ten French colonial administrators spoke an African language. Cohen, *Rulers of Empire: The French Colonial Service in Africa*, p. 126.

20 Ibid., p. 127.

21 Buell, *The Native problem in Africa*, p. 990.

22 Schachter-Morgenthau, *Political Parties in French-Speaking West Africa*, p. 128.

23 In his report accompanying the 1912 naturalization decree, the French Minister of colonies declared that French citizenship should be given to those "who approach us in education, adopt our civilization and our customs, or distinguish themselves by their service." Cited by Buell, *The Native Problem in Africa*, p. 946.

24 Cohen, *Rulers of Empire*, p. 147.

25 Buell, *The Native Problem in Africa*, pp. 1008–1009.

26 Klein, *Islam and Imperialism in Senegal*, pp. 214–216.

27 Diouf, *Sénégal: Les Ethnies et la Nation* (Dakar: Les Nouvelles Editions Africaines du Sénégal, 1998), pp. 82–95.

28 Weinstein, *The Civic Tongue*, pp. 30–31.

29 Vincent Foucher, "Les 'évolués', la migration, l'école: pour une nouvelle interprétation de la naissance du nationalisme casamançais," in Momar-Coumba Diop (ed.), *Le Sénégal Contemporain* (Paris: Karthala, 2002), p. 385.

30 Weinstein, *The Civic Tongue*, pp. 166–174.

31 For example, see FEANF, *Francophonie et Néo-Colonialisme: Le Combat Linguistique dans la Lutte de libération du Peuple Sénégalais* (Paris: August 1979).

32 Momar-Coumba Diop and Mamadou Diouf, *Le Sénégal sous Abdou Diouf*, pp. 274–281.

33 For more details about the États Généraux, see Abdou Sylla, "l'École: quelle réforme," in Momar-Coumba Diop (ed.), *Sénégal: Trajectoires d'un État* (Paris: Karthala, 1992), pp. 385–389.

34 Donal Cruise O'Brien, "The Shadow-politics of Wolofisation," *The Journal of Modern African Studies*, Vol. 36, No. 1 (1991), p. 36.

35 Ibid., p. 49.

36 Ibid., p. 41.

37 Wade in 1988 chose *Sopi* for the name of his PDS party newspaper. Wade, however, was not the first to use this term. After his 1974 release from prison, Mamadou Dia published *And-Sopi*, a newspaper whose title could be translated as working together for change.

38 For an analysis of the intermingling of French and Wolof concepts of democracy and their different meanings, see Schaeffer, *Democracy in Translation*, pp. 35–53.

39 For Wade's use of urban Wolof, see Leigh Swigart, "Cultural Creolisation and Language Use in Post-Colonial Africa: The Case of Senegal," *Africa*, Vol. 64, No. 2 (1994), pp. 183–186.

40 For examples as to how Wolof words has influenced French language usage in Senegal, see Jacques Blondé, Pierre Dumont, and Dominique Gontier, *Lexique français du Sénégal* (Dakar: Nouvelles Editions Africaines, 1979).

41 In 2002, Diouf became the secretary-general of the Francophone community.

42 For a discussion of the Islamo-Wolof model as the dominant one in Senegal, see Mamadou Diouf, *Histoire du Sénégal: Le Modèle Islamo-Wolof et ses Périphéries*, pp. 7–9.

43 For more on this theme, see Souleymane Bachir Diagne, "La Lecon de Musique: Réflexions sur une politique de la culture," in Momar-Coumba Diop (ed.), *Le Sénégal Contemporain* (Paris: Karthala, 2002), pp. 243–259. Diagne speaks of the informalization of the state following Senghor and his policy of tight control over Senegalese culture.

44 For analysis of Senegal's urban youth culture, see Mamadou Diouf, "Des cultures urbaines entre traditions et mondialisation," in Momar-Coumba Diop (ed.), *Le Sénégal Contemporain*, pp. 261–287.

45 ENDA, *Set Setal: des murs qui parlent, nouvelle culture urbaine à Dakar* (Dakar: ENDA, 1991) and Mamadou Diouf, "Des cultures urbaines entre traditions et mondialisation," pp. 266–270.

46 For the evolution of Senegalese world music, see Mark Hudson, Jenny Cathcart, and Lucy Duran, "Senegambian Stars are Here to Stay," in Simon Broughton, Mark Ellingham, and Richard Trillo (eds.), *World Music: Africa, Europe and the Middle East, The Rough Guide Volume 1* (London: The Rough Guides, 1999), pp. 617–633.

47 Renaissance of Pulaar associations in Mauritania also sprung up in Mauritania during the late 1970s and early 1980s, to protest efforts by the Moor-dominated government to impose Arabic as the official language.

48 In the 1990–1991 school year, the region of Ziguinchor had 100 percent of school-age children attending primary school. For the impact of universal primary schooling on the Diola, see

Vincent Foucher, "Les 'Évolués,' la migration, l'école: pour une nouvelle interprétation de la naissance du nationalisme casamançais," pp. 375–424.

49 Ibid., pp. 389–390. Migrants from the Ziguinchor region where the Diola are in the majority represented 12.8 percent of the total number of migrants established in Dakar. Seasonal migrations were also extremely high. One 1984 survey showed that 80 percent of women and 82 percent of men between the ages of twenty and forty in Mlomp, a large village east of the regional capital, had participated in seasonal migrations during the course of their lives.

50 Ibid., pp. 409–410

51 For the development of plurilinguistic traditions and identities in Ziguinchor, see Caroline Juillard, "Ville plurielle? Indices de la wolofisation en cours," in François George Barbier-Wiesser (ed.), *Comprendre la Casamance: Chronique d'une intégration contrastée* (Paris: Karthala, 1994), pp. 401–412 and Marie-Louise Moreau, "Demain, la Casamance trilangue? Valeurs associées au diola, au français, et au wolof," in Barbier-Wiesser, *Comprendre la Casamance*, pp. 413–428.

Chapter Ten   Equality

1 Tocqueville, *Democracy in America*, p. 12.

2 Ibid., p. 11.

3 Johnson, *The Emergence of Black Politics in Senegal*, p. 157.

4 For the social background of elected officials and party leaders in Senegal and other French West African territories during the postwar era, see Schachter-Morgenthau, *Political Parties in French-Speaking West Africa*, pp. 404–411.

5 Ndiaye, *L'Ethique Ceddo et la Société d'Accaparement*, pp. 158–160.

6 Martin Klein, *Slavery and Colonial Rule in French West Africa*, p. 256.

7 Ibid., p. 23.

8 Ibid., pp. 22–26.

9 For Tocqueville's analysis of slavery in America and why it would be difficult to abolish, see *Democracy in America*, pp. 340–363.

10 Racial prejudices played a greater role in places like Mauritania where light-skinned Moors enslaved Black Africans and maintained attitudes of racial superiority.

11 Portuguese visitors to Senegambia in the sixteenth century referred to artisans and griots as Jews because like the Jews, they were segregated from the rest of the population. For a discussion of the social taboos among the Wolof related to caste, see Abdoulaye-Bara Diop, *La Société Wolof*, pp. 38–46.

12 Linda J. Beck, "Democratization and the Hidden Public: The Impact of Patronage Networks on Senegalese Women," *Comparative Politics*, Vol. 35, No. 2 (January 2003) p. 152.

13 Pathé Diagne, *Pouvoir Politique Traditionnel en Afrique Occidentale*, p. 110.

14 See, for example, Christian Coulon, "Women, Islam and *Baraka*," in Donal B. Cruise O'Brien and Christian Coulon (eds.), *Charisma and Brotherhood in African Islam* (Clarendon: Oxford University Press, 1988), pp. 113–126. For a more critical attitude toward Senegalese Islam's treatment of women, see Lucy E. Creevey, "The Impact of Islam on Women in Senegal," *Journal of Developing Areas*, Vol. 25, No. 3 (April 1991), pp. 347–368.

15 Jean Bethke Eistain, "Women, Equality, and the Family," *Journal of Democracy*, Vol. 11, No. 1 (2000), pp. 157–158.

16 Lucy E. Creevey, "Impact of Islam on Women in Senegal," pp. 356–357.

17 For more on this theme, see Jane L. Parpart, "Women and the State in Africa," in Naomi Chazan and Donald Rothchild (eds.), *The Precarious Balance: State and Society in Africa* (Boulder: Westview Press, 1988), pp. 210–215.

18 Linda J. Beck, "Democratization and the Hidden Public," p. 153.

19 Paul Mercier, "La vie politique dans les centres urbains du Sénégal: Étude d'une période de transition," *Cahiers Internationaux de Sociologie*, Vol. 27 (1959), p. 72.

20 For an account of the role of women in this strike, see Ousmane Sembène's epic novel, *God's Bits of Wood* (Garden City, NY: Anchor Books, 1970).

21 Services des Statistiques d'Outre-Mer, *Outre-Mer 1958: Tableau économique et social des états et territories d'outre-mer à la veille de la mise en place des nouvelles institutions* (Paris: Presses Universitaires de France, 1960), p. 729.

22 See the Preamble to the new Senegalese Constitution adopted by referendum on January 7, 2001.

23 See L.B.Venema, *The Wolof of Saloum: Social Structure and Rural Development in Senegal* (Wageningen: Centre for Agricultural Publishing and Documentation, 1978). For his analysis of later developments, see Bernhard Venema and Mayke Kaag, *Le Savoir Local et la Gestion des Ressources Naturelles dans les Communautés Rurales Sénégalaises: Le cas de l'Arrondissement de Médina-Sabakh* (Amsterdam:Université Libre d'Amsterdam, 1997) and Bernhard Venema,"The Rural Councillor as Development Agent:An Uneasy Connection?:A Report from Senegal," *APAD-Bulletin*, No. 12 (1999), pp. 83–101.

24 For Halpulaar political leadership patterns in Futa Toro and Dakar, see Ismaila Dia, "Halpulaar Political Leadership with Political Parties and the Dynamics of Clan Politics in Dakar and the Senegal River Valley." Dakar, unpublished manuscript, 1997.

25 Cécile Laborde, *La Confrérie Layenne et les Lébou du Sénégal: Islam et culture traditionnnelle en Afrique* (Bordeaux: Centre d'Étude d'Afrique Noire, 1995), p. 41.

26 Statistical analysis is based on profiles of all ministers serving in the government between 1957 and 2000 presented in Babacar Ndiaye and Waly Ndiaye, *Présidents et Ministres de la République du Sénégal* (Dakar: La Sénégalaise de l'Imprimerie, 2000).

27 For a detailed discussion of Tocqueville's views on gender equality, see Cheryl Welch, *De Tocqueville* (New York: Oxford University Press, 2001), pp. 190–216. Although Tocqueville recognized women as equals, he believed that men were the natural heads of families and that women should not become involved in the rough and tumble of democratic politics.

28 Tocqueville, *Democracy in America*, p. 600.

29 For the notion of *femme phare* and a detailed analysis of the role played by women in Senegal's patronage politics, see Linda J. Beck, "Democratization and the Hidden Public: The Impact of Patronage Networks on Senegalese Women," pp. 147–169.

30 Ibid., p. 155.

31 Ibid., p. 165.

32 *Le Soleil*, May 14, 2001.

33 For the 1962–1963 academic year, the University of Dakar had only thirty female students out of a total of over 700 Senegalese students. Fatou Sow, *Les Fonctionnaires de l'Administration Centrale* (Dakar: IFAN, 1972), p. 66.

34 While 34 percent of women in the survey declared that they preferred to stay at home, 58 percent expressed a preference for working outside the home, mostly in the modest occupations generally reserved for women. Pierre Fougeyrollas, *Où va le Sénégal? Analyse Spectrale d'une nation africaine* (Paris: Éditions anthropos, 1970), p. 165.

35 Mohammed Mbodj, "Le Sénégal entre ruptures et mutations: Citoyennetés en construction," in Momar-Coumba Diop (ed.), *Le Sénégal Contemporain*, p. 583.

Chapter Eleven   Democracy in Senegal: A Balance Sheet

1 Tocqueville, *Democracy in America*, p. 686.

2 For more on this phenomenon, see Michael Bratton and Nicolas Van Der Walle, "Neopatrimonial Regimes and Political Transitions in Africa," *World Politics*,Vol. 46, No. 4 (1994), pp. 453–489.

3 Following the French example, all of Senegal's presidents since independence have had secret slush funds used for political purposes and "*raisons d'état*."

4 Abdou Latif Coulibaly's *Wade, un opposant au Pouvoir* and Parti de l'Indépendance et du Travail au Sénégal, *Radioscopie d'une alternance confisquée* (Dakar: Parti de l'Indépendance, Augus 2002).

5 Marina Ottaway, *Democracy Challenged: The Rise of Semi-Authoritarianism* (Washington, DC: Carnegie Endowment for International Peace, 2003), pp. 91–108.

6 Margaret A. Novicki, "Abdoulaye Wade: Democracy's Advocate," *Africa Report*, Vol. 36, No. 2 (March–April 1991), pp. 41–44. In December 2004, Wade received the Harriman award from the National Democratic Institute for his lifelong work in promoting the cause of democracy.

7 Linda Beck,"Le Clientelisme au Sénégal," in Momar-Coumba Diop (ed.), *Le Sénégal Contemporain*, (Paris: Karthala, 2002), pp. 529–547.

8 Mamadou Diarra, *Justice et Développement au Sénégal* (Dakar: Nouvelles Éditions Africaines, 1973), pp. 179–183.

9 The noncommunal nature of the conflict in the Casamance is cogently argued in Diouf, Sénégal: *Les Ethnies et la nation*.

10 For a description of the cause and the events leading to the conflict, see Michael Horowitz, "Victims of Development," *IDA Development Anthropology Network*, Vol. 7, No. 2 (Fall 1989), pp. 1–8 and John V. Magistro, "Crossing Over: Ethnicity and Transboundary Conflict in the Senegal River Valley," *Cahiers D'Études Africaines*, Vol. 33, No. 2 (1993), pp. 201–232.

11 République du Sénégal, Service de la Statistique et de la Mécanographie, *Situation Économique du Sénégal (1962)* (Dakar, 1963), p. 12. The Moor communities who dwelled in the Ferlo in the traditional gum-producing areas of Senegal generally lived in peace with their Senegalese neighbors.

12 For Senghor's philosophy on these themes, see Léopold Sédar Senghor, *Le Dialogue des Cultures* (Paris: Seuil, 1993) and *Ce que je crois: négritude, francité et civilization de l'universelle* (Paris: B. Grasset, 1988).

13 Senegal received large numbers of Pulaar-speaking immigrants from Guinea who fled Sékou Touré's repressive regime. Guineans settled primarily in Dakar and in what is now Kolda region. Smaller numbers of Bambara-speaking Malians also settled in Senegal and took Senegalese citizenship shortly after independence. During the revolt against Portuguese rule in Guinea-Bissau that began in 1962, many from that country crossed the border into Senegal to flee the fighting and settled there.

14 For an in-depth analysis of French society in Senegal, see Rita Cruise O'Brien, *White Society in Black Africa: The French of Senegal* (Evanston: Northwestern University Press, 1972).

15 For Lebanese adaptation strategies, see Said Boumedouha, "Adjustment to African Realities: The Lebanese in Senegal," *Africa*, Vol. 60, No. 4 (1990), pp. 538–549.

16 Moustapha Tambadou (ed.), *Les Convergences Culturelles au sein de la Nation Sénégalaise, Actes du colloque de Kaolack (8–13 juin 1994)*, (Dakar: Imprimérie Saint-Paul, 1996), p. 8.

17 *Sud Quotidien*, July 10, 2003.

18 For the text of the proposed legislation and a detailed critique of the Family Code, see *Le Quotidien*, May 19, 2003.

19 *Le Soleil*, May 19, 2003.

20 *Sud Quotidien*, May 19, 2003.

21 A few months later, Wade reversed his position and established a commission to study the issue.

22 Institut Panos Afrique de l'Ouest, *Médias et Élections au Sénégal: La Presse et les nouvelles technologies de l'information dans le processus electoral* (Dakar: Panos, 2002), p. 55.

23 Ibid., pp. 77–80.

24 The *Haut Conseil de l'Audiovisuel*, which now oversees access to the media has criticized the state media for not giving enough time and space to coverage of opposition party events. *Le Soleil*, July 29, 2003. Also see Jacques Habib Sy, *Crise de l'audio-visuel au Sénégal* (Dakar: Aide Transparence, 2003).

25 Nine newspapers, including nearly all of Dakar's independent press, published a joint editorial condemning Diagne's arrest, which they denounced as an effort to muzzle the press. *Sud Quotidien*, July 7, 2004.

26 "Situation politique, une nouvelle Coalition sort de la société civile," *Walfadjri*, January 28, 2004.

27 For detailed coverage of this event, see *Sud Quotidien*, January 27, 2003.

28 ARC/Sénégal, *Note d'Information*, Dakar, December 29, 2003.

29 République du Sénégal, *Le Sénégal en Chiffres* (Dakar: Société Africaine d'Edition, 1979).

30 Leonardo Villalòn, "Islamism in West Africa: Senegal," *African Studies Review*, Vol. 47, No. 2 (September 2004), pp. 68–71.

31 Linda Beck, "Brokering Democracy in Africa: Political Competition, Participation and Stability in Senegal," Paper presented to American Political Science Association, September 5, 2004, pp. 22–25.

Chapter Twelve   The Future of Democracy in Africa

1 Tocqueville, *Democracy in America*, p. 9.

2 For a monumental study of the negative consequences of the colonial legacy, see Crawford Young, *The African Colonial State in Comparative Perspective* (New Haven: Yale University Press, 1994).

3 For examples, see James S. Coleman and Carl G. Rosberg, Jr. (eds.), *Political Parties and National Integration in Tropical Africa* (Berkeley: University of California Press, 1964) and Aristide R. Zolberg, "Patterns of National Integration," *Journal of Modern African Studies*, Vol. 10, No. 4 (December 1967), pp. 449–467.

4   For an excellent collection of essays on this theme, see Donald Rothchild and Naomi Chazan (eds.), *The Precarious Balance: State and Society in Africa* (Boulder: Westview Press, 1988).

5   For a survey of this literature, see Clark C. Gibson, "Of Waves and Ripples: Democracy and Political Change in Africa in the 1990s," *Annual Review of Political Science*, Vol. 5 (2000), pp 201–221. For an excellent collection of essays on democracy in Africa drawn from the *Journal of Democracy* during the 1990s, see Larry Diamond and Marc, F. Plattner (eds.), *Democratization in Africa*. Also see René Lemarchand, "African Transitions to Democracy: An Interim (and Mostly Pessimistic) Assessment," *Africa Insight*, Vol. 22, No. 3 (1992), pp. 178–185.

6   Michael Bratton, "Second Elections in Africa," in Larry Diamond and Marc F. Plattner (eds.), *Democratization in Africa* (Baltimore: Johns Hopkins University Press, 1999), p. 22.

7   On the eve of the 1994 genocide, Rwanda was receiving the highest per capita financial assistance in Africa from the international donor community. Peter Uvin, *L'Aide Complice?: Coopération Internationale et Violence au Rwanda* (Paris: L'Harmattan, 1999).

8   For of the oppressiveness of the regime in Rwanda preceding the 1994 genocide and a call for an alternative to the central state, see Timothy Longman, "Rwanda: Chaos from Above," in Leonardo A. Villalòn and Phillip A. Huxtable (eds.), *The African State at a Critical Juncture: Between Disintegration and Reconfiguration* (Boulder: Lynne Rienner Publishers, 1998), pp. 75–91.

9   See Bratton, "Second Elections in Africa," pp. 22–33.

10 Fareed Zakaria, "The Rise of Illiberal Democracies," pp. 181–195.

11 For one of the early pieces seeing civil society as comprising more than just urban Western-educated elites, see Jean-François Bayart, "Civil Society in Africa," in Patrick Chabal (ed.), *Political Domination in Africa: Reflections on the Limits of Power* (Cambridge: Cambridge University Press), pp. 109–125. Also see his *L'État en Afrique: La Politique du Ventre* (Paris: Fayard, 1989) for a critique of the ahistorical approach of most political scientists writing on Africa.

12 The original concept of patrimonialism comes from Max Weber. For a detailed discussion of this concept see, Reinhard Bendix, *Max Weber: An Intellectual Portrait* (Garden City, NY: Doubleday, 1962), pp. 329–384.

13 For a broad survey of indigenous African political institutions in precolonial Africa, see George B.N. Ayittey, *Indigenous African Institutions* (New York: Transnational Publications, 1991), pp. 1–272.

14 Crawford Young, "Itineraries of Freedom in Africa: Precolonial to Postcolonial," in Robert H. Taylor (ed.), *The Idea of Freedom in Asia and Africa* (Stanford: Stanford University Press, 2003), pp. 12–15.

15 On this point, see Chisanga N. Siame, "Two Concepts of Liberty through African Eyes," *The Journal of Political Philosophy*, Vol. 8, No. 1 (2000), pp. 53–67.

16 For analysis of the attributes of the inheritance elite, their inheritance that is, control over the institutions of the colonial state, and the inheritance situation, see J. P. Nettl and Roland Robertson, *International Systems and the Modernization of Societies* (London: Faber and Faber, 1968), pp. 63–127.

17 For a pioneering study examining linkages between institutional arrangements and differences in the physical environment, see Boone, *Political Topographies of the African State*.

18 For examples of African success stories in building effective rural self-governing associations, see Pierre Pradervand, *Listening to Africa: Developing Africa from the Grassroots* (New York: Praeger, 1989).

19 Simon Fass and Gerrit M. Desloovere, "Chad: Governance by the Grassroots," in Dele Olowu and James S. Wunsch (eds.), *Local Governance in Africa: The Challenges of Democratic Decentralization* (Boulder: Lynne Rienner Publishers, 2004).

20 For one of the best studies of the relationships and differences between local and decentralization, see Dele Olowu and James S. Wunsch (eds.), *Local Governance in Africa: The Challenges of Democratic Decentralization*.

21 For the stances of Christian and Animist religious institutions vis-à-vis the colonial and postcolonial state, see Achille Mbembe, *Afriques indociles: Christianisme, pouvoir et Etat en société postcoloniale* (Paris: Karthala, 1988).

22 A poll taken in Nigeria, Mali, Tanzania, and Uganda indicates that Muslims overwhelmingly support democracy with 71 percent of the Muslims polled agreeing that democracy was preferable to any other form of government. Afrobarometer, "Islam, Democracy and Public Opinion in Africa," (Afrobarometer Briefing Paper No. 3, September 2002).

23 For Muslim–Christian relations in Sierra Leone, see Lamin Sanneh, *Piety and Power: Muslims and Christians in West Africa* (Maryknoll, NY: Orbis Books, 1996).

24 Nearly 95 percent of the population in Mali is Muslim with most Muslims belonging to Sufi orders. For a detailed study of Islam in Mali and its traditions of religious tolerance and respect for the

Other, see Hamidou Magassa and Moussa Guindo, *Etats des Lieux de l'Islam au Mali* (Bamako: Fondation Fredrich Ebert, December 2003).

25 Mbembe, *Afriques indociles*, pp.14–34.

26 Amos Sawyer, "Social Capital, Survival Strategies and their Implication for Post-Conflict Governance in Liberia." Unpublished paper, prepared for Third Workshop on the Workshop Conference, Bloomington, Indiana, July 2–July 6, 2004.

27 On this point, see Michael Bratton and Robert Mattes, "How People View Democracy: Africans' Surprising Universalism," *Journal of Democracy*, Vol. 12, No. 1 (January 2001), pp. 108–111.

28 See Tocqueville's preface to the twelfth edition of *Democracy in America*, p. xiv, written in 1848 following the 1848 Revolution.

BIBLIOGRAPHY

Abun-Nasr, Jamil, *The Tijaniyya: A Sufi Order in the Modern World*. New York: Oxford University Press, 1965.

Afrobarometer, "Islam, Democracy and Public Opinion in Africa," *Afrobarometer Briefing Paper No. 3*, 2002.

Almond, George A. and James S. Coleman (eds.), *The Politics of Developing Areas*. Princeton, NJ: Princeton University Press, 1960.

Amin, Samir, *Le Monde des Affaires sénégalais*. Paris: Editions du Minuit, 1969.

——, *Accumulation on a World Scale*. New York: Monthly Review Press, 1974.

Avineri, Shlomo (ed.), *Karl Marx on Colonialism and Modernization*. New York: Doubleday, 1969.

Ayittey, George B.N., *Indigenous African Institutions*. Dobbs Ferry, NY: Transnational Publishers, 1991.

Ba, Abdourhamane, *La Takrur, des origins à la conquête par le Mali (VIe-XIII siècle)*. Nouakchott: Imprimerie Nouvelle, 2002.

Babou, Cheikh Anta Mbacké, "Autour de la Génèse du Mouridisme," *Islam et Sociétés au sud du Sahara*, Vol. 13, No. 1 (1999):5–38.

Balans, Jean-Louis, Christian Coulon, and Jean-Marc Gastellu, *Autonomie Locale et Intégration Nationale au Sénégal*. Paris: A. Pedone, 1975.

Barbier-Wiesser, François George (ed.), *Comprendre la Casamance: Chronique d'une Intégration Contrastée*. Paris: Karthala, 1994.

Barry, Boubacar, *La Sénégambie du XVe au XIXe siècle Traite négrière, Islam, et conquête coloniale*. Paris: Editions L'Harmattan, 1988.

Bathily, Abdoualye, *Mai 68 à Dakar ou la révolte universitaire et la démocratie*. Paris: Editions Chaka, 1992.

Bayart, François, "Civil Society," in *Political Domination in Africa: Reflections on the Limits of Power*, edited by Patrick Chabal, 109–125. Cambridge: Cambridge University Press, 1987.

——, *L'État en Afrique: la politique du ventre*. Paris: Fayard, 1989.

Beck, Linda J., "Patrimonial Democrats: Incremental Reforms and the Obstacles to Consolidating Democracy in Senegal." *Canadian Journal of African Studies*, Vol. 31, No. 1 (1998):1–31.

——, "Reining in the Marabouts?: Democratization and Local Governance in Senegal," *African Affairs*, No. 100 (2001):601–621.

——, "Le clientélisme au Sénégal: un adieu sans regrets?," in *Le Sénégal Contemporain*, edited by Momar-Coumba Diop, 529–547. Paris: Karthala, 2002.

——, "Democratization and the Hidden Public: The Impact of Patronage Networks on Senegalese Women," *Comparative Politics*, Vol. 35, No. 2 (2003):47–169.

——, "Clientelist Democracy." Unpublished paper, April 2003.

——, "Brokering Democracy in Africa: Political Competition, Participation and Stability in Senegal." Unpublished paper presented to the American Political Science Association, September 5, 2004.

Behrman, Lucy C., *Muslim Brotherhoods and Politics in Senegal*. Cambridge: Harvard University Press, 1970.

Bendix, Reinhard, *Max Weber: An Intellectual Portrait*. Garden City, NY: Doubleday, 1962.

Berg, Elliot J., "The Economic Basis of Political Choice in French West Africa," *American Political Science Review*, Vol. 54, No. 2 (June 1960):391–405.

Bernard-Duquente, Nicole, *Le Sénégal et le Front Populaire*. Paris: L'Harmattan, 1985.

Blanchet, Gil, "L'évolution des dirigeants du Sénégal: De l'Indépendance à 1975," *Cahiers d'Etudes Africaines*, Vol. 18, Nos. 1–2 (1978):49–78.

Blondé, Jacques, Pierre Dumont, and Dominique Gontier, *Lexique du français au Sénégal*. Dakar: Nouvelles Editions Africaines, 1979.

Boilat, David, *Esquisses Sénégalaises*. Paris: Editions Karthala, 1984.

Boone, Catherine, *Political Topographies of the African State: Territorial Authority and Institutional Choice*. New York: Cambridge University Press, 2003.

Boulégue, Jean, *Le Grand Jolof (XIII–XVIe siècle)*. Blois: Editions Facades, 1987.

Boumedouha, Said, "Adjustment to African Realities: The Lebanese in Senegal." *Africa*, Vol. 60, No. 4 (1990):538–549.

Bratton, Michael, "Second Elections in Africa," in *Democratization in Africa*, edited by Larry Diamond and Marc F. Plattner, 18–33. Baltimore, MD: Johns Hopkins Press, 1999.

Bratton, Michael and Robert Mattes, "How People View Democracy: Africans' Surprising Universalism," *Journal of Democracy*, Vol. 12, No. 1 (2001):108–111.

Bratton, Michael and Nicolas Van der Walle, "Neopatrimonial Regimes and Political Transition in Africa," *World Politics*, Vol. 46, No. 4 (1994):453–489.

Brooks, George E., *Landlords and Strangers: Ecology, Society, and Trade in Western Africa, 1000–1630*. Boulder, CO: Westview Press, 1993.

Brunsweig, Henri, *Mythes et Réalités de l'Impérialisme Colonial Français, 1871–1914*. Paris: Armand Colin, 1960.

Buell, Raymond Leslie, *The Native Problem in Africa*. New York: Macmillan, 1928.

Casswell, Nim, "Autopsie de l'ONCAD: La politique arachidière du Sénégal, 1966–1980." *Politique Africaine*, No. 14 (1984):38–73.

Chantornvong, Sombat, "Tocqueville's *Democracy in America* and the Third World," in *Rethinking Institutional Analysis and Development: Issues, Alternatives and Choices*, edited by Vincent Ostrom, David Feeny, and Harmut Picht, 69–99. San Francisco, CA: Institute for Contemporary Studies Press, 1988.

Club Nation et Développement, *Club Nation et Développment*. Paris: Présence Africaine, 1972.

Cohen, William B., *Rulers of Empire: The French Colonial Service in Africa*. Stanford, CA: Stanford University Press, 1971.

Coleman, James S. and Carl G. Rosberg, Jr. (eds.), *Political Parties and National Integration in Tropical Africa*. Berkeley: University of California Press, 1964.

Collier, David and Steven Levitsky, " 'Democracy' with Adjectives: Conceptual Innovation in Comparative Research," *World Politics*, Vol. 49 (April 1997):430–451.

Conklin, Alice L., *A Mission to Civilize: The Republican Idea of Empire in France and West Africa, 1895–1930*. Stanford, CA: Stanford University Press, 1998.

Copans, Jean, *Les marabouts de l'arachide*. Paris: Le Sycomore, 1980.

Coulibaly, Abdou Latif, *Wade, un opposant au pouvoir: L'Alternance Piégée*. Dakar: Les Éditions Sentinelles, 2003.

Coulon, Christian, *Le marabout et le prince: Islam et pouvoir au Sénégal*. Paris: Pedone, 1981.

———, *Les musulmans et le pouvoir en Afrique noire: Religion et contre-culture*. Paris: Karthala, 1983.

———, "Women, Islam and *Baraka*," in *Charisma and Brotherhood in African Islam*, edited by Donal B. Cruise O'Brien and Christian Coulon, 113–126. Clarendon: Oxford University Press, 1988.

Coulon, Christian and Odile Reveyrand, *L'Islam au feminine, Sokhna Magat Diop, Cheikh de la confréries mouride et les paysans (Sénégal)*. Bordeaux-Talence, Centre d'étude d'Afrique noire, 1990.

Cowan, L. Gray, *Local Government in West Africa*. New York: Columbia University Press, 1958.

Creevey, Lucy E., "The Impact of Islam on Women in Senegal," *Journal of Developing Areas*, Vol. 25 (1991): 347–348.

Crowder, Michael, *Senegal: A Study of French Assimilationist Policy*. New York: Oxford University Press, 1967.

Cruise O'Brien, Donal B., *The Mourides of Senegal: The Political and Economic Organization of an Islamic Brotherhood*. Oxford: Oxford University Press, 1971.

———, "Charisma Comes to Town: Mouride Organization, 1945–1986," in *Charisma and Brotherhoods in African Islam*, edited by Donal B. Cruise O'Brien and Christian Coulon, 135–155. Oxford: Clarendon Press, 1988.

Cruise O'Brien, Donal B., "The Shadow-politics of Wolofisation," *The Journal of Modern African Studies*, Vol. 36, No. 1 (1998):25–46.

Cruise O'Brien, Rita, *White Society in Black Africa: The French of Senegal*. Evanston, IL: Northwestern University Press, 1972.

Curtin, Philip D., *Economic Change in Precolonial Africa: Senegambia in the Era of the Slave Trade*. Madison: University of Wisconsin Press, 1975.

Darbon, Dominque, *L'Administration et le Paysan en Casamance: Essai d'Anthropologie Administrative*. Paris: Pedone, 1988.

David, Philippe, *Les Navétanes: Histoire des migrants saisonniers de l'arachide en Sénégambie des origins à nos jours*. Dakar: Les Nouvelles Editions Africaines, 1980.

Davidson, Basil, *A History of West Africa to the Nineteenth Century*. Garden City, NY: Doubleday, 1966.

———, *The Black Man's Burden: Africa and the Curse of the Nation-State*. New York: Random House, 1992.

Delavignette, Robert, *Freedom and Authority in French West Africa*. London: Oxford University Press, 1950.

Descendre, Danielle, *L'Autodétermination Paysanne en Afrique: Solidarité ou tutelles des O.N.G. parténaires?* Paris: L'Harmattan, 1986.

Dia, Ismaila, "Halpulaar Political Leadership with Political Parties and the Dynamics of Clan Politics in Dakar and the Senegal River Valley." Dakar, unpublished manuscript, 1997.

Diagne, Pathé, *Pouvoir Politique Traditionnel en Afrique occidentale*. Paris: Présence Africaine, 1967.

———, "Le Pouvoir en Afrique," in UNESCO, *Le Concept de Pouvoir en Afrique*, 28–55. Paris: Les Presses de l'UNESCO, 1981.

———, "Pluralism and Plurality in Africa," in *Democracy and Pluralism in Africa*, edited by Dov Ronen, 65–85. Boulder, CO: Lynne Rienner, 1986.

———, "La Liberté des candidatures: un imperative de la démocratisation de l'État-Parti," *Prospective Alternative Africaine*, Bulletin No. 3 (1988):4–10.

Diagne, Souleymane Bachir, "La Lecon de Musique: Réflexions sur une politique de la culture," in *Le Sénégal Contemporain*, edited by Momar-Coumba Diop, 243–259. Paris: Karthala, 2002.

Diamond, Larry and Marc. F. Plattner (eds.), *Democratization in Africa*. Baltimore, MD: Johns Hopkins University Press, 1999.

Diané, Charles, *La FEANF et les grandes heures du movement syndical étudiant noir*. Paris: Éditions Chaka, 1990.

Diarra, Mamadou, *Justice et Développement au Sénégal*. Dakar: Nouvelles Éditions Africaines, 1973.

Diop, Abdoulaye, "Une Expérience Associative du Foyer de Ronkh à l'Amicale Economique du Walo," *Archives des Sciences Sociales de la Coopération et du Développement*, No. 62 (October–December 1982):108–127.

Diop, Abdoualye-Bara, *La Société Wolof, Tradition et Changement:Les Systèmes d'Inégalité et de Domination*. Paris: Karthala, 1981.

Diop, Cheikh Anta, *Nations Négres et Culture*. Paris: Présence Africaine, 1959.

———, *L'Unité Culturelle de l'Afrique Noire*. Paris: Présence Africaine, 1959.

———, *L'Afrique Noire pré-coloniale*. Paris: Présence Africaine, 1960.

———, *Les Fondements économiqueet culturelle d'un État féderal d'Afrique noire*. Paris: Présence Africaine, 1961.

———, *Civilisation et Barbarie*. Paris: Présence Africaine, 1981.

Diop, Majhemout, *Histoire des classes socials dans l'Afrique de l'Ouest: Le Sénégal*. Paris: Francois Maspero, 1972.

Diop, Momar-Coumba, *La Lutte contre la pauvrété à Dakar: Vers une définition d'une politique municipale*. Dakar: Nouvelles Impriméries du Sénégal, 1996.

Diop, Momar-Coumba and Mamadou Diouf, *Le Sénégal sous Abdou Diouf:État et Société*. Paris: Karthala, 1990.

———, "Pouvoir Central et pouvoir local: la crise de l'institution municipale," in *Pouvoirs et cités d'Afrique noire: Décentralisation en question*, edited by Sylvy Jaglin and André Dubresson, 101–125. Paris: Karthala, 1993.

Diouf, Makhtar, *Sénégal: Les Ethnies et la Nation*. Dakar: Les Nouvelles Editions Africaines du Sénégal, 1998.

Diouf, Mamadou, *Le Kajoor au XIXe siècle: Pouvoir Ceddo et Conquête Coloniale*. Paris: Karthala, 1990.

————, "Le clientelisme, la 'technocratie' et après," in *Sénégal: Trajectoires d'un État*, edited by Momar-Coumba Diop, 233–278. Paris: Karthala, 1992.

————, "Les Intellectuals et l'État au Sénégal: La Quête d'un paradigme," in *Liberté Académique en Afrique*, edited by Mamadou Diouf and Mahmoud Mamdani, 241–271. Paris: Karthala, 1994.

————, *Histoire du Sénégal: Le Modéle Islamo-Wolof et ses Péripheries*. Paris: Maisonneuve & Larose, 2001.

————, "Des cultures urbaines entre traditions et mondialisation," in *Le Sénégal Contemporain*, edited by Momar-Coumba Diop, 261–287. Paris: Karthala, 2002.

Dupuy, Claude, "Les Associations Villageoises au Sénégal: Fonctions Économiques et Modalités de financement." *Revue Tiers Monde*, Vol. 31, No. 122 (April–June 1990):351–375.

Eistain, Jean Bethke, "Women, Equality, and the Family," *Journal of Democracy*, Vol. 11, No. 1 (January 2000):157–163.

Emerson, Rupert, *From Empire to Nation*. Cambridge, MA: Harvard University Press, 1960.

ENDA *Set Setal: des murs qui parlent, nouvelle culture urbaine à Dakar*. Dakar: ENDA, 1991.

Fass, Simon and Gerrit M. Desloovere, "Chad: Governance by the Grassroots," in *Local Governance in Africa: The Challenges of Democratic Decentralization*, edited by Dele Olowu and James S. Wunsch, 155–180. Boulder, CO: Lynne Rienner, 2004.

Fatton, Robert, Jr., "Clientelism and Patronage in Senegal," *African Studies Review*, Vol. 29, No. 4 (December 1986):61–78.

————, *The Making of a Liberal Democracy: Senegal's Passive Revolution, 1975–1985*. Boulder, CO: Lynne Rienner, 1987.

Féderation des Étudiants d'Afrique Noire en France, *Francophonie et Néo-Colonialsime: Le Combat Linguistique dans la lutte de liberation du Peuple Sénégalais*. Paris: FEANF, 1979.

Foltz, William J., *From French West Africa to the Mali Federation*. New Haven, CT: Yale University Press, 1965.

————, "Social Structure and Political Behavior of Senegalese Elites," in *Friends, Followers and Factions*, edited by Steffen W. Schmidt, James C. Scott, and Laura Gusti, 242–250. Berkeley: University of California Press, 1977.

Forment, Carlos A., *Democracy in Latin America, 1760–1900*. Chicago: University of Chicago Press, 2003.

Foucher, Vincent, "Les 'évolués', la migration, l'école: pour une nouvelle interpretation du nationalisme casamançais," in *Le Sénégal Contemporain*, edited by Momar-Coumba Diop, 375–424. Paris: Karthala, 2002.

Fougeyrollas, Pierre, *Où va le Sénégal?: Analyse spectrale d'une nation africaine*. Paris: Editions Anthropos, 1970.

Frank, André Gunder, *Capitalism and Underdevelopment in Latin America*. New York: Monthly Review Press, 1967.

Gade, Henry, *Proverbes et Maximes, Peuls et Toucouleurs traduits, expliqués et annotés*. Paris: Institut d'Ethnologie, 1931.

Gamble, David P., *The Wolof of Senegambia*. London: International African Institute, 1957.

Gannett, Robert T., Jr., "Bowling Ninepins in Tocqueville's Township," *American Political Science Review*, Vol. 97, No. 1 (February 2003):1–14.

Gellar, Sheldon, "State-Building and Nation-Building in West Africa," in *Building States and Nations: Models, Analyses, and Data across Three Worlds*, Vol. 2, edited by Schmuel N. Eisenstadt and Stein Rokkan, 384–426. Beverly Hills, CA: Sage Publications, 1973.

————, *Structural Changes and Colonial Dependency: Senegal, 1885–1945*. Beverly Hills, CA: Sage Publications, 1976.

————, "Circulaire 32 Revisited: Prospects for Revitalizing the Cooperative Movement in the 1980s," in *The Political Economy of Risk and Choice in Senegal*, edited by Mark Gersowitz and John Waterbury, 123–159. London: Frank Cass, 1987.

————, "State Tutelage Vs. Self-Governance: The Rhetroric and Reality of Decentralization in Senegal," in *The Failure of the Centralized State: Institutions and Self-Governance in Africa*, edited by James S. Wunsch and Dele Olowu, 130–147. Boulder, CO: Westview Press, 1990.

————, "Pluralisme ou jacobinisme: quelle démocratie pour le Sénégal," in *Le Sénégal Contemporain*, edited by Momar-Coumba Diop, 507–528. Paris: Karthala, 2002.

Gellar, Sheldon, Robert A. Charlick, and Yvonne Jones, *Animation Rurale and Rural Development: The Experience of Senegal*. Ithaca, NY: Cornell University, 1980.

Gentil, Dominique, *Les Mouvements Coopératifs en Afrique de l'Ouest: Intervention de l'État ou organizations paysannes?* Paris: L'Harmattan, 1986.

Gibson, Clark C. "Of Waves and Ripples: Democracy and Political Change in Africa in the 1990s," *Annual Review of Political Science*, Vol. 5 (2000):201–222.

Glickman, Harvey, "Frontiers of Liberal and Non-Liberal Democracy in Tropical Africa," *Journal of Asian and African Studies*, Vol. 22, Nos. 3–4 (1988):235–254.

Gomez-Perez, Muriel, "Associations Islamiques à Dakar," *Islam et Sociétés au Sud du Sahara*, Vol. 5 (November 1991):5–19.

Gray, John Milner, *A History of the Gambia*. London: Frank Cass, 1966.

Guèye, Cheikh, "Touba: les marabouts urbanisants," in *Petites et Moyennes villes d'Afrique Noire*, edited by Monique Bertrand and Alain Dubresson, 179–203. Paris: Karthala, 1997.

Harrison, Carol E., *The Bourgeois Citizen in Nineteenth Century France: Gender, Sociability, and Uses of Emulation*. Clarendon: Oxford University Press, 1999.

Herbst, Jeffrey, *States and Power in Africa: Comparative Lessons in Authority and Control*. Princeton, NJ: Princeton University Press, 2000.

Hereth, Michael, *Alexis de Tocqueville: Threats to Freedom in Democracy*. Durham, NC: Duke University Press, 1986.

Hesseling, Gerti, *Histoire Politique du Sénégal: Institutions, droit et société*. Paris: Karthala, 1985.

Hodgkin, Thomas, *Nationalism in Colonial Africa*. New York: New York University Press, 1957.

———, *African Political Parties*. London: Penguin Books, 1961.

Horowitz, Michael, "Victims of Development." *IDA Anthropology Network*, Vol. 7, No. 2 (Fall 1989):1–8.

Hudson, Mark, Jenny Cathcart, and Lucy Duran, "Senegambian Stars are Here to Stay," in *World Music: Africa, Europe and the Middle East, The Rough Guide*, Vol. 1, edited by Simon Broughton, Mark Ellingham, and Richard Trillo, 617–633. London: The Rough Guides, 1999.

Huntington, Samuel P., *Political Order in Changing Societies*. New Haven, CT: Yale University Press, 1968.

———, *The Third Wave: Democratisation in the Late Twentieth Century*. Norman: University of Oklahoma Press, 1990.

Hymans, Jacques, *Léopold Sédar Senghor*. Edinburgh: Edinburgh University Press, 1971.

Institut Panos, *Médias et Élections au Sénégal: La Presse et les nouvelles technologies de l'information dans le processus electoral*. Dakar: Panos, 2002.

Jacob, James E., "Language Policy and Political Development in France," in *Language Policy and Political Development*, edited by Brian Weinstein, 43–65. Norwood, NJ: Ablex Publishing, 1990.

Jacob, Jean-Pierre and Phil Lavigne Deville (eds.), *Les Associations Paysannes en Afrique: Organisation et dynamiques*. Paris: Karthala, 1994.

Johnson, G. Wesley, Jr., *The Emergence of Black Politics in Senegal: The Struggle for Power in the Four Communes, 1900–1920*. Stanford, CA: Stanford University Press, 1971.

Juillard, Caroline, "Ville plurielle?: Indices de la wolofisation en cours," in *Comprendre la Casamance: Chronique d'une intégration contrastée*, edited by FrançoisGeorges Barbier-Wiesser, 401–412. Paris: Karthala, 1994.

Kaba, Lansiné, *The Wahabiyya: Islamic Reform and Politics in French West Africa*. Evanston, IL: Northwestern University Press, 1974.

Karlstrom, Mikael, "Imagining Democracy: Political Culture and Democratisation in Uganda," *Africa*, Vol. 66, No. 4 (1996):485–505.

Klein, Martin A., *Islam and Imperialism in Senegal: Sine-Saloum 1847–1914*. Stanford, CA: Stanford University Press, 1968.

———, *Slavery and French Colonial Rule in French West Africa*. New York: Cambridge University Press, 1998.

Konaté, Abdourahmane, *Le cri du mange-mil: Mémoires d'un Préfet Sénégalais*. Paris: L'Harmattan, 1990.

Laborde, Cécile, *La Confrérie Layenne et les Lébou du Sénégal: Islam et culture traditionnelle en Afrique*. Bordeaux: Centre d'Étude d'Afrique Noire, 1995.

Lachenmann, Gudrun, "Civil Society and Social Movements in Africa," in *Les Associations paysannes en Afrique: Organisation et dynamiques*, edited by Jean-Pierre Jacob and Philippe Lavigne Deville, 61–95. Paris: Karthala, 1994.

Lambert, Michael C., *Longing for Exile: Migration and the Making of a Translocal Community in Senegal, West Africa*. Portsmouth, NH: Heinneman, 2002.

Lemarchand, René, "African Transitions to Democracy: An Interim (and Mostly Pessimistic) Assessment," *Africa Insight*, Vol. 22, No. 3 (1992):178–185.

Levtzion, Nehemia, *Ancient Ghana and Mali*. London: Methuen, 1973.

Lewis, M.D., "One Hundred Million Frenchmen: The Assimilation Theory in French Colonial Policy," *Comparative Studies in Society and History*, Vol. 4, No. 9 (1962):48–61.

Leys, Colin, *Underdevelopment in Kenya: The Political Economy of Underdevelopment*. London: Heinneman, 1975.

Lipset, Seymour, *The First New Nation: The United States in Historical and Comparative Perspective*. London: Heinneman, 1963.

Lo, Magatte, *Syndicalisme et Participation Responsable*. Paris: L'Harmattan, 1987.

Loimeier, Roman, "The Secular State and Islam in Senegal," in *Questioning the Secular State: The Worldwide Resurgence of Religion in Politics*, edited by David Westurlund, 183–202. London: Hurst & Co., 1996.

———, *Islamic Reform and Political Change in Northern Nigeria*. Evanston, IL: Northwestern University Press, 1997.

Longman, Timothy, "Rwanda: Chaos from Above," in *The African State at a Critical Juncture: Between Disintegration and Reconfiguration*, edited by Leonardo A. Villalòn and Phillip A. Huxtable, 75–91. Boulder, CO: Lynne Rienner, 1998.

Ly, Abdoulaye, *Le Regroupement des partis politiques au Sénégal (1956–1970)*. Paris: Karthala, 1992.

Magassa, Hamidou and Moussa Guindo, *États des Lieux de l'Islam au Mali*. Bamako: Fondation Fredrich Ebert, December 2003.

Magassouba, Moriba, *L'Islam au Sénégal: Demain les Mollahs?* Paris: Karthala, 1985.

Magistro, John V., "Crossing Over: Ethnicity and Transboundary Conflict in the Senegal River Valley," *Cahiers d'Etudes Africaines*, Vol. 33, No. 2 (1993):201–232.

Mamdani, Mahmood, *Citizen and Subject: Contemporary Africa and the Legacy of Late Colonialism*. Princeton, NJ: Princeton University Press, 1996.

Marfaing, Laurence and Mariam Sow, *Les Opérateurs économiques au Sénégal: Entre le formel et l'informel (1930–1996)*. Paris: Karthala, 1999.

Markowitz, Irving L., *Léopold Sédar Senghor and the Politics of Negritude*. New York: Atheneum, 1969.

Marty, Paul, *Etudes sur l'Islam*, 2 vols. Paris: Leroux, 1917.

Mbacké, Khadim, *Soufisme et Confréries Religieuses au Sénégal*. Dakar: Publifan, 1995.

Mbacké, Serigne Salihou, *Touba(Sénégal): Du "Ndiguel" de Cheikh Ahmadou Bamba Mbacké aux Réalisations de ses Khalifes ou une Voie Communautaire vers la Maitrise de la Croissance Urbaine Rapide* (Istanbul, Turkey, June 1996).

Mbembe, Achille, *Afriques indociles: Christianisme, pouvoir et État en société postcoloniale*. Paris: Karthala, 1988.

Mbodj, Mohammed, "Le Sénégal entre ruptures et mutations: Citoyennetés en construction," in *Le Sénégal Contemporain*, edited by Momar-Coumba Diop, 575–600. Paris: Karthala, 2002.

Meillasoux, Claude, *The Urbanization of an African Community: Voluntary Associations in Bamako*. Seattle: University of Washington Press, 1968.

Michels, Robert, *Political Parties: A Sociological Study of the Oligarchical Tendencies of Modern Democracies*. New York: Free Press, 1966.

Moreau, Marie-Louise, "Demain, la Casamance trilangue?: Valeurs associées au diola, français, et au wolof," in *Comprendre la Casamance: Chronique d'une Intégration contrastée*, edited by François George Barbier-Wiesser, 413–428. Paris: Karthala, 1994.

Ndiaye, Augustin Simmel, "Une Minorité confessionnelle dans l'État laic: Point de vue d'un Chrétien," in *Le Sénégal Contemporain*, edited by Momar-Coumba Diop, 601–616. Paris: Karthala, 2002.

Ndiaye, Babacar and Waly Ndiaye, *Présidents et Ministres de la République du Sénégal*. Dakar: La Sénégalaise de l'Imprimérie, 2000.

Ndiaye, Jean-Pierre, *Enquête sur les étudiants noirs en France*. Paris: Editions Réalités Africaines, 1962.

Ndiaye, Malick, *L'Ethique Ceddo et la Société d'Accaparement ou les conduits culturelles des Sénégalais d'audjourd'hui*. Dakar: Presses Universitaires de Dakar, 1996.

———, *Les Móodu-Móodu ou l'ethos du développement au Sénégal*. Dakar: Presses Universitaires de Dakar, 1998.

Ndione, Emmanuel, *Dynamique Urbaine d'une Société en Grappe: Un Cas*. Dakar: ENDA, 1987.

———, *Avenir des Terroirs: La Ressource Humaine*. Dakar: Enda-Editions, 1992.

Ndione, Emmanuel, *Le Don et le Recours: Ressorts d'une Économie Urbaine*. Dakar: ENDA, 1992.

Nettle, J.P. and Roland Robertson, *International Systems and the Modernization of Societies*. London: Faber and Faber, 1968.

Niane, Djibril Tamsir, *Le Soudan Occidentale au temps des grands empires (XIe-XVIe siécles)*. Paris: Présence Africaine, 1975.

Niasse, Sidy Lamine, *Un arabisant entre presse et pouvoir*. Dakar: Editions Groupe Wal Fadjri, 2003.

Novicki, Margaret A., "Abdoulaye Wade: Democracy's Advocate," *Africa Report*, Vol. 36, No. 2 (March–April 1991): 41–44.

Nzouankeu, Jacques Mariel, *Les Partis Politiques Sénégalais*. Dakar: Editions Clairafrique, 1984.

O'Dèye-Finzi, Michèle, *Les Associations en Villes Africaines, Dakar-Brazzaville*. Paris: Editions L'Harmattan, 1985.

Ostrom, Vincent, *The Intellectual Crisis in American Public Administration*, 2nd ed. Tuscaloosa: University of Alabama Press, 1989.

———, *The Meaning of Democracy and the Vulnerability of Democracies: A Response to Tocqueville's Challenge*. Ann Arbor: University of Michigan Press, 1997.

Ottaway, Marina, *Democracy Challenged: The Rise of Semi-Authoritarianism*. Washington, DC: Carnegie Endowment for International Peace, 2003.

Owusu, Maxwell, "Democracy and Africa—A View from the Village," *The Journal of Modern African Studies*, Vol. 30, No. 3 (1992):369–396.

Parpart, Jane L., "Women and the State in Africa," in *The Precarious Balance: State and Society in Africa*, edited by Naomi Chazan and Donald Rothchild, 208–230. Boulder, CO: Westview Press, 1988.

Paye, Moussa, "La Presse et le Pouvoir," in *Sénégal: Trajectoires d'un État*, edited by Momar-Coumba Diop, 331–377. Paris: Karthala, 1992.

Pélissier, Paul, *Les Paysans du Sénégal: Les Civilszations agraires du Cayor à la Casamance*. Saint Yvrieux: Imprimerie Fabreque, 1966.

Perry, Donna, "Rural Weekly Markets and the Dynamics of Time, Space and Community in Senegal," *Journal of Modern African Studies*, Vol. 38, No. 3 (2000):461–486.

Pradervand, Pierre, *Listening to Africa: Developing Africa from the Grassroots*. New York: Praeger, 1989.

Programme des Nations Unies pour le Développement, *Rapport National sur le Développement Humain au Sénégal*, 2001.

Putnam, Robert D., *Making Democracy Work: Civic Traditions in Modern Italy*. Princeton, NJ: Princeton University Press, 1993.

———, *Bowling Alone: The Collapse and Revival of American Community*. New York: Simon & Schuster, 2000.

Pye, Lucian W., *Aspects of Political Development*. Boston: Little, Brown, 1966.

Quinn, Charlotte, *Mandingo Kingdoms of the Senegambia: Traditionalism, Islam, and European Expansion*. London: Longman, 1972.

Reboul, Claude, "Les Associations de Village de la Vallée du Fleuve Sénégal," *Revue Tiers Monde*, Vol. 28, No. 10 (April–June 1987):435–440.

République de France, Services des Statistiques d'Outre-Mer, *Outre-Mer 1958: Tableaux économique et social edes états et territoires d'outre-mer à la veille de la mise en place des nouvelles institutions*. Paris: Presses Universitaires de France, 1966.

République du Sénégal, *Textes et Lois sur la Décentralisation*. Dakar, 1966.

Robinson, David, *Chiefs and Clerics: The History of Abdul Bokar Kane and the Fouta Toro*. Oxford: Clarendon Press, 1975.

———, "French Islamic Policy and Practice in Late Nineteenth Century Senegal," *Journal of African History*, Vol. 29, No. 3 (1988):185–211.

———, *Paths of Accommodation: Muslim societies and colonial societies in Senegal and Mauritania, 1880–1920*. Athens: Ohio University Press, 2000.

Robinson, Kenneth, "Senegal," in *Five Elections in Africa*, edited by W.J.K. Mackensie and Kenneth Robinson, 281–390. London: Oxford University Press, 1960.

Rodney, Walter, *How Europe Underdeveloped Africa*. Washington, DC: Howard University Press, 1974.

Ross, Eric, "Touba: A Spiritual Metropolis in the Modern World," *Canadian Journal of African Studies*, Vol. 29, No. 2 (1995):222–259.

Roth, Guenther, "Personal Rulership, Patrimonialism, and Empire-Building in the New States," *World Politics*, Vol. 20, No. 22 (January 1968):194–206.

Rothchild, Donald and Naomi Chazan (eds.), *The Precarious Balance: State and Society in Africa*. Boulder, CO: Westview Press, 1988.

Samb, Amadou Makhtar, *Introduction à la Tariqah ou voie spirituelle de Cheikh Ahmad Tijani*. Dakar: Imprimérie Saint-Paul, 1994.

Sanneh, Lamin, *Piety and Power: Muslims and Christians in West Africa*. Maryknoll, NY: Orbis Books, 1996.

Sawyer, Amos, "Social Capital, Survival Strategies and their Implication for Post-Conflict Governance in Liberia." Bloomington: Indiana University, Workshop in Political Theory and Policy Analysis. Unpublished paper, July 2004.

Schachter-Morgenthau, Ruth, *Political Parties in French-Speaking West Africa*. New York: Oxford University Press, 1964.

Schaeffer, Frederick C., *Democracy in Translation: Understanding Politics in an Unfamiliar Culture*. Ithaca, NY: Cornell University Press, 1998.

Schliefer, James T., *The Making of Tocqueville's Democracy in America*. Chapel Hill: University of North Carolina Press, 1980.

Schmitz, Jean, "Cités Noires: Les Républiques villageoises du Fuuta Tooro (Vallée du Flueve Sénégal)," *Cahiers d'Études Africaines*, Vol. 34, Nos. 1–3 (1994):419–461.

Schumacher, Edward J., *Politics, Bureaucracy, and Rural Development in Senegal*. Berkeley: University of California Press, 1975.

Searing, James E., *God Alone is King: Islam and Emancipation in Senegal, The Wolof Kingdoms of Kajoor and Bawol, 1859–1914*. Portsmouth, NH: Heinneman, 2002.

Sembène, Ousmane, *God's Bits of Wood*. Garden City, NY: Anchor Books, 1970.

Senghor, Léopold Sédar, *On African Socialism*. New York: Frederick A. Praeger, 1964.

———, *Ce que je crois: négritude, francité et civilization de l'universelle*. Paris: B. Grasset, 1988.

———, *Le Dialogue des Cultures*. Paris: Seuil, 1993.

Siame, Chisanga N., "Two Concepts of Liberty through African Eyes," *Journal of Political Philosophy*, Vol. 8, No. 1 (2000):53–67.

Siedentop, Larry, *Tocqueville*. New York: Oxford University Press, 1994.

Smith Deric, Bably Sall, and Mady Dansonko, *Liberalisme, Patrimonialisme, ou authoritarianisme Attenué: Variations autour de la Démocratie Sénégalaise*. Washington: Afrobarometer, December 2002.

Snyder, Francis G., *Capitalism and Legal Change: An African Transformation*. New York: Academic Press, 1981.

Sow, Fatou, *Les Fonctionnaires de l'Administration Centrale Sénégalaise*. Dakar: IFAN, 1972.

Suret-Canale, Jean, *L'Afrique Noire: l'Ere Colonial, 1900–1945*. Paris: Editions Sociales, 1964.

Swigart, Leigh, "Cultural Creolisation and Language Use in Post-Colonial Africa: The Case of Senegal," *Africa*, Vol. 64, No. 2 (1994):175–189.

Sy, Cheikh Tidjiane, *La Confrérie sénégalaise des Mourides*. Paris: Présence Africaine, 1969.

Sylla, Abdou, "L'École: quelle réforme?," in *Sénégal: trajectories d'un État*, edited by Momar-Coumba Diop, 379–429. Paris: Karthala, 1992.

Sylla, Assane, *La philosophie morale des Wolof*. Dakar: Sankoré, 1978.

Tall, Cheikh Omar, *Islam: Engagement Politique et Démocratie*. Dakar: Les Presses de la Sénégalaise de l'Imprimerie, 1997.

Tamari, Tal, *Les castes de l'Afrique occidentale: Artisans et musiciens endogames*. Nanterre: Société d'ethnologie, 1997.

Tambadou, Moustapha (ed.), *Les Convergences Culturelles au sein de la Nation Sénégalaise, Actes du colloque de Kaolack, 8–13 juin 1994*. Dakar: Imprimérie Saint-Paul, 1996.

Thioub, Ibrahima, Momar-Comba Diop, and Catherine Boone, "Economic Liberalization in Senegal: Shifting Politics of Indigenous Business Interests," *African Studies Review*, Vol. 41, No. 2 (September 1998):63–89.

Tignor, Robert L., "Senegal's Cooperative Experience, 1907–1960," in *The Political Economy of Risk and Growth in Senegal*, edited by Mark Gersovitz and John Waturbury, 90–122. London: Frank Cass, 1987.

Tocqueville, Alexis de, *The Old Régime and the French Revolution*. Garden City, NY: Doubleday, 1955.

———, *Recollections*. Garden City, NY: Doubleday, 1970.

———, *Democracy in America*. New York: Harper & Rows, 1988.

Triaud, Jean-Louis and David Robinson (eds.), *La Tijaniyya: Une Confrérie Musulmane à la conquête de l'Afrique*. Paris: Karthala, 2000.

Turpin, Dominque, *Droit de la Décentralisation: Principes-Institutions-compétences*. Paris: Gualino Éditeur, 1998.

Uvin, Peter, *L'Aide Complice?: Coopération Internationale et Violence au Rwanda*. Paris: L'Harmattan, 1999.

Van Chi-Bonnardel, Regina, *Vie de Relations au Sénégal: La circulation des biéns*. Dakar: IFAN, 1978.

Venema, L.B., *The Wolof of Saloum: Social Structure and Rural Development in Senegal*. Wageningen: Centre for Agricultural Publishing and Documentation, 1978.

———, "The Rural Councillor as Development Agent: An Uneasy Connection?: A Report from Senegal," *APAD-Bulletin*, No. 12 (1999):83–101.

Venema, L.B. and Mayke Kaag, *Le Savoir Local et la Gestion des Resources Naturelles dans les Communautés Rurales Sénégalaises: le cas de l'Arrondissement de Médina-Sabakh*. Amsterdam: Free University of Amsterdam, 1997.

Vengroff, Richard and Alan Johnston, *Senegal's Rural Councils: Decentralization and the Implementation of Rural Development*. Dakar: CAIDS, 1985.

Villalòn, Leonardo A., *Islamic Society and State Power in Senegal: Disciples and Citizens in Fatick*. New York: University of Cambridge Press, 1995.

———, "Senegal: The Crisis of Democracy and the Emergence of an Islamic Opposition," in *Critical Juncture: The African State between Disintegration and Reconfiguration*, edited by Leonardo Villalòn and Philip Huxtable, 143–166. Boulder, CO: Lynne Rienner, 1998.

———, "Islamism in West Africa: Senegal," *African Studies Review*, Vol. 47, No. 2 (September 2004):61–71.

Villalòn, Leonardo and Ousemane Kane, "Entre confrérisme, réformisme, et Islamisme, les mustarchidin du Sénégal," in *Islam et Islamismes au Sud du Sahara*, edited by Ousemane Kane and Jean-Louis Triaud, 263–310. Paris: Karthala, 1998.

Vuarin, Robert, "L'Enjeu de la misère pour l'Islam Sénégalais." *Revue Tiers Monde*, Vol. 31, No. 123 (July–September 1990):601–604.

Wade, Abdoulaye, "La doctrine économique Mouride," *Annales Africaines* (1967):175–208.

Wallerstein, Emmanuel, "Voluntary Associations," in *Political Parties and National Integration in Tropical Africa*, edited by James S. Coleman and Carl Rosberg, Jr., 318–339. Berkeley: University of California Press, 1964.

Weinstein, Brian, *The Civic Tongue: Political Consequences of Language Choices*. New York: Longman, 1983.

Welch, Cheryl, *De Tocqueville*. New York: Oxford University Press, 2001.

Wunsch, James S., "Refounding the African State and Local Self-Governance: The Neglected Foundation," *Journal of Modern African Studies*, Vol. 38, No. 3 (2000):487–509.

Wunsch, James S. and Dele Olowu (eds.), *The Failure of the Centralized State: Institutions and Self-Governance in Africa*. Boulder, CO: Westview Press, 1990.

———, *Local Governance in Africa: The Challenges of Democratic Decentralization*. Boulder, CO: Lynne Rienner, 2003.

Young, Crawford, *The African Colonial State in Comparative Perspective*. New Haven: Yale University Press, 1994.

———, "Itineraries of Freedom in Africa: Precolonial to Postcolonial," in *The Idea of Freedom in Asia and Africa*, edited by Robert H. Taylor, 9–39. Stanford, CA: Stanford University Press, 2002.

Young, Crawford and Babacar Kanté, "Governance, Democracy, and the 1988 Senegalese Elections," in *Governance and Politics in Africa*, edited by Goren Hyden and Michael Bratton, 57–74. Boulder, CO: Lynne Rienner, 1992.

Zakaria, Fareed, "The Rise of Illiberal Democracy," *Foreign Affairs*, Vol. 76, No. 6 (1997):181–195.

Zolberg, Aristide, *Creating Political Order: The Party-States of West Africa*. Chicago: Rand McNally, 1966.

———, "Patterns of National Integration," *Journal of Modern African Studies*, Vol. 10, No. 4 (December 1967):449–467.

Zuccarelli, Francois, *La vie politique Sénégalaise (1789–1940)*, Vol. 1, Paris: CHEAM, 1988.

———, *La vie politique Sénégalaise (1940–1988)*, Vol. 2, Paris: CHEAM, 1989.

INDEX